Mastering Woodworking Machines

Mastering Woodworking Machines

MARK DUGINSKE

The Taunton Press

Cover photo: CRAIG UMANOFF

First printing: April 1992
Printed in the United States of America

A FINE WOODWORKING Book

FINE WOODWORKING ® is a trademark of The Taunton Press, Inc.,
registered in the U.S. Patent and Trademark Office.

The Taunton Press, 63 South Main Street, Box 5506, Newtown,
CT 06470-5506

Library of Congress Cataloging-in-Publication Data

Duginske, Mark.
    Mastering woodworking machines / Mark Duginske.
        p.   cm.
    "A Fine Woodworking book"—T.p. verso.
    Includes index.
    ISBN 0-942391-98-5
    1. Woodworking tools. I. Title. II. Series.
TT186.D85   1992   91-44709
684'.083—dc20   CIP

This book is dedicated to my brothers and sisters.

CONTENTS

ACKNOWLEDGMENTS

Producing a book reminds me of Edison's remark that creativity is 1% inspiration and 99% hard work. I was fortunate to have help with this book from a large number of people. First and foremost, this book exists because of the tremendous effort on the part of my editor, Andy Schultz. He gave good constructive criticism and suggestions and kept track of the thousands of details that go into producing a book. I especially appreciated his positive attitude when dealing with the frustrations and pressures that accompany this kind of project. I would also like to thank John Kelsey and Deborah Cannarella, publisher and senior editor at The Taunton Press.

My wife, Kate Morris, was always there to help me with editing and photographs. My brother, Gene, also helped with the photography. My nephew, Chris Morris, did the preliminary drawings and provided assistance on many levels.

I must also thank Sue Barr, Kelly Mehler and Sandor Nagyszalanczy. A number of individuals from various companies were also helpful: Lee Franck (Franck Photography), Garry Chinn and Peter Segal (Garrett Wade), Brad Witt (Woodhaven), Ron Bechen (Workbench), David Draves (Woodcraft Supply), Gene Sliga and Steve Holly (Delta), Paul Thoms (Belsaw), Brad Packard, Zach Etheridge and Chris Bagby (Highland Hardware), Bill Biesemeyer (Biesemeyer Company), Tim Hewitt (H.T.C.), Dr. Chen Sun (Sunhill), John McConegly (J.D.S.), Torben Helshoj (Laguana Tools), Tim Silvers (Shopsmith), Chris Schamb (Wisconsin Knifeworks), Jesse Barragon (Eagle Tools), Deborah Schmid and Rod Nelson (Jet) and Chuck Olson (Olson Saw Company).

INTRODUCTION

Many woodworkers are frustrated by machinery. A good woodworker is not always a good mechanic, and some don't have the confidence to change the adjustment of a machine no matter how poorly it is performing. On many machines the owner's manual is so confusing that you're lucky to get the table right side up. All of this can lead to frustration and a feeling of helplessness.

The goal of this book is to help you acquire the skills of machine woodworking. The book covers the use, setup, maintenance and troubleshooting of the eight most common woodworking machines, and emphasizes two things. First, you develop the confidence and skill needed to keep your machinery well tuned. As with any other new technique, proper machine setup will initially be time-consuming and perhaps a little frustrating. Once you develop the habits and awareness, you will do better woodworking easily and with more control. Second, the book gives you an in-depth understanding of the principles involved in machine woodworking.

More than just explaining how to use and tune your woodworking machines, this book enables you to develop and master a system of machine woodworking. You need a system because woodworking is more complicated than it at first appears. It's a series of steps in which proper sequencing is critical and the quality of every step depends on the accuracy of the previous step. Any error, sloppiness or poor judgment at an early stage compounds exponentially to haunt you at a later stage.

Fundamentals are incredibly important. Once you can make a square box you can build just about any piece of carcase furniture. Making the first perfectly square box is the hard part. The second box takes less time and less mental energy. By the tenth box you have developed a system.

This book is an attempt to pass on to others the systematic approach to woodworking that I inherited from my father, who in turn learned from his father.

About safety:

I've thought a great deal about the accuracy and safeness of the information I've provided in this book. As it says at the beginning of *Fine Woodworking* magazine, "Working wood is inherently dangerous....Don't try to perform operations you learn about here (or elsewhere) until you're certain that they are safe for you and your shop situation." Many advanced procedures require you to modify safety equipment on your machinery. You do so at your own risk.

CHAPTER 1
The Table Saw

Of all the machine tools in a woodworking shop, the table saw is the workhorse. With it, you can make virtually any straight cut. Fitted with a dado head, the table saw is the tool of choice for cutting grooves, dadoes and rabbets. Although I prefer to use the router or shaper for making moldings, many craftsmen have shaped thousands of board feet with molding heads on their table saws. When equipped with shopmade jigs, the table saw is the most efficient tool for finger joints, tenons and even dovetails. In fact, with my spacer-block dovetail technique (see pp. 219-230), you'll be able to make variable-spaced dovetails (the best-looking kind) faster than with even the most expensive jigs at virtually no cost.

Though undeniably handy, the table saw also has its dark side. It is probably responsible for more injuries than any other woodworking tool. Many of those injuries, particularly those caused by kickback, can be traced directly to an incorrectly adjusted saw or accessory. To run well and safely, the table saw must be kept in a tuned condition.

By "tuned," I mean all working parts must be properly adjusted and aligned. These parts include the trunnions, the table and undercarriage, the square and bevel stops (see the drawing on p. 6), and the miter gauge and rip fence. Some critical tune-up techniques are given short shrift in the owner's manual, and sometimes the information is incomplete or just plain wrong. Fortunately, tuning is simple. It doesn't

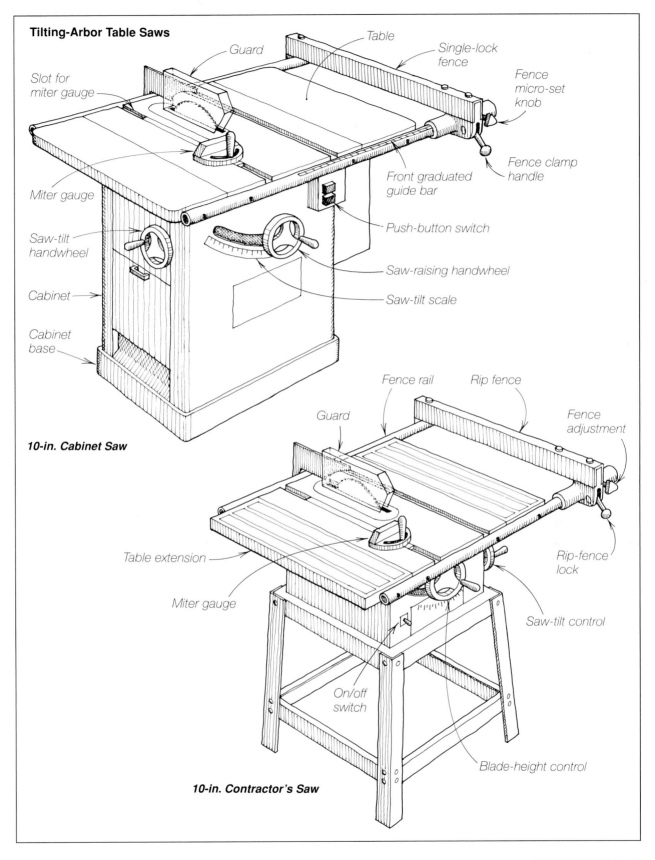

Tilting-Arbor Table Saws

Slot for miter gauge

Guard

Table

Single-lock fence

Fence micro-set knob

Miter gauge

Saw-tilt handwheel

Cabinet

Cabinet base

Front graduated guide bar

Fence clamp handle

Push-button switch

Saw-raising handwheel

Saw-tilt scale

10-in. Cabinet Saw

Fence rail

Rip fence

Guard

Fence adjustment

Table extension

Miter gauge

Rip-fence lock

Saw-tilt control

On/off switch

Blade-height control

10-in. Contractor's Saw

require any special tools, esoteric knowledge or superhuman strength. Even a cheap saw can be tuned to perform well, and the brief time that you invest in a tune-up is amply repaid in highly accurate work.

There is no such thing as the perfect table saw. Every design has advantages and disadvantages. By the end of this chapter, you should be able to tune and operate your own saw to its best advantage and minimize its disadvantages. Before we start working on your saw, let's look at some of the different types of saws and discuss some design features and differences.

Table-saw design

The first table saws were owner-built. The arbor and bearings were purchased, and the rest of the saw was made out of wood. It was simplest to make the arbor fixed and then tilt the table for making bevel cuts, so this design became known as the tilting-table table saw. Until the early 20th century, most table saws had tilting tables.

During the 1920s and 1930s sheet materials such as plywood became more popular, particularly in production settings. Large sheets of plywood on tilting tabletops were a recipe for disaster. Manufacturers responded by creating the tilting-arbor table saw. On this machine the table is stationary and the arbor tilts. Also, the table is usually bigger to handle 4-ft. by 8-ft. sheets. For years both styles were manufactured, but the tilting-table design has been largely discontinued in the United States. The Shopsmith multiple-use machine, however, retains a tilting-table design, and European manufacturers still make a number of tilting-table machines. These machines are often fitted with collets on the external end of the arbor so that they can mortise or drill. A tilting table is less troublesome and perhaps more accurate, but the tilting arbor is handier for sheet goods. I prefer a tilting-arbor table saw, but it's a minor preference.

Two styles of tilting-arbor table saw predominate in North America (see the drawing on p. 3). The *cabinet saw* is a large industrial saw with a solid base or cabinet. The *contractor's saw* is usually lighter and has an open base. The cabinet saw also has a larger and heavier tilt mechanism. The motor is enclosed in the base and often drives the arbor with three belts. The contractor's saw, on the other hand, has a lighter undercarriage, and the motor hangs off the back of the saw on one belt. On cheaper models the motor shaft may also be the arbor. Machines like these are called direct-drive table saws. Although these cheaper saws have tarnished the reputation of the direct-drive design, some of the finest large industrial table saws are direct-drive machines.

Blade-tilt direction

There is an ongoing controversy over which way the table-saw blade should tilt. On the Delta, European and Taiwanese saws the blade tilts to the right. On the industrial Powermatic and Sears saws the blade tilts to the left. No saw tilts both ways.

Blade-tilt direction has important safety implications. Since most people crosscut with the miter gauge in the left table slot, it's best to have the blade tilt to the right for crosscutting bevels. However, most people rip with the fence on the right side of the blade, which makes the left-tilting saw better for ripping bevels. Thus, the best design for ripping bevels is not usually the best design for crosscutting bevels, and vice versa. To get around this problem, move the rip fence to the left side of the blade when making a bevel cut on a right-tilting saw. This way the workpiece won't bind between the fence and the blade and kick back. Use the right miter slot when crosscutting a bevel on a left-tilting saw.

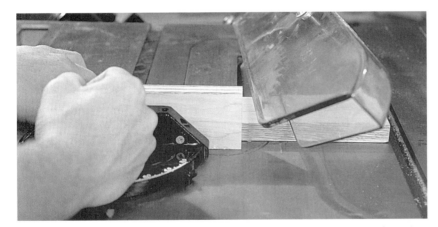

For a bevel crosscut, the blade should tilt away from the operator's hand.

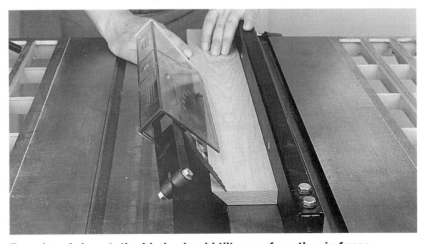

For a bevel rip cut, the blade should tilt away from the rip fence.

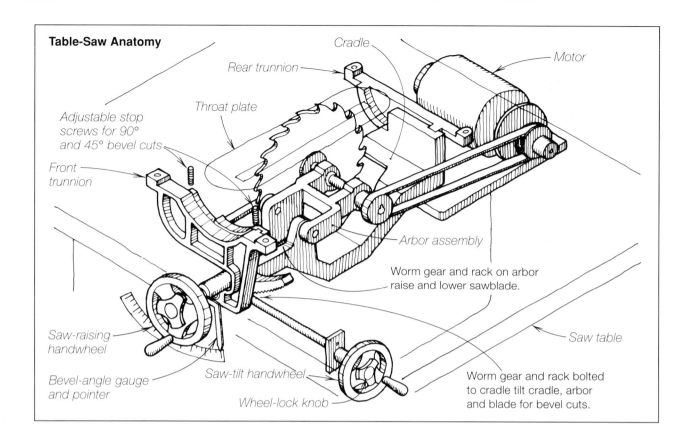

Table-Saw Anatomy

Cradle

Rear trunnion

Motor

Throat plate

Adjustable stop
screws for 90°
and 45° bevel cuts

Front
trunnion

Arbor assembly

Worm gear and rack on arbor
raise and lower sawblade.

Saw-raising
handwheel

Saw table

Bevel-angle gauge
and pointer

Saw-tilt handwheel

Worm gear and rack bolted
to cradle tilt cradle, arbor
and blade for bevel cuts.

Wheel-lock knob

Table-saw anatomy

The drawing above shows the internal components of a typical tilting-arbor table saw. The saw cradle (or carriage), trunnions and arbor assembly are bolted to the underside of the saw table. The cradle supports the arbor assembly, which holds the arbor. The arbor assembly consists of a shaft held in place by either sleeve bearings or ball bearings (the latter are far superior). The arbor has a pulley on one end for the V-belt, and the sawblade is secured by a flange and nut on the other end. The cradle also supports the motor, which is in the back of the saw on the contractor design and below the cradle on the cabinet saw.

Two trunnions, one at each end of the assembly, support and align the cradle and the motor. The semicircular trunnions make it possible for the cradle to be tilted for bevel cuts. Two crank wheels change the height and angle of the blade. The tilt wheel on the side of the saw adjusts the angle of the blade to the table. The tilt mechanism generally has a worm gear that engages a semicircular rack on the front trunnion. Two adjustable stop screws, which are usually set at 90° and 45°, limit the range of trunnion travel. Another handwheel at the front of the saw drives another worm gear, which pivots the arbor to raise and lower the blade.

Sawblades

No discussion of table-saw anatomy would be complete without mention of circular sawblades. The two largest categories of sawblades are carbide-tipped blades and high-carbon steel blades. At one time steel blades were the only choice for the table-saw owner. With the advent of tungsten carbide, steel blades have been virtually replaced in the woodshop except for a few specialized applications.

A sawblade with carbide teeth can cut smoothly up to 50 times longer between sharpenings when cutting hardwoods and up to 400 times longer when cutting man-made materials such as particleboard. The initial cost of a quality carbide blade is much higher than that of a steel blade, but this expense is offset by the blade's longevity, low maintenance and superior cutting performance. There are four common tooth grinds in sawblades and several blade configurations that combine different grinds.

Flat-top grind (FTG)   The flat-top grind, which has a flat face and a flat top, is primarily a rip tooth. Like a chisel, it cuts well with the grain and poorly across the grain. The rip blade generally has between 10 and 30 teeth, has deep gullets to eject the larger chips and takes more power to run than the other types of blades. The FTG is the blade to use if you have a lot of ripping to do quickly.

Alternate-top bevel (ATB)   The teeth on an ATB blade slice through wood like a knife by means of a steep bevel across the top of the tooth. The slicing action is good for crosscutting and keeps tearout to a minimum. The steeper the bevel, the sharper the cut; the less steep the bevel, the more general purpose the blade and the longer it stays sharp. A high-quality, 40-tooth ATB blade is good for both crosscutting and ripping. It is my favorite blade to use.

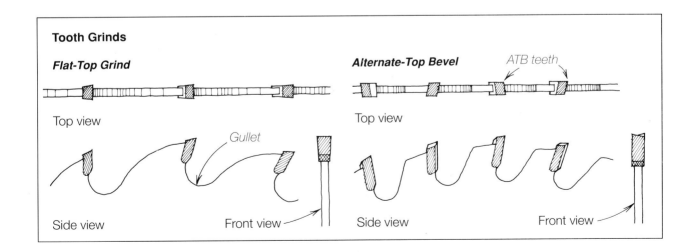

Tooth Grinds

Flat-Top Grind

Top view

Gullet

Side view

Front view

Alternate-Top Bevel

ATB teeth

Top view

Side view

Front view

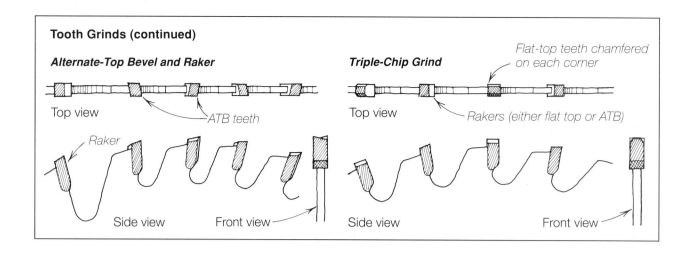

Tooth Grinds (continued)

Alternate-Top Bevel and Raker

Top view

ATB teeth

Raker

Side view   Front view

Triple-Chip Grind

Flat-top teeth chamfered
on each corner

Top view

Rakers (either flat top or ATB)

Side view   Front view

Alternate-top bevel and raker This blade is also commonly known as a combination blade because of the combination of ATB and raker (flat top) teeth. The general configuration is 4 ATB teeth and 1 raker tooth. On a 10-in. blade there are usually 10 sets or 50 teeth. The gullets are shallow for the ATB teeth and deep for the raker tooth. This general-purpose blade (used for both ripping and crosscutting) is probably the most commonly used blade in the woodshop.

Triple-chip grind This blade also uses a combination of two different tooth grinds: flat-top teeth that are chamfered on each corner and rakers that can be either ATB or flat top. The chamfered teeth are ground so as to be a little taller than the rakers. They plow a center cut, while the rakers clean up any tearout and establish the sides of the cut. Although this blade is fairly good on solid wood, I save it for cutting materials such as particleboard, aluminum and plastics.

Choosing a sawblade

A sawblade must be flat and stay stiff when in use. The body of the blade is cut or stamped from steel plate and then ground flat. (The appearance of that grind is a good indicator of quality: Cheaper blades are merely polished or ground quickly, whereas better blades will show finer circular grind marks from the arbor hole to the rim of the blade.) The gullets are ground to dimension; the teeth are bent and ground, or brazed carbide teeth are attached.

Given that the blade is spinning parallel to the fence and miter slots, the flatter the blade the smoother the cut and the quieter it will run. Any error in the blade causes runout. The arbor on the table saw invariably will have some runout, too. Sometimes the error in the blade and arbor can be minimized by placing the blade on the arbor at a place where the arbor runout cancels out the blade runout.

The arbor hole on the blade should fit as snugly as possible on the arbor. This snug fit helps the blade run true. Manufacturers can stamp an oversize hole more cheaply than they can ream a correct fit. If you look at the arbor hole of a lower-quality blade, you can see a metal lip or burr where the hole has been punched out.

A blade with more teeth is not necessarily better than a blade with fewer teeth. More important is to to use a blade with the optimum number of teeth for the job. Blades with many teeth become dull faster because they run hotter, cut more slowly and require more feed pressure. A blade with a lot of teeth may produce a smoother cut, but a smoother cut may not be necessary. For example, I usually joint the edges of my boards before gluing so the smoothness of the cut is not important. Ripping cuts require from 10 to no more than 40 teeth. Blades with more than 50 teeth are only necessary for smoothness when crosscutting or cutting plywood and man-made materials.

Tuning the table saw

With use, machinery always slips out of adjustment. The vibration of operation, the hammering of sawteeth against hickory or the slap of several hundred board feet of oak against the fence all take a toll on the accuracy of your table saw. Just moving the saw around in your shop can lose a critical few thousandths of an inch in accuracy. It is quite possible (even probable) that your saw was not properly tuned at the factory. Timely adjustments make big differences in your saw's performance and will be reflected in your work.

A well-tuned table saw exhibits the following characteristics:
• The saw arbor is solid and turns smoothly (without endplay or wobble).
• The table and the table extensions are flat.
• The cradle and the arbor assembly are secure while running and at rest.
• The table slots are parallel to the sawblade.
• The blade is at 90° to the table.
• The miter gauge is at 90° to the blade and the table.
• The rip fence is parallel to the blade and at 90° to the table.

Think of your table saw as a kit—it is your job to put it together correctly. The first step is to test the alignment of the various parts of the saw. It is very important that you go through this tune-up process in the proper sequence, because each step builds on the completion of the previous step.

Adjusting the table

Not too long ago, cast parts were well aged before machining, but manufacturers can no longer afford to age castings as long. As a result, warped table tops are more frequently found on new machines. A new saw should be checked for flatness with a straightedge and a flat, automotive-type feeler gauge as soon as you get it home. The table top should not be more than 1/32 in. out of level. You should recheck the saw every few months, but particularly while it is still under warranty.

If the saw is still under warranty, the simplest solution for a warped table top is to replace it. Filing, scraping and even belt sanding are other options if you have the skill. A friend of mine solved the problem by covering the low spot with epoxy paint and flattening it with a piece of glass. The paint didn't help the appearance of the saw, but the table top was perfectly flat. The most expensive solution is to have the top reground at a machine shop.

Check and adjust the saw's throat plate, or table insert, periodically. It should be a couple of thousandths of an inch lower than the saw table in front, and about the same amount higher in back. This slight difference in height prevents the workpiece from hitting the plate before the cut or binding on the table after it. Throat plates on some saws are

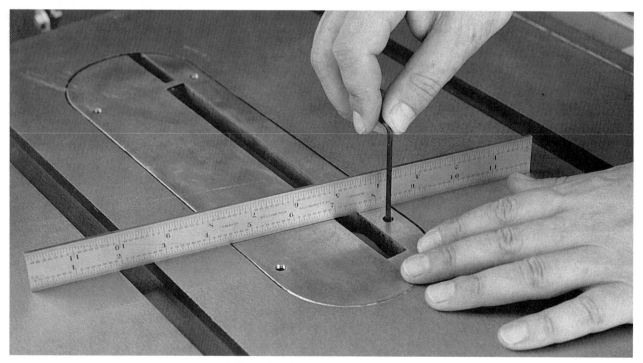

Adjust the throat-plate height by turning the leveling screws with a hex wrench.

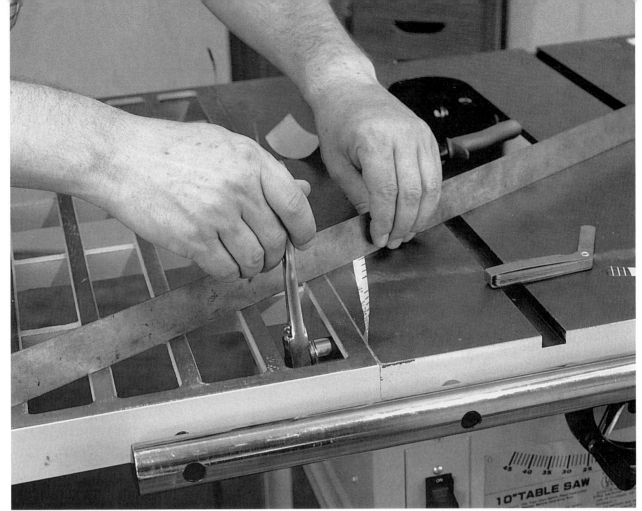

Check the extension alignment with a straightedge. Insert metal shim stock between the table and the extension to adjust.

drilled and tapped for Allen screws to allow adjustment of height. On saws without screws, you may have to file, tape or glue shims to change the level of the plate. If your adjustment screws vibrate loose, roughen the threads with a file.

Most saws have extensions attached to the table that expand the surface area of the table. They are usually cast iron or stamped sheet steel. The extension tables should be adjusted so that they are level with the table. Check the alignment with a straightedge. If the outside of the extension table is either too high or too low, insert a metal shim between the main table and the extension table. If you do not have any shim stock, cut up an aluminum soda can.

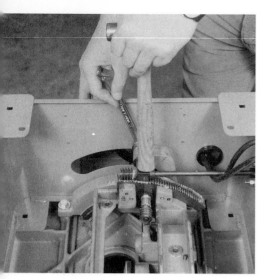

To remove backlash between the worm gear and rack on a Delta 10-in. tilting-arbor bench saw, use the handle of a hammer to press down on the block that supports the worm gear.

Adjusting the tilt mechanism

During both square and bevel cutting operations, the trunnions and cradle are ultimately responsible for keeping the sawblade running straight and true. Excess play in the tilt mechanism makes the whole cradle shift, causing the blade's angle to shift during the cut. This movement decreases the accuracy of the cut and increases the likelihood of kickback. You have a problem if the cut is square at the beginning of each cut but not at the end. The problem shows up even more with beveled cuts in thick stock.

The best check for cradle play is to feel for it. Unplug the saw. Turn the tilt mechanism until it is up against the 90° stop. Grab the motor and try to shake it back and forth. If the cradle is solid, make one more test. Tilt the saw to 70° and shake the motor again. It may be that the cradle is solid when it is against the 90° stop, but loose in the angled position. If the cradle is loose in either position, you need to work on your saw.

Depending on the design of your saw, there are several ways to adjust the tilt mechanism. If you have a contractor's saw, you have the option of removing the motor assembly and flipping it upside-down on a low table or blocks. Be sure to unplug the saw; you'll want to leave it unplugged for most of the tune-up. Now grab the cradle by the motor-mounting plate and wiggle it back and forth to determine the amount of play.

Most saws have a mechanism for getting the slop or backlash out of the tilt system. If you don't have an owner's manual, you should be able to figure out what kind of tilting mechanism your saw has by looking into the machine's interior. The most common tilting mechanism found on Delta, Powermatic and many Taiwanese clones relies on a worm gear and rack mechanism. With this design, the solidity of the cradle depends on the fit between the worm gear on the tilt mechanism and the rack on the front trunnion. Tightening the lock knob at the center of the tilt wheel only locks the position of the tilt mechanism—it doesn't tighten anything inside the saw. Although the basic design of the tilt mechanism is shared by many saws, there are several ways to snug up the fit between the worm and rack gear.

Before making an adjustment of the saw, clean the worm gear and rack with a dry rag. After cleaning be sure to lubricate all mating surfaces of moving parts. Make sure you get the front and back ends of the cradle and the trunnions. Manufacturers lubricate with oil or grease, but these collect dust. The best lubricant is silicone, Teflon® or graphite.

On most contractor's saws, reducing backlash is a matter of pivoting the tilt-adjustment wheel's shaft. Loosen the two screws that hold the tilt wheel's mounting plate to the outside of the saw housing and shift the wheel downward. A fulcrum inside the saw forces the worm gear up against the teeth on the bottom of the front trunnion, creating a tighter fit. Once you make the adjustment, tilt the blade a couple of times to make sure the tilt mechanism operates smoothly. If it doesn't, the gears may fit too snugly, which can cause premature wear. In this case, loosen the backlash adjustment a little.

On some saws, such as the Delta 10-in. tilting-arbor bench saw, there's no fulcrum mechanism for moving the gear and the rack closer together. On these machines a locknut secures the position of the block that houses the worm-gear shaft. By loosening the locknut and pressing down on the block, backlash is reduced.

Boice-Crane and some Sears models have a separate tilt lock that clamps the front trunnion and the cradle together. Once the angle of the blade has been set with the tilt wheel, a spring-loaded handle (similar to a ratchet) on the front of the saw locks the front trunnion and cradle. On these saws, gear mesh isn't crucial and requires no adjustment because the trunnion-lock handle secures the cradle. Remember to loosen the lock before changing the blade angle and then retighten. Note that tightening the lock can change the blade angle slightly, so recheck the blade angle after the lock is tightened.

On most cabinet saws, such as the Powermatic 66, an adjustment bolt on the front of the saw moves the worm gear into the rack on the trunnion. On Shopsmith saws, some Inca saws and most older saws, the table tilts instead of the blade for angle cuts.

Not all saws have an adjustment to make the cradle solid. Even after adjusting, the saw cradle may still have play after the gear mesh has been set and/or the tilt lock has been tightened. In this case, clamp a small C-clamp or Vise-grip®-type adjustable wrench as a homemade trunnion lock to secure the cradle to the rear trunnion, as shown in the photo above. A word of caution: Vibration may loosen the clamp, so make sure it can't fall into the belt or pulley. After adding the clamp, recheck the blade angle to ensure that the locking action didn't change it. Once you've made these adjustments and are satisfied with the firmness of the cradle, you're ready to flip the saw back over and perform the remaining adjustments from the top of the saw.

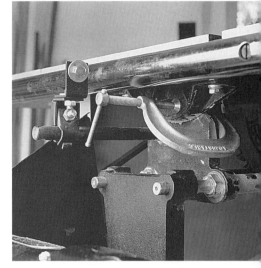

Make the cradle more secure by clamping the back trunnion and cradle together. Make sure the clamp cannot loosen and fall into the belt or pulley.

Adjusting the raising mechanism

The raising worm gear and the teeth on the arbor-assembly bracket wear slightly over time. Some saws have a provision for making an adjustment to remove this play. The adjustment is usually a nut that is located behind the saw-raising handwheel. Consult your owner's manual.

Check the squareness of the blade and table. Take this measurement on the side of the table with the least amount of insert.

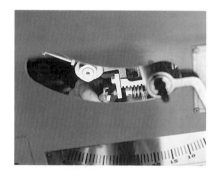

On cabinet-style saws, adjust the trunnion stop screw through the slot in the front of the saw.

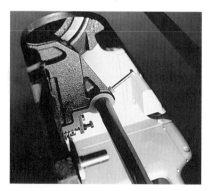

The stop screw on the contractor's saw is at the end of the front trunnion. It is often easiest to reach the stop from the back of the saw.

Squaring the blade

The next step in the tune-up process is to square the blade to the table. Release the saw's tilt lock and remove the rear trunnion clamp, if you're using one. Raise the blade as high as it will go. Check the blade's squareness with a reliable, high-quality metal or plastic square. (Avoid wooden squares because their accuracy changes with heat and humidity.) Place the blade of the square vertically against the saw-blade, making sure you're not on a tooth, and look for a gap between the square and blade. Put the handle of the square on the side of the table that has the least amount of space between the blade and the table edge. This gives the most accurate reading of the surface of the table and the blade. Turn the saw's tilt-adjustment handwheel until the gap of light between the blade and the square disappears. Don't force it. If the blade won't tilt far enough, you may have to loosen the stop screw. Next, secure the cradle with the trunnion lock or clamp, as described on p. 13, and recheck the blade for squareness.

Now that the blade is square, adjust the stop for 90°. Once again, make sure the saw is unplugged and consult your manual. On some saws tilt stops are screws that are accessible through the saw top, but on most saws you'll have to reach up under the saw to loosen the locknut and screw the stop in or out. On cabinet saws the stops are usually accessible through the opening behind the blade-raising wheel through the side door or table-insert hole. On contractor's saws the stop may be accessible from the front, but it may be easiest to reach the stop from the back or under the saw.

Ideally, the blade should reach 90° just as you feel resistance at the tilt wheel, which is a sign that the trunnion is hitting the stop. Never apply excess pressure in an effort to square the blade. If the blade goes past 90°, reset the stop. Even after the stop is set perfectly, don't depend on it; for critical cuts recheck with an accurate square. (It's a good idea to keep an accurate square just for squaring up equipment.)

Follow the same procedure for setting the 45° stop, but use an inexpensive plastic triangle for checking the angle. An adjustable drafting square or a bevel gauge is handy for setting blade angles other than 45° or 90°.

Finally, realign the pointer on the front of the saw. This adjustment makes the angle scale fairly accurate for setting bevel cuts quickly. Never assume that the angle scale is precise, however. To set the saw accurately, always check angles with a square, a bevel gauge or an adjustable drafting square against the blade.

Check the 45° setting on your saw with a plastic triangle. Once the saw is at the correct angle, adjust the saw stop (if there is one).

Once the blade is square to the table, set the pointer on the saw-angle scale. On most saws, you have to remove the saw-raising handwheel to make the adjustment.

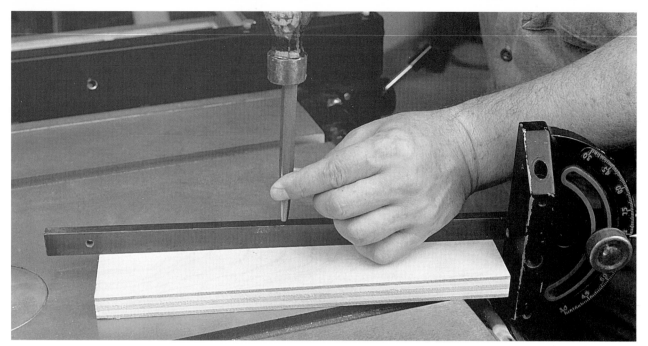

If the miter bar is loose in the slot, expand it slightly by dimpling the bar with a sharp center punch or prick punch.

Adjusting the miter gauge

The miter-gauge bar usually fits too loosely in the slot of the saw table to yield accurate crosscuts. To adjust the bar to fit more snugly, dimple the side of the bar with a center or prick punch. The dimples expand the metal around each indentation, effectively making the bar wider. Dimple only on the side of the bar nearest the blade every inch or so. Stagger the dimples width-wise on the bar so they won't wear a groove in the side of the slot.

When you're finished, the bar should slide smoothly along the length of the slot without hanging up. There should be a minimal amount of side-to-side play. Check the fit in the table slot you use most often; most right-handed people put the miter gauge in the left slot for crosscutting. Unless the slots on your saw are identical, the bar probably won't fit as well in both slots. If the dimples in any one area cause the bar to stick in the slot, smooth them with a flat mill file. Use a non-silicone wax to lubricate the table slot and the bar. (Silicone wax may transfer to the workpiece and later cause finishing problems.)

Squaring the miter head

Next, square the head of the miter gauge perpendicular to its bar. I like to lay pennies in the miter-gauge slot to elevate the bar slightly. Simply loosen the lock knob on the protractor head, butt the handle of an accurate square against the bar of the miter gauge and align the protractor head with the blade of the square. Be sure you don't square against the edge with the dimples in it. Tighten the gauge's lock screw/handle and set the adjustment screw on the 90° stop if your miter gauge has one. Don't trust these stops for fine work though. Like the tilt stops, they're not always perfectly accurate, and the setting should be frequently rechecked with an accurate square.

On some saws you can flip the miter gauge upside-down and press the head against the front of the saw; this is convenient, but it may not be accurate. Although you may be tempted to square the miter head to the sawblade, don't do it. You won't get accurate crosscuts unless the miter slot and the blade are parallel to each other, and we haven't checked that alignment yet.

Checking arbor runout

The foundation of the table saw is the arbor. With the exception of the wobble dado head, which is sometimes affectionately called a drunken saw because it wobbles to and fro, visible wobbling in a sawblade spells disaster. Most runout problems are small in magnitude, but no less important. You can't see 0.015-in. runout in a blade spinning at 3,450 rpm, but you will certainly notice it in your work.

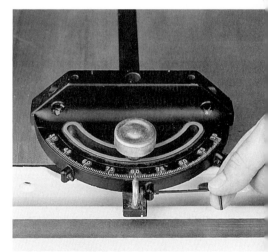

After squaring the miter head, adjust the stop and recheck.

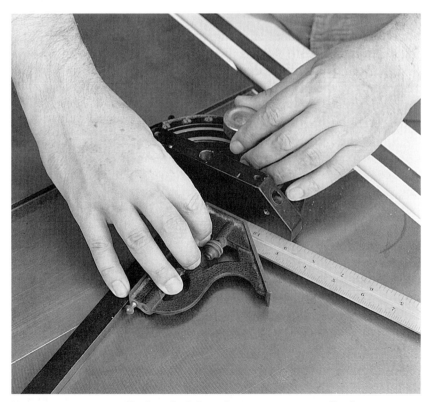

Use a square to set the head of the miter gauge perpendicular to its bar.

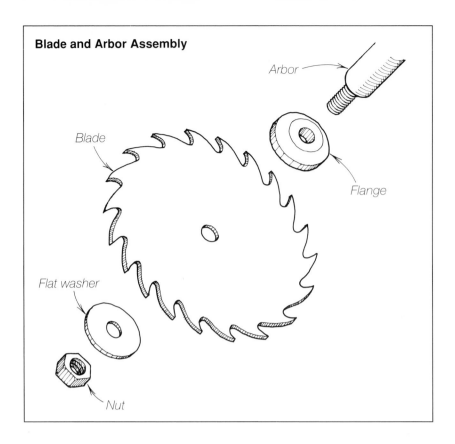

Blade and Arbor Assembly

Arbor

Blade

Flange

Flat washer

Nut

The problem of runout is complex. The blade is clamped to a flange by the arbor nut and a washer. The arbor spins supported by two bearings, which are held in place by the arbor assembly. This whole assembly has to run precisely true to the table, fence and miter slots through the saw's full range of blade angle and height adjustments. Runout causes the blade to cut a wider kerf than the width of the blade. It increases blade wear, vibration and inaccuracy, and it degrades surface quality. A slight amount of runout is normal, but it should never exceed 0.012 in. on a 10-in. blade.

Since runout is inevitable if the bearings are loose or worn or if the arbor is bent or worn, you should check these parts first. Check by trying to wiggle the arbor shaft. If it's loose or moves in or out, it needs repair or adjustment. Rotate the shaft by hand. If it turns smoothly, the bearings are probably acceptable. However, if the shaft is rough or difficult to turn or if you hear any noise or feel resistance, the bearings should be replaced. If the arbor is in good shape (that is, the threads are okay and the shaft is not bent or scored), you can get by just by replacing the bearings. When the arbor is bent or damaged in some other way, it should also be replaced. Check for a bent arbor by rolling it on a flat surface.

A less obvious cause of runout is a slight imperfection in the arbor or flange. I recently fixed a serious persistent runout problem just by locating and filing a flaw on the flange rim. A dirty flange can also cause runout.

It's possible to replace the shaft, flange or bearings yourself, especially if you have mechanical experience. Buy new parts from the manufacturer. If you have an old saw and the arbor or flange is no longer available, any competent machinist can make a new one for you. There's a good chance that your neighborhood bearing-supply house will stock exactly the size bearing you need, too. But some bearings can be difficult to remove, in which case it may be better to take the whole assembly to a machine shop or bearing house.

A dial indicator is handy for checking runout in the arbor, flange and blade. To check runout in the flange, secure the dial-indicator base on the table and adjust the indicator so that the contact point is slightly depressed against the outer edge of the flange. Adjust the indicator to 0 and rotate the arbor. The flange and the arbor should be out of true by no more than 0.003 in. Check blade runout with the dial indicator on the blade blank, not on the teeth. Test for runout at eight locations around the blade. Reset the contact point for each reading.

Use a dial indicator to check for runout on the flange. Ideally, runout should be less than 0.003 in.

The dial indicator can also be used to check for runout on the blade. Set the dial indicator against the blade blank, not the teeth.

In all probability, the runout in your saw is an accumulation of small errors in the arbor assembly and the blade. It's very likely that the blade is dished or has a bend in it. Sometimes you can eliminate much of the runout just by rotating the blade to a different location on the arbor.

I've devised a method for measuring runout that does not require use of a dial indicator. My low-tech method involves four sets of four observations. The objective is to find the location with the least runout. Make a checklist like the one shown on p. 22 to record your results. The most runout occurs when inaccuracies of the blade and the saw are combined, as shown at A in the drawing below. The least runout occurs when arbor and blade imperfections nearly cancel each other out (D in the drawing). There are two combinations between the worst- and the best-case scenarios when the blade and arbor imperfections are moderate, as shown at B and C in the drawing.

My low-tech method gives me a reading of the actual amount of runout at the outside edge of the blade. Here's how it works: Raise the blade as high as it will go. Clamp a small piece of wood (say, a piece 1x3x15) to the miter head and crosscut it. Unplug the saw. Now rotate the blade (with the belt) against the freshly cut piece of wood. Listen carefully when the teeth touch the wood. If the sound remains the same as the blade rotates, there is no runout. Usually, there will be one point in the rotation where the sound is the loudest. This is where the saw teeth rub hardest against the sawn surface. I call this the high spot. Using a felt-tip pen, mark the high spot with the numeral "1." (If you are using a dial indicator, mark the high spot in the same way.) Remove the throat plate and mark the corner of the arbor on the same side as the mark on the blade. Then mark the numerals 2, 3 and 4 around the blade at 90° intervals.

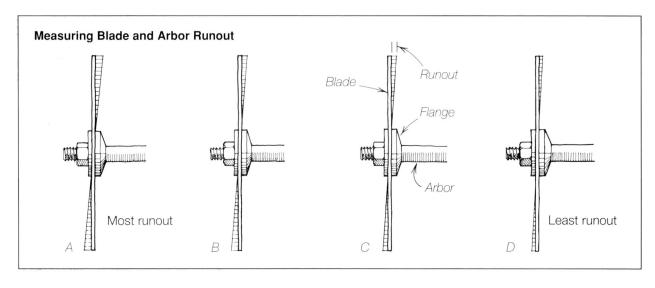

Measuring Blade and Arbor Runout

Blade — Runout

Flange

Arbor

A — Most runout
B
C
D — Least runout

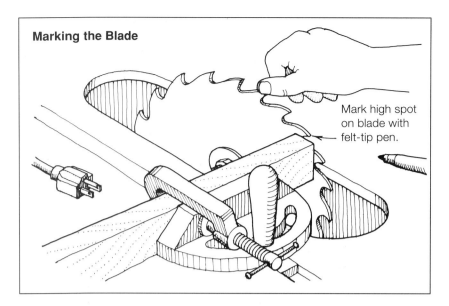

Marking the Blade

Mark high spot on blade with felt-tip pen.

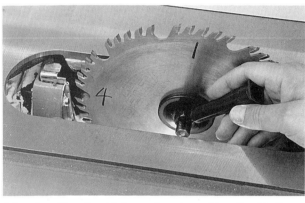

After locating the high spot and marking it with the numeral '1,' mark the blade with the numerals 2, 3 and 4 at 90° intervals.

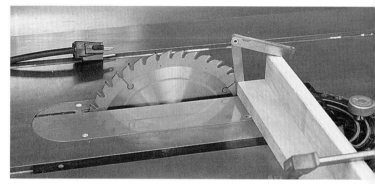

The edge of the board marks the high spot. The difference between the low spot on the blade and the board is the amount of runout. Measure this distance with a feeler gauge.

Now check the blade for the amount of runout. You've already established 1 as the high spot or 0.000, so rotate the blade to each of the other numerals and take a reading. If you use a dial indicator, retract the probe each time you rotate the blade. If you use the low-tech method, rotate the blade to each numeral and insert the appropriate blade of an automotive-type feeler gauge between the wood and the saw tooth. Note the amount of runout for each numeral on the checklist shown on p. 22.

The amount of runout is the difference between the high spot and the low spot. The greatest amount of runout will usually be opposite the high spot (numeral 3 in this case), but this is not always the case with a warped blade.

In Test A (see the drawing below) the alignment of the 1 on the blade with the mark on the arbor corresponds to one of the four possible scenarios shown in the drawing on p. 20. For Test B loosen the blade and rotate the blade 90° so that the mark on the arbor is aligned with the numeral 2. Tighten the blade and measure and record the runout at each of the four numerals on the blade on the checklist. If you are using a dial indicator, check the runout at 1, 2, 3 and 4. If you are using the low-tech method, turn the saw on and make another cut. The sawblade may or may not cut the wood. If the blade does not touch the wood during the test, it means that there is less runout than in Test A. If the blade cuts the wood, there is more runout than in Test A. In either case, unplug the saw and test positions 1, 2, 3 and 4 with a feeler

Checklist for Measuring Runout					
	Measurement at position				
	1	2	3	4	Runout
Test A					
Test B					
Test C					
Test D					

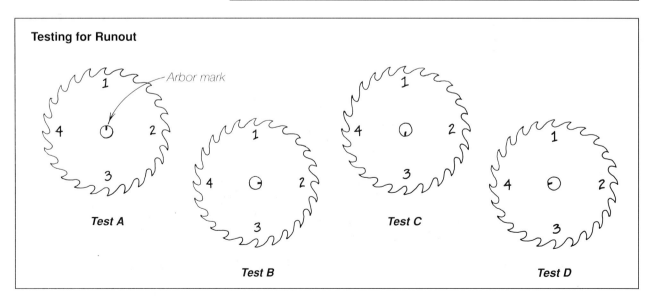

Testing for Runout

Arbor mark

Test A

Test B

Test C

Test D

gauge. Record the results on the checklist. Repeat the procedures for Tests C and D and record your results. Remember that you have to record all of the combinations even when there is less runout than in Test A.

When the four tests are complete, analyze your results to determine which combination causes the most runout. Ideally, runout will have been caused by a combination of the blade and the saw-arbor assembly. If the numeral 1 on the blade is always the high spot, your blade is bent and that could be the only problem. Try the test with another blade. If the high spot always corresponds to the mark on the arbor, it means that the saw assembly is the biggest cause of your problem. In that case, if the runout is more than 0.03 in. in all of the four test positions, you need a new arbor or new flange, and most probably both.

If you have a bent blade, you may want to use a dampener, which is a piece of heat-treated machined steel that rests next to the blade. The dampener stiffens the blade and gives it extra support. It decreases the bend or dishing of the blade.

One of the problem areas with modern table saws is the flange. On top-quality saws the flange is a large machined piece of steel that fits snugly on the arbor; it can be replaced independent of the arbor. On most American saws, however, the arbor and the flange are a unit. Most flanges are pressed onto the arbor, and you have to remove the arbor assembly to change the flange. In certain situations a dampener fitted on each side of the blade can make up for shortcomings of a small flange. Adding a dampener may require adjustments to the throat plate and recalibration of the fence scale. It is imperative that the mating surfaces of the flange and blade be as clean as possible.

A dampener fitted next to the blade on the arbor helps reduce runout and limits the depth of the saw cut.

Aligning the blade to the miter slots

For your table saw to crosscut accurately, the blade must be parallel to the miter slot. When the blade and the slot aren't parallel, the sawblade "heels" and has a tendency to recut the workpiece at the back of the blade. This double cut is not only inaccurate but also dangerous because the back of the sawblade can lift the binding workpiece and cause kickback.

The first step in adjustment is to test the saw's alignment. To do this, you can use a dial indicator or a combination square, but as with checking for runout, I think the best reading comes directly from a real saw cut. Raise the blade as high as it will go and clamp a piece of wood to the miter gauge; a 1x3x15 piece of common pine is plenty big enough. Crosscut the test piece and unplug the saw. Now, slide the miter gauge with the test piece still clamped to it next to the front of the sawblade. Rotate the blade by hand-turning the belt or using a motor pulley. Don't grab the blade because your hand may deflect it.

As you rotate the blade, one or two teeth will rub against the wood the hardest, making the loudest sound. Mark those teeth and slide the test piece to the back of the blade. The same teeth that rubbed against the

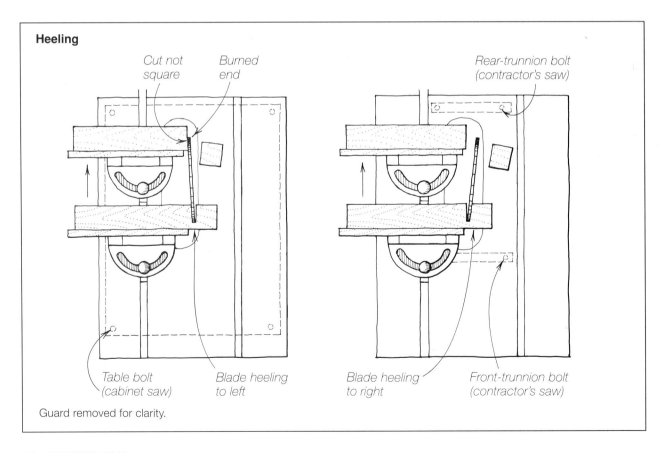

Heeling

Cut not square

Burned end

Rear-trunnion bolt (contractor's saw)

Table bolt (cabinet saw)

Blade heeling to left

Blade heeling to right

Front-trunnion bolt (contractor's saw)

Guard removed for clarity.

To test the alignment of the blade to the miter slot, rotate the blade against a test piece clamped to the miter gauge. If the blade is parallel to the slot, the board will make the same sound against the blade at the front and back positions.

workpiece at the front should rub against it at the back, making the same sound. You may want to move the piece to the front and back several times to test the sound. If the sound is the same, the table slot and the blade are in alignment and you will not have to make any adjustments. If you get a louder or softer sound at the front than at the back, the distance between the blade and the slot will have to be increased or decreased accordingly.

Realigning the blade parallel to the miter slot is fairly straightforward. On contractor's saws you simply rotate the trunnions relative to the table. Most contractor's saws have four bolts, two in front and two in back, that secure the trunnions to the underside of the table. On cabinet saws the saw table is usually secured directly to the saw's shell or frame, and the adjustment is made by changing the table position. In either case, the bolts must be loosened on the trunnion or the table. Leave one of the front bolts a bit snug so that it acts as a pivot point. Also, the trunnion lock (if your saw has one) should be tightened and the back trunnion should be clamped, as described on p. 13, to keep the two trunnions in alignment during the operation. If you do not have a trunnion lock on your table saw, clamp the front trunnion to the cradle if possible. The objective is to rotate the cradle and both trunnions as a unit.

To realign the blade with the miter slot, loosen the bolts on the trunnion or the table with a ratchet and extension. Keep one bolt snug to act as a pivot point.

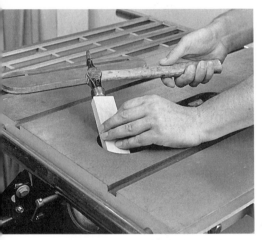

To rotate the trunnion/cradle assembly on a contractor's saw, tap a wooden wedge between the trunnion and the frame. Use the trunnion lock if your saw has one.

On some saws the throat-plate slot allows access to the back trunnion. Insert a piece of wood to cushion the blow of the hammer.

To rotate the trunnion assembly on the contractor's saw, drive a wooden wedge between the trunnion and the table casting at the back of the saw, as shown in the photo at left. This is the most civilized method, but if there isn't room for a wedge, you can use a prybar or a rubber mallet to move the trunnion. If the mallet isn't effective, try a hammer. Don't hammer directly on the saw or you could crack the castings; put a piece of wood on the trunnion and pound the wood. You may have luck using a piece of wood against the trunnion through the table-saw slot.

Make a slight adjustment and slide the test piece by the blade as you did earlier. Keep rotating the trunnions until the sawblade bears against the test piece and sounds the same at the front and back. When you are satisfied, tighten the bolts, plug in the saw and make another test cut. It may take several attempts, but stay calm and take your time. Once the slot in the top is aligned with the blade, you should, theoretically, be able to crosscut with the miter gauge in either slot. Unfortunately, it's my experience that the slots in many saws aren't perfectly parallel to each other. Pick the slot you use most often to make the final test cut.

Rip-fence alignment

For virtually all rip cuts the work must be guided by the rip fence. In theory, the rip fence is perfectly parallel to the blade. If it is out of parallel, the workpiece will wedge between the back of the blade and the fence or you'll constantly rip tapers. In practice, it's best if the fence is slightly canted away from the back of the blade. This prevents the wood from binding between the blade and the fence, particularly if the workpiece warps slightly as it is ripped.

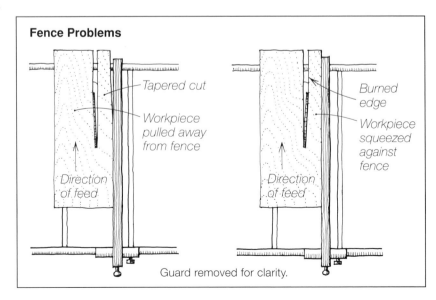

Fence Problems

Tapered cut

Workpiece pulled away from fence

Direction of feed

Burned edge

Workpiece squeezed against fence

Direction of feed

Guard removed for clarity.

Adjust the angle of the rip fence after loosening the two bolts on the top of the fence.

Position the miter gauge with the test piece at the front of the saw and bring the rip fence in contact with the board. Lock the fence.

Set the rip fence slightly wider at the back of the blade to prevent binding. Insert a feeler gauge between the board and the rip fence at the back of the saw to gauge the amount of clearance.

To set the rip fence, take the same test piece you used to check for crosscut alignment. Lower the sawblade below the table. Loosen the bolts that lock your fence's angle relative to the guide rail, then move the miter gauge with the test piece to the front of the saw and lock the rip fence against it. Tighten the bolts, but not all the way. Allow for slight movement of the back end fence with firm pressure. Then, slide the test piece until it's over the back of the saw's throat plate. There should be about 0.015 in. (about 1/64 in.) clearance between the piece and the fence. To gauge the amount of clearance, slide a feeler gauge or a dollar bill folded over twice between the fence and the test piece. Finally, tighten the fence bolts and recheck the settings before making a test cut.

Feedback from the workpiece

Once you've tuned your table saw, get into the habit of checking its accuracy often, particularly when you have an important job that requires great precision or when you've had to move the saw. This accuracy check takes only a few seconds and a single cut on a scrap of wood. Just clamp a test piece to the miter gauge. Before making the cut, mark the piece with an X where the cut will be made. After the cut, unclamp the piece and put the two halves back together the way they were before the cut. They should fit perfectly. Now, flip one piece so that it faces the opposite direction and match the two pieces back together, as shown in the drawing below. This test determines whether the blade is square to the table. The saw cut should match as well as it did before the piece was reversed. Any error that is present will be doubled.

Next rotate both pieces 90° so that they lie on the adjacent side. This tests the squareness of the miter gauge to the blade. Here again, any error will be doubled. The test piece also shows the direction in which you'll need to make corrections, as well as how much of an adjustment is needed.

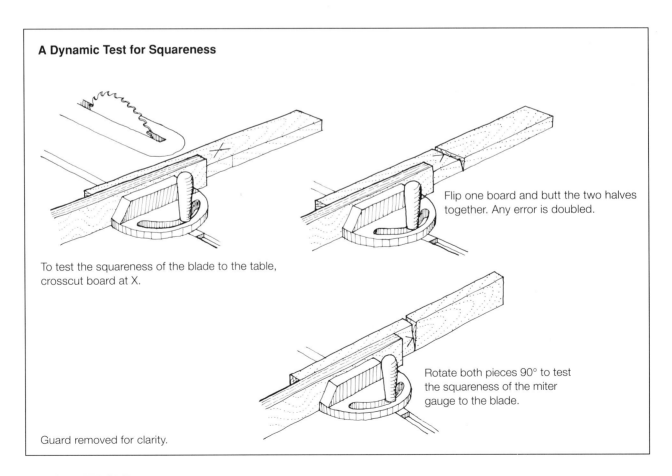

A Dynamic Test for Squareness

To test the squareness of the blade to the table, crosscut board at X.

Flip one board and butt the two halves together. Any error is doubled.

Rotate both pieces 90° to test the squareness of the miter gauge to the blade.

Guard removed for clarity.

Safety equipment

Table saws have a bad reputation for safety. Statistics show that the table saw is the most dangerous machine in the workshop, and there's no doubt that any accident on it is perilous. I'm constantly searching for ways to minimize shop dangers. For example, although you can shape on the table saw with a molding head, I choose not to. One of my agreements with my fingers is that I shape only on the shaper or router. As you gain experience working wood with machines, you'll soon decide which operations are not for you. Respect your decisions, and either design a way to make the operations safer or approach the problem in a different way.

Manufacturers spend hundreds of thousands of dollars and years in research developing guards and accessories to make their machines safer. Some of this safety equipment is discussed on the pages that follow. Remember, however, that no guard is a guarantee of safety—your vigilance is always your best safety equipment.

The splitter

Wood is unpredictable. While a tree is growing, stresses (tension and compression) develop in its woody tissues. Drying also causes stresses. You won't be able to see these pressures, but as you saw, the wood may change form and distort. You'll find that the thicker the stock, the greater the problem.

Stresses in wood are relieved anytime you cut wood, but particularly when ripping. Then, one of three things can happen. One possibility is that the wood will keep its shape during the saw cut and the resulting two pieces will remain straight. This causes no particular safety hazard because the wood is not binding against the fence or the blade. Alternatively, the release of tension inside the workpiece can cause it to spread apart during the saw cut. The wood binds against the fence and the blade. (This problem can be diminished by using a shorter fence when cutting solid stock, thereby giving the wood a place to spread after the cut.) A third possibility is that the forces of compression inside the wood cause it to close back together after the cut, pinching the back of the blade. As the pressure on the back of the blade increases, kickback becomes more likely.

To help solve kickback problems caused by wood pinching the sawblade as it is ripped, table saws are equipped with a splitter, a thin piece of metal directly behind the sawblade. If the wood shuts after the cut, it pinches the splitter rather than the back of the blade, thus keeping the kerf open.

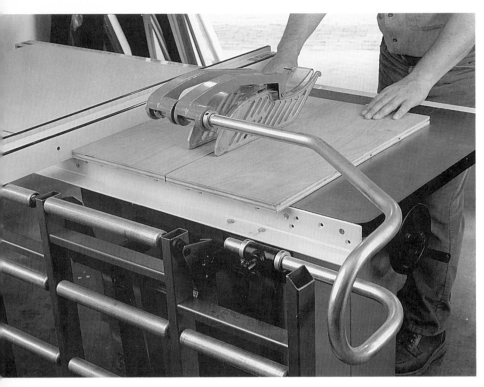

The Delta Uniguard (left), which features a retractable splitter (above), is a European-style overhead guard.

Most guards incorporate a toothed antikickback mechanism. Make sure that this piece swings back freely and is not bent or damaged.

There are two designs for splitters. One type of splitter, a small piece of metal attached to the back trunnion, is independent of the guard. Independent splitters are common features on European saws and are often found on machines with overhead guards. The Delta Uniguard is similar to this European standard and also features an independent splitter. On some European saws a guard is mounted on top of the splitter. The second type of splitter incorporates the splitter into the guard. This is the most common type of splitter found on American table saws.

The saw guard

Most table saws sold in North America are equipped with a cage guard, which is a see-through plastic or metal guard with a sheet-metal spine. The metal spine also serves as the splitter. It is connected to the saw in two places, behind the saw and to the back trunnion, which allows the guard to tilt when the blade is tilted. A toothed antikickback mechanism swings backward over the workpiece.

This type of guard offers a high degree of protection, but it is unwieldy in some situations. It's hard to rip narrow pieces, or slide a push stick past the guard if the fence is close to the blade. Sometimes, when you are crosscutting thick stock, the piece will wedge under the antikickback fingers and it will be difficult to pull it backwards after the cut.

Also, the cage guard must be removed if an incomplete cut such as a dado or rabbet is made, and it's time-consuming to replace. Because of these drawbacks, guards are often left off the saw, in spite of the operator's and manufacturer's best intentions.

Adjusting the guard and the splitter

The guard and splitter must be perfectly adjusted or they will be difficult and dangerous in operation. The flange, splitter and guard bracket must lie in the same plane as the blade. Check this alignment as shown in the photo at right. If the front of the guard bracket does not line up with the flange, readjust the cradle bracket at the back of the table hole.

Lay the sheet-metal cage flat on the saw table to make sure that it isn't warped or bent. Mount the guard, leaving the adjustment nut on the back support loose. Check the alignment of the blade and the guard plate using a straightedge, then make the final adjustment of the back support and tighten the guard in place. Finally, check that the guard is square to the table.

Optional guards

Some manufacturers make high-quality guards to retrofit older machines. Most of these guards are similar to the suspended European design. The Biesemeyer guard, for example, is a suspended guard that has an alarm that rings if the guard is not in place during a saw cut. The

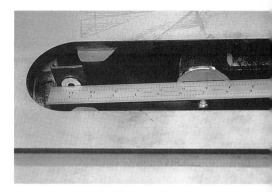

To work properly, the guard bracket must be perfectly aligned with the flange. Check this alignment with a straightedge.

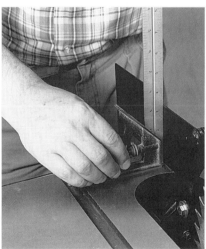

Tighten the front bolt first when attaching the guard (left). Check to make sure that the guard plate is square to the table (above).

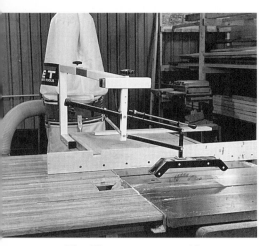

The Biesemeyer guard is an overhead guard with an alarm system.

Brett guard is clear plastic and also functions as a hold-down. Both of these auxiliary guards can also be wired into the switch, so that you can't start the saw if the guard isn't in place. One design features a guard suspended from the ceiling. Ceiling-mounted guards are typically found in industrial settings where the huge table saws are permanently positioned.

Using the rip fence

The rip fence is a straightedge aligned parallel to the blade. The distance between the blade and the fence, which is adjustable, determines the width the workpiece will be cut to. To rip safely and accurately, the workpiece must lie flat on the table with a straight edge against the rip fence. If the edge is not straight, joint it straight before making the cut or make a jig to hold the wood securely while making a straight cut. One option is to screw or nail a wood straightedge to the workpiece (as shown in the drawing on p. 191). If the wood is not flat,

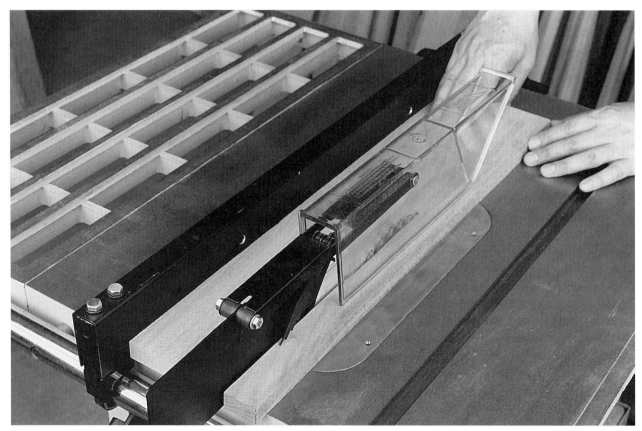

The workpiece remains in contact with the fence during ripping. The rip cut proceeds with the grain.

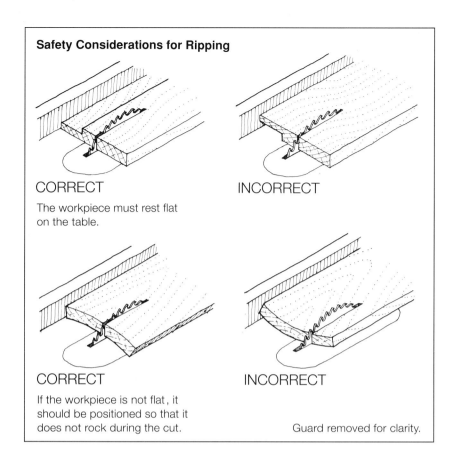

Safety Considerations for Ripping

CORRECT

The workpiece must rest flat on the table.

INCORRECT

CORRECT

If the workpiece is not flat, it should be positioned so that it does not rock during the cut.

INCORRECT

Guard removed for clarity.

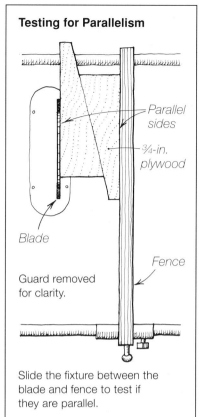

Testing for Parallelism

Parallel sides

¾-in. plywood

Blade

Guard removed for clarity.

Fence

Slide the fixture between the blade and fence to test if they are parallel.

face-joint it to establish a flat surface or position the workpiece so that it doesn't rock during the saw cut. Never rip a badly twisted board because it will bind and may kick back. Sometimes you can salvage a badly twisted piece of wood by cutting it into smaller lengths.

To ensure that the fence locks parallel to the blade, always adjust the fence toward the blade rather than away from it. Apply pressure on the front of the fence before it is locked in place. Periodically check the alignment of the fence and the blade with a ruler. Measure the distance between the blade and the fence at the front of the blade and then at the back of the blade. The distance should be no more than ¼₄ in. greater at the back of the blade.

A faster and more accurate way to check whether the blade and fence are parallel is with sliding wedges (see the drawing at right above). Take a piece of plywood with parallel sides and cut it at a 70° angle. Slide the two pieces between the fence and the blade to test for parallelism. It is good to have different sizes for different workpiece widths. Make one pair of wedges for each of the following widths: 6 in., 9 in., 12 in. and 18 in. On cutting widths wider than 18 in. you can use more

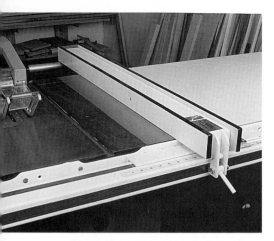

Replacement fences have large front rails and wide T-fences that maintain consistent alignment.

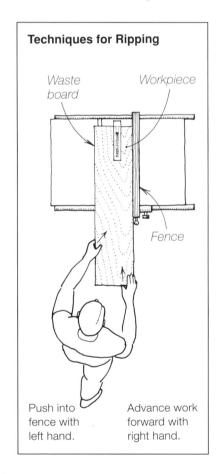

Techniques for Ripping

Waste board

Workpiece

Fence

Push into fence with left hand.

Advance work forward with right hand.

than one pair of wedges. Although there is a plastic device on the market that does the same thing, this is one accessory you can easily make yourself and it will work better too.

The standard fence that comes with your saw is probably the best possible compromise between economy, safety and performance. In the early 1980s, Bill Biesemeyer of Mesa, Arizona, manufactured the first replacement rip fence, and there are now a number of different models available. Replacement fences are heavier and stiffer than standard fences. They have large front rails and wide T-fences that maintain consistent alignment. On some cabinet saws these fences are now standard equipment.

Ripping

Before making either a rip cut or a crosscut, raise the blade so that the highest sawtooth is positioned about ¼ in. above the work. With carbide-tipped blades, all of the highest carbide tooth should be above the work. The guard should be in place and functional.

Most woodworkers prefer to work with the fence on the right side, so the text and illustrations show it in that position. If you prefer to rip with the fence on the left side of the blade, reverse the arrangement. Never stand in line with the sawblade. Stand to the side of the saw opposite the fence. Push the work along the fence applying side and forward pressure, holding the work with both hands initially. Apply forward pressure on the workpiece with your right hand and sideways pressure against the fence with your left. As you near completion of the cut, continue to push the workpiece past the blade with your right hand, but remove your left hand from the work. I like to put my left hand on my hip.

It is a good idea to have the pushing hand in contact with the fence if the workpiece is wider than 3 in. (Some people prefer to hook a couple of fingers over the fence.) The fence provides a safe path past the front and back of the blade. The left hand should not touch the waste board at the completion of the cut, and you should never reach past the front of the blade with your left hand. Resist the temptation to try to control the workpiece or the waste piece at the back of the blade, too. Many accidents happen when a person fumbles with the wood at the conclusion of a cut and a kickback pulls their hand into the back of the blade.

Long boards must be supported at the back of the table saw. A support keeps the board from falling off the back of the table or from binding between the blade, guard or fence. Stand-alone roller units and fold-down roller systems that attach to the back of the saw are available. Auxiliary tables are good options, too, if you have the floor space. Both rollers and auxiliary tables are commercially available or you can build your own. The simplest solution is a plywood auxiliary table on a pair of sawhorses.

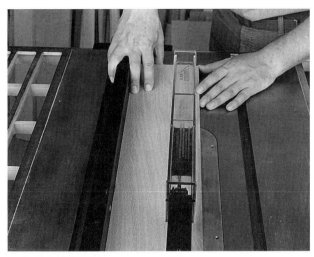

The fence provides a safe path past the front and the back of the blade if the board is wider than about 3 in. Note that the operator has looped two fingers over the fence for additional safety.

As the cut nears completion, the hand at the fence continues to push the workpiece while the other hand is placed on the operator's hip or in a pocket.

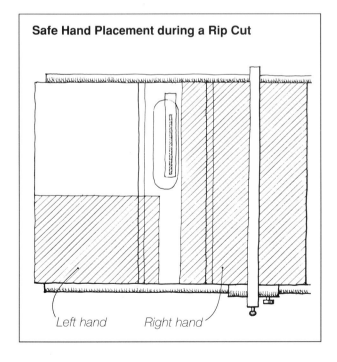

Safe Hand Placement during a Rip Cut

Left hand   Right hand

Commercially built or home-made auxiliary tables greatly enlarge the table-saw surface.

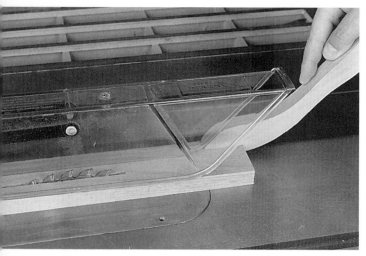

Use a push stick if the distance between the blade and the rip fence is less than 3 in.

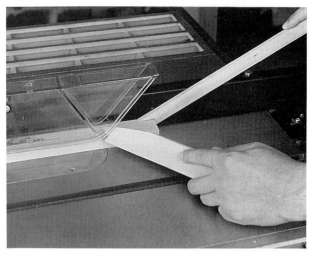

Use two push sticks when ripping narrow stock. To avoid kickback, don't allow the push stick that applies the side pressure to move past the front of the blade.

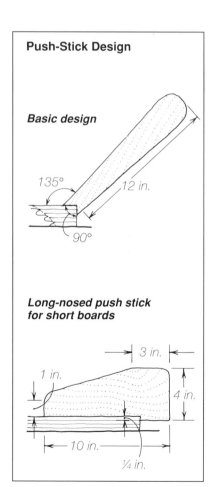

Push-Stick Design

Basic design

135°

12 in.

90°

Long-nosed push stick for short boards

3 in.

1 in.

4 in.

10 in.

¼ in.

Push sticks   If the distance between the blade and the rip fence is less than 3 in., push the workpiece past the blade with a push stick rather than your hand. As a new push stick begins to pick up the inevitable war wounds, you really start to appreciate it. Push-stick designs are quite varied, but all have in common a notch that hugs the corner of the workpiece. The notch allows you to push the workpiece forward and hold the back of the workpiece down on the table. For most of the rip cut, the push stick should rest on the table on the opposite side of the fence. About 6 in. before the end of the cut, pick up the push stick with your right hand and complete the cut.

On narrow boards, feed the work with two push sticks. Never allow the push stick that applies the side pressure to move past the front of the blade, however, because you would be applying side pressure on the blade, which could cause kickback. For short boards, you may want to make a long-nosed push stick that holds down the front of the board (see the bottom drawing at left). This kind of push stick counteracts the upward force from the back of the blade, which has a tendency to lift the board off the table.

Featherboards   A featherboard applies side pressure to the workpiece. Clamp the featherboard to the table so that light pressure is applied just in front of the sawblade. It works best to make the featherboard out of softwood, with cuts spaced about ¼ in. apart to provide flexibility and allow some latitude for adjustment. You can use a featherboard and a push stick in conjunction to hold the workpiece, and two featherboards working in tandem also make a good team.

Wheel hold-downs   Spring-loaded wheel hold-downs attach to a fence or a board mounted to the fence. The spring tension is adjustable for the height of the workpiece, and the wheels rotate in only one direction to provide antikickback protection. Although hold-downs are purchased in pairs, I like to install just one at the back of the saw. The single hold-down controls the wood at the back of the saw and allows me to use a push stick at the front.

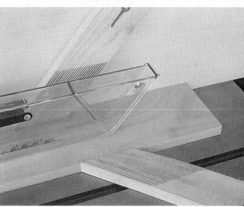

Top: A featherboard can be used in conjunction with a push stick. Above: Two featherboards work well together, too. The top featherboard is clamped to a high fence.

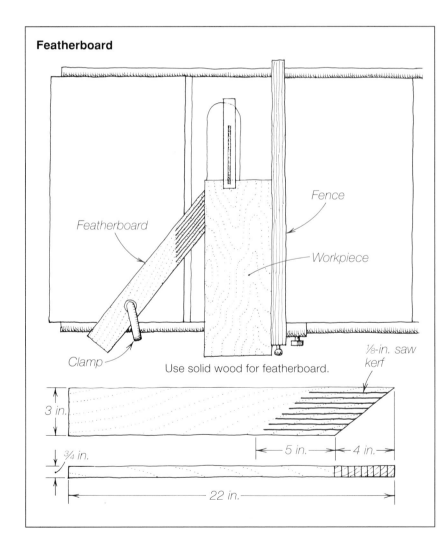

Featherboard

Featherboard

Fence

Workpiece

Clamp

Use solid wood for featherboard.

⅛-in. saw kerf

3 in.

¾ in.

5 in.

4 in.

22 in.

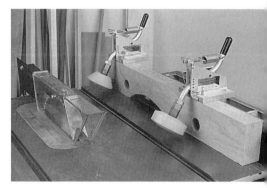

Spring-loaded wheel hold-downs attach to a fence or a board mounted to the fence.

A wooden fence protects both the blade and the rip fence. It can be bolted or screwed to the metal fence.

An auxiliary fence

The sawblade must not come in contact with the metal fence, so it's a good idea to make a wooden fence that protects both the blade and the saw. Different techniques require different types of wooden fences. Most standard fences are drilled so that you can attach a wooden fence, either with bolts or screws. It is best if the auxiliary fence is made of plywood or another manufactured product that will not warp. If you use solid wood, choose quartersawn rather than flatsawn wood, because it is more stable. Finish both sides to prevent warping and apply plastic laminate to provide a good wear surface. Wax the fence often.

Occasionally the metal fence is twisted or not straight. By attaching a wooden fence and shimming it with paper, you can make the setup perfectly straight and accurate. Check the relationship of the fence to the table with a square, and check its straightness with a straightedge.

The high fence   When cutting the edge of a board (as with raised-panel doors), it's safest to use a high fence to support the work. Make your high fence out of plywood if possible. Position the fence and raised panel so that the blade tilts away from the piece. If you are making a cut that separates a small piece, it should not be captured between the rest of the workpiece and the fence.

The low fence When ripping a bevel or a chamfer, you should position the fence so that the blade tilts away from it. At times this may not be possible because of the position of the fence rails at the front of the saw. A good solution when you must make a cut with the piece captured between the fence and the blade is to use a low fence. This fence can be a separate two-piece fence or a board that is attached to your regular wooden fence. Because the cut workpiece is trapped between the fence and the blade, a kickback is likely. Use a long push stick to move the workpiece past the blade. I often prefer to use a low fence when I am ripping narrow pieces, because I find it easier to control the workpiece without a high rip fence in the way.

The long fence The long fence, which extends the entire length of the rip fence, makes it easier to cut sheets of man-made materials. Because sheet materials are dimensionally stable, pinching or spreading after the cut is not usually a problem.

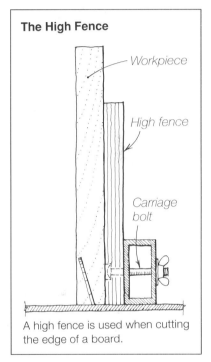

The High Fence

A high fence is used when cutting the edge of a board.

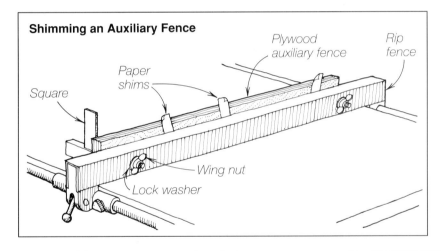

Shimming an Auxiliary Fence

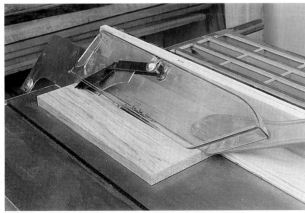

Use a low fence when you must make a cut with the piece captured between the fence and the blade.

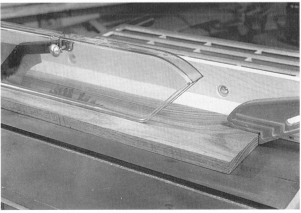

The low fence is good for square cuts, too. It allows more room between the fence and the blade.

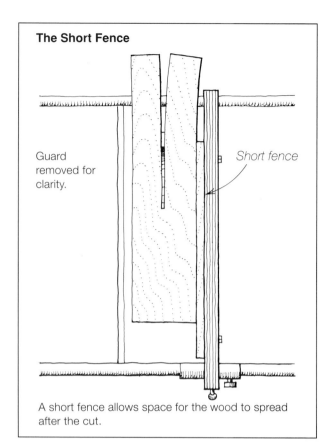

Guard removed for clarity.

Short fence

A short fence allows space for the wood to spread after the cut.

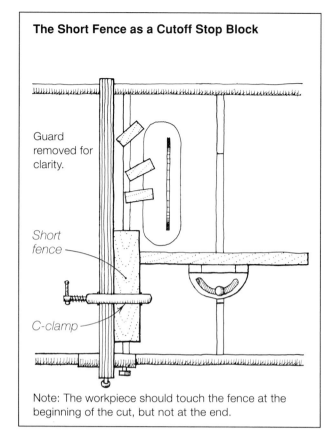

Guard removed for clarity.

Short fence

C-clamp

Note: The workpiece should touch the fence at the beginning of the cut, but not at the end.

When using a dado blade or molding head, house the cutter within the arch of the auxiliary fence.

The short fence   When cutting solid wood, there is always the possibility that the wood will either pinch or spread during the cut. The splitter is designed to eliminate the problem of the wood pinching the back of the blade. The short fence is designed to eliminate the problem of the wood spreading apart after the cut. The short fence ends at the back of the blade at its full height to allow space for the wood to spread into after the cut. When cutting multiple small pieces to the same length, a short fence works well as a stop. The workpiece should touch the fence at the beginning of the cut, but not at the end.

The dado and molding fence   The dado blade and the molding head often cut the edge of a board, which means that the cutter or blade is near the fence. The fence for these cuts should have a round arch for the cutter. Whenever possible the cutter should be housed within the arch. Never cut a rabbet or make a molding with the workpiece between the fence and the cutter, because of the potential for kickback.

Because molding heads and dadoes require more hold-down pressure, it is a good idea to add a guide strip to the wooden fence for molding and rabbeting. Make the molding and rabbets on wide boards and then rip them to width.

Incomplete cuts

An incomplete cut is a cut that doesn't go completely through the board. Examples are a groove (with the grain), a dado (across the grain) and a rabbet (either with or across the grain). Incomplete cuts can be made with a standard blade by making multiple passes, but take extra care because the standard guard must be removed.

Intersecting cuts

Although a rabbet can be made with a series of cuts, it is much faster to make two intersecting cuts to remove the waste. The second cut separates the waste, which should be on the side of the blade opposite the fence. If the waste falls between the blade and the fence, it can bind and eject backwards with lightning speed.

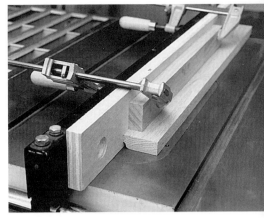

Add a hold-down strip to the wood fence for cutting molding and rabbeting.

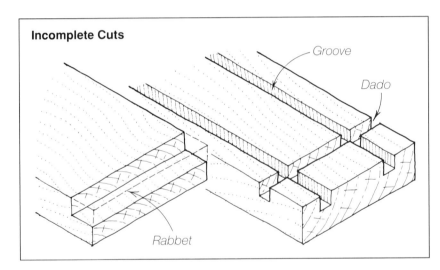

Incomplete Cuts

Groove

Dado

Rabbet

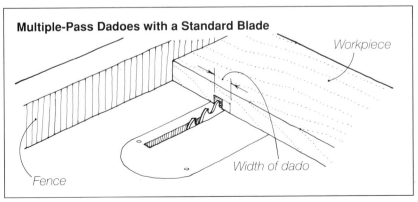

Multiple-Pass Dadoes with a Standard Blade

Workpiece

Width of dado

Fence

Intersecting Cuts

First cut

Second cut

Second cut separates waste to form rabbet.

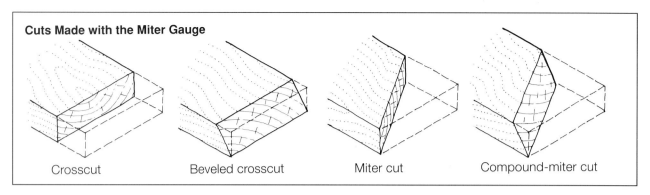

Cuts Made with the Miter Gauge

Crosscut   Beveled crosscut   Miter cut   Compound-miter cut

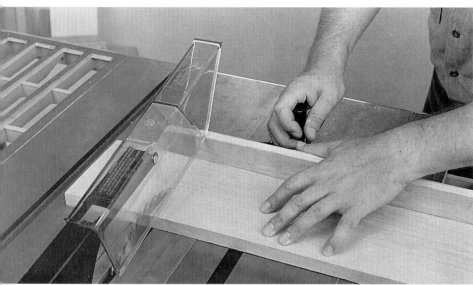

To crosscut, place the workpiece against the face of the miter gauge and advance both the gauge and the wood forward into the blade. Use both hands to control the wood and the gauge.

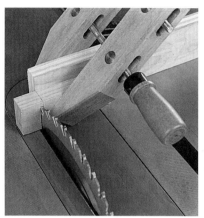

Clamp small pieces to the miter gauge for increased accuracy and safety.

Using the miter gauge

The miter gauge is an adjustable protractor that slides in the miter slot. The gauge supports the work as it is crosscut. The face of the miter gauge remains square to the bar for the square crosscut and the bevel crosscut, but is angled in relation to the blade for the miter cut and the compound-miter cut.

Crosscutting

To crosscut, press the workpiece against the face of the miter gauge and down onto the miter bar. After making sure your fingers are clear of the blade, advance both the gauge and the wood into the blade. Most people prefer the left miter slot for crosscutting, but either slot works. When the blade is angled, use the slot opposite the direction of the tilt.

Use both hands to control the wood and the gauge, and hold the wood tightly against the face of the gauge so that it doesn't slip during the cut. Once the wood is cut into two pieces, stop the forward movement of the miter gauge and pull the wood and the miter gauge backward to the front of the saw. As you retract the wood and the gauge, maintain the same pressure that you used as you cut—relaxing too soon can cause accidents. Never touch a cut-off piece while the saw is running. As a safety precaution, clamp small pieces to the miter gauge.

The auxiliary miter fence Most miter gauges have holes so that a wooden fence can be screwed to the face of the miter head. A longer auxiliary fence gives the workpiece more support. Use plywood for the auxiliary fence, because it is more dimensionally stable than solid wood. Extend the wood past the blade and crosscut it to establish the exact location of the sawblade.

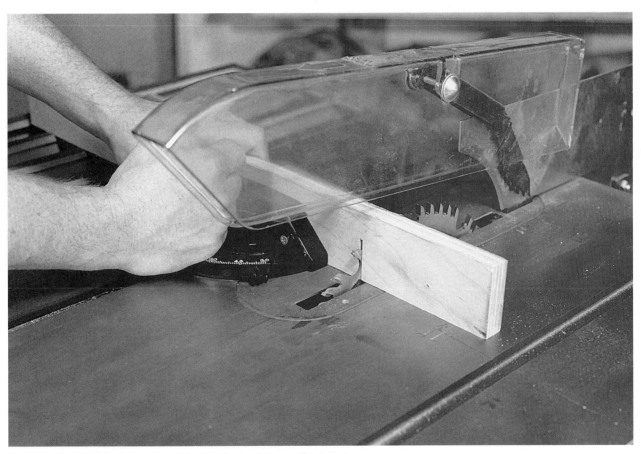

The auxiliary fence is screwed to the face of the miter head.

Align the mark on the back of the workpiece with the kerf cut on the auxiliary fence.

Marking the work Before making the crosscut, it's best to draw at least one edge mark when the wood is lying flat because the edge contacts the blade first. The final positioning of the workpiece lines up the mark with an outside tooth of the sawblade. (Make sure the kerf is on the waste side of the line.) It's faster and more accurate to scribe a line on the back of the board and align it with the saw cut on the auxiliary fence of the miter gauge.

Miter-gauge stops A stop block clamped to the wooden fence automatically measures the required length of board. This simple technique offers both efficiency and accuracy, particularly when you need several pieces exactly the same length. Keep gentle pressure against the stop as the wood is fed into the blade. After the cut is made, maintain the pressure against the stop as the wood and miter gauge are being retracted to lessen the likelihood of contact with the blade.

Clamp a stop block to the auxiliary fence for cutting multiple pieces to the same length.

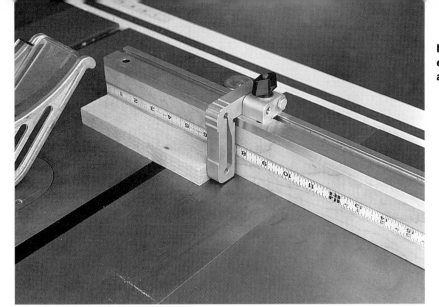

Miter gauges on European saws are equipped with an auxiliary fence and metal stops.

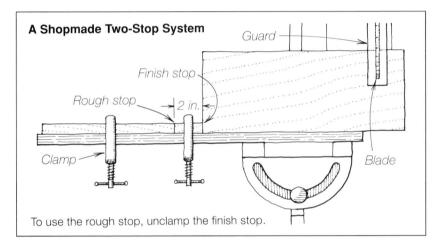

A Shopmade Two-Stop System

Guard

Finish stop

Rough stop

2 in.

Clamp

Blade

To use the rough stop, unclamp the finish stop.

European miter gauges have been equipped with auxiliary fences and metal stops as standard equipment for years. The advantage of the metal stops is that they have hinges that allow them to flip out of way. European-style miter gauges are now available in North America.

Dual stops Sometimes it may be desirable to have several precise stops. For example, when you must trim a rough end and then cut several boards exactly the same length, two stop blocks are efficient. The stop nearer the blade is the finish stop, the stop farther from the blade is the rough stop. If you do not have a miter gauge with hinged stops, two wood pieces clamped to the fence work almost as well. Cut a piece of wood about 2 in. long for the finish stop, and clamp another piece opposite the blade for a rough stop. When you need to use the rough stop just unclamp the finish stop block. Reclamp it when you need the finish stop.

Another job for the two-stop system is to space standard sawblade cuts when making a dado without installing the dado head. The finish stop block is the width of the dado minus the width of the saw cut.

Multiple stops Stack multiple stop blocks to space a series of cuts, such as dadoes. The spacing block width is the distance from the corner of one dado to the corner of the next dado.

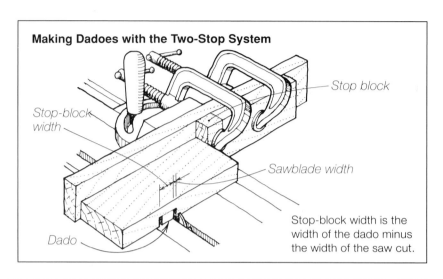

Making Dadoes with the Two-Stop System

Stop block

Stop-block width

Sawblade width

Dado

Stop-block width is the width of the dado minus the width of the saw cut.

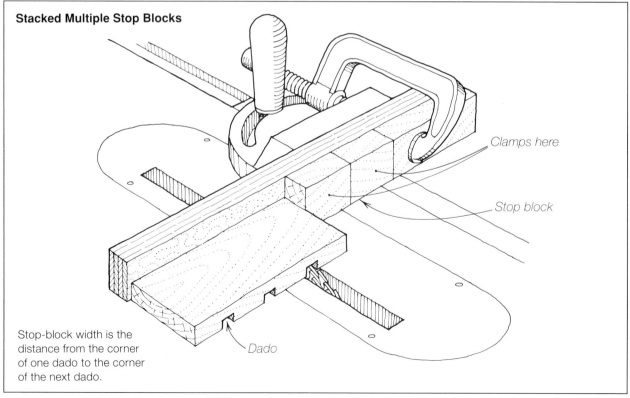

Stacked Multiple Stop Blocks

Clamps here

Stop block

Dado

Stop-block width is the distance from the corner of one dado to the corner of the next dado.

Paper shims are the low-tech approach to making very fine adjustments.

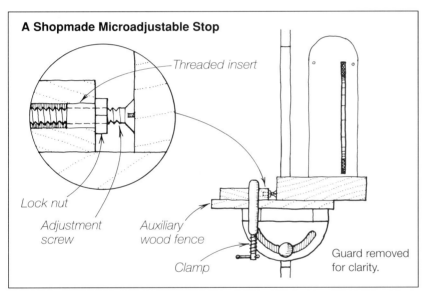

A Shopmade Microadjustable Stop

Threaded insert

Lock nut

Adjustment screw

Auxiliary wood fence

Clamp

Guard removed for clarity.

Microadjustable stops   For very precise work it's essential to be able to make very fine adjustments of the stops. One low-tech approach is to put paper shims between the rough stop block and the finish stop block. A dollar bill or sheet of typing paper is 0.004 in. thick. By folding it you can stack the measurement; for example, a dollar bill folded twice is four thicknesses of paper or 0.016 (1/64) in.

Another technique is to make a block that has a threaded insert and an adjustment screw, as shown in the drawing above. Make the block out of plywood for stability and finish it with oil. Every full turn of a 1/4-in., 20 threads-per-inch machine screw adds or subtracts 0.05 in. to the length of the stop block. The locknut makes this measurement reliable for repeated operations.

CHAPTER 2
The Radial-Arm Saw

While the table saw is the premier ripping machine, the radial-arm saw has traditionally been dubbed king of crosscuts. I say traditionally because the radial-arm saw is currently being challenged for the title by a couple of newcomers: the electric miter saw and the sliding compound-miter saw. I'll cover both of these upstarts briefly at the end of this chapter (see pp. 76-77).

The strength of the radial-arm saw is its great versatility. You might call it the Cuisinart® of woodworking; it slices, it dices, it.... This versatility is also the source of some of its weaknesses. Many woodworkers think of the radial-arm saw as an inaccurate machine, and it does take more care and attention to make it accurate. To add injury to insult, it is a more dangerous machine than the table saw, especially when used for ripping. The radial-arm saw requires frequent cleaning and care, particularly if it has to be moved. Adjusting the saw is initially more time-consuming, because it has a number of parts and its adjustments must be made in proper sequence. However, if the saw is properly adjusted and cared for, it will give years of faithful service.

Radial-Arm-Saw Anatomy

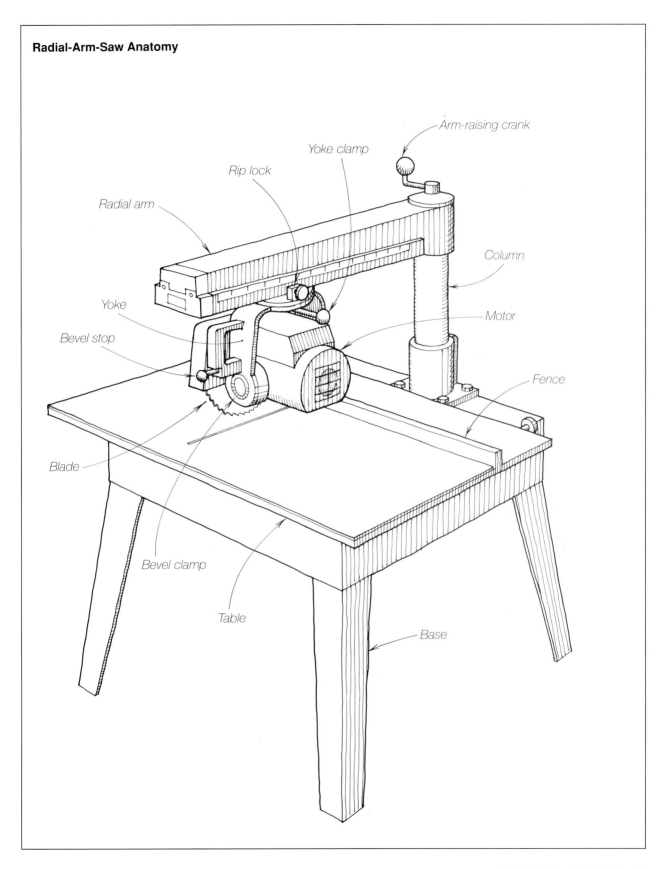

Arm-raising crank

Yoke clamp

Rip lock

Radial arm

Column

Yoke

Motor

Bevel stop

Fence

Blade

Bevel clamp

Table

Base

Radial-arm-saw design

The radial-arm saw, which was developed in the late 1920s by Raymond DeWalt, is like an upside-down table saw that you pull across the workpiece. The design is skeletal—all of the working parts are visible to the user. Like the table saw, the radial-arm saw is a stationary machine, but the motor and blade assembly is suspended over the work. The machine is designed for straight crosscuts and angled or compound-angled crosscuts, but it can also be used for rip cuts. For crosscutting, the workpiece remains stationary and the blade is pulled through it to make the cut. For ripping, the motor/blade assembly is rotated 90° and locked in a stationary position on the arm and the workpiece is fed into the blade.

Crosscutting on the Radial-Arm Saw

Crosscuts are made by pulling the saw through the workpiece.

Compound cuts

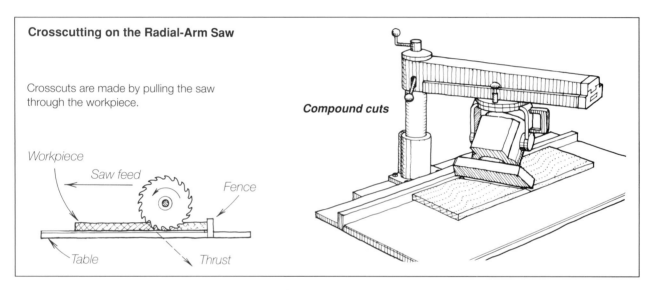

Ripping on the Radial-Arm Saw

For rip cuts, the saw is locked in a stationary position on the arm and the workpiece is fed into the blade.

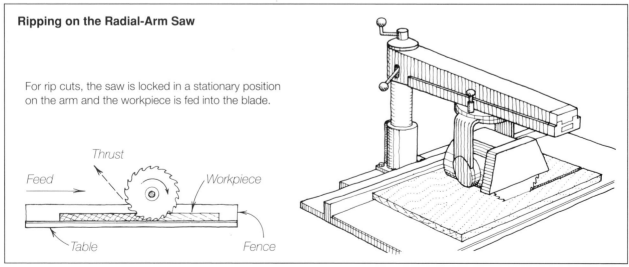

Radial-arm-saw anatomy

The radial-arm saw is named for the arm that supports the motor. The arm is secured to the column by a locking mechanism, which when loosened allows the arm to rotate through 360°. The angle of the arm to the fence determines the angle of the saw cut. The column telescopes in and out of the base, which supports the table and always remains stationary.

The motor mechanism that slides on the track on the underside of the arm is usually referred to as the head. It comprises the motor, the yoke and the roller-mechanism casting. The cast-iron yoke holds the motor in place and allows it to be rotated and tilted. The yoke is suspended from the roller head, which has four bearings mounted on top of it. The roller bearings run along the arm track, providing the vehicle by which the head moves back and forth.

The blade used on the radial-arm saw is very similar to the blade used on the table saw. A crosscut blade should be used for crosscutting, and a rip blade for ripping. Avoid aggressive hook angles to minimize the radial-arm saw's tendency to self-feed.

General maintenance

To get precise cuts the sawblade must be held securely by the arm, table frame and yoke. The radial saw incorporates several different parts, and if there is any movement in any of the parts, the accuracy of the cut suffers. The greater the movement, the greater the inaccuracy.

Except for the positive stops at 45° and 90°, critical adjustments are held by the pressure of friction clamps. These adjustments must hold securely without being too tight. If they are too tight, the parts will bind or wear prematurely. If they are too loose, the parts will move and the equipment will be sloppy and imprecise.

Removing the slack in the saw's parts often means that you tighten clamps and adjust factory settings beyond recommendations. To work well at these tighter tolerances, the saw must be well lubricated and very clean. Cleanliness and lubrication are especially important for the rolling mechanism.

Cleaning and lubricating the saw

The single most important thing that you can do for your radial-arm saw is to keep it clean. Dirt and rust are the enemies of precision on any machine, but particularly on the radial-arm saw. If there is dirt or rust on the saw's moving parts, it will cause you to overtighten the clamps and locks, and the machine will still be too loose.

The column, head bearings and roller track require constant surveillance for cleanliness. I like to use an ammonia solution for cleaning and light machine oil or WD-40® for lubrication. Unfortunately, there is no solution that both cleans and lubricates. WD-40® is widely used in industry because it lubricates, leaves a thin protective film and prevents rust. The drawback is that this film attracts dirt, can ruin a board for finishing and can build up into a sticky layer if it is too thick. Wipe most of the WD-40® off after you spray it on.

The other lubricant of choice is a light machine oil. It too attracts dust, but if you wipe the rollers and track with an oily rag every time you use the saw, the buildup of dirt is minimized.

I use a 50:50 ammonia/water solution to keep the bearings and the track clean as I am cutting. A rag soaked in an ammonia solution helps to remove sawdust or residue. Usually an hourly cleaning will do, but if you start to feel the action of the roller getting rough or choppy, take half a minute to remove the buildup. You should also clean the rollers at the end of each working session, because the buildup is much harder to remove after it has dried.

Cotton rags are better cleaning tools than paper towels because they are more abrasive. For rougher cleaning pick up some plastic abrasive pads (the Teflon®-safe type). Avoid using Scotch Brite Abrasive Pads® and their ilk because they have enough grit to actually remove metal. You should also avoid steel wool because it leaves undesirable iron fragments behind. Don't allow oily rags to pile up in your shop—it's a sure recipe for fire. Always store oil and ammonia rags in closed containers: I use a plastic Ziploc® bag attached to my saw.

To clean the column, raise the arm as high as it will go. Clean it with a Teflon®-safe plastic abrasive pad to remove any buildup or rust. Then lubricate it with WD-40®, but be sure to wipe it off before lowering the arm. Lubricate the column with a light coating of machine oil every month for intermittent use or, if you cut with the saw every day, spray WD-40® on the column and track about once a week. With the oil on the column, raise and lower the arm three or four times to help spread oil to the inside of the base. Finally, raise the mechanism as high as it will go and wipe it down before sawing.

There's an art to cleaning the roller track so that you don't pinch your fingers. Push the head all the way back. Apply the ammonia solution to the rag. Wipe the exposed track first, then pull the head forward and wipe the back of the track. To clean the four ball bearings that serve as rollers, hold the rag against one and move the head so that the rag doesn't pinch between the track and the roller. After cleaning each roller clean the track one final time, and then give the track and rollers a light coating of machine oil.

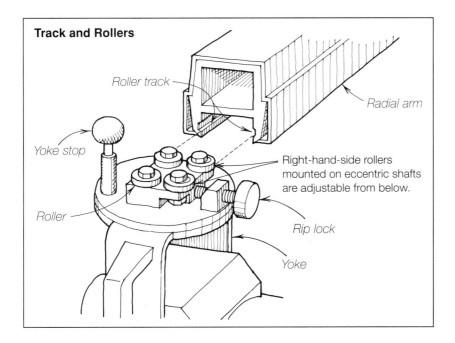

Track and Rollers

Roller track

Radial arm

Yoke stop

Right-hand-side rollers
mounted on eccentric shafts
are adjustable from below.

Roller

Rip lock

Yoke

Because cleanliness is so important on the radial-arm saw, it's a good idea to install a dust-collecting system if you can afford one. It will catch most of the sawdust, you'll breathe better and your saw will be healthier too.

Initial setup

All woodworking machines work best when they sit flat. If possible, secure the saw to the floor using appropriate fasteners. Level the saw with shim stock.

Tuning the radial-arm saw

The process of tuning the radial-arm saw can be divided into two main stages. The first stage — making the preliminary adjustments — entails testing and adjusting the column, roller bearings and yoke for tightness. The second stage involves aligning and squaring the machine.

Each brand and model of saw is slightly different, so refer to your owner's manual for specific information on tuning. If you don't have a manual, you may want to pick up a copy of *Fine Tuning Your Radial-Arm Saw* by Jon Eakes (Lee Valley Tools, Ltd., 1987). Even if you do have a manual, the book will still be useful, since Eakes goes into more detail than the Sears, Delta or DeWalt manuals.

Initially, it's best to take nothing for granted each time you tune your radial-arm saw, and start at the very beginning. After spending some time with your saw, you will be able to test it with a single crosscut and adjust it in a matter of minutes.

Column adjustments

The column, a machined cylindrical tube with a square piece of metal either bolted or welded to the back, is the bridge that connects the top and the bottom of the saw. It must fit snugly in the base at the bottom and also in the arm at the top. If there's any noticeable play, the parts must be tightened. If the column is hard to move up and down, it is either too tight or needs to be cleaned and lubricated (see p. 52). You should clean and lubricate the column before making any adjustment.

There are three adjustments to make, one between the arm and the column and two between the column and base.

Arm-to-column adjustment The arm is designed to rotate at the top of the column. There are stops that lock the column at both 45° and 90°. An arm-to-column clamp holds the arm securely in place. This clamp should be adjusted so that the arm fits snugly on the column but loosely enough to allow movement from side to side for making angled cuts. Test your machine for looseness by releasing the clamp and by shoving upward and then downward on the front of the arm. You may be able to flex the arm slightly but you should not be able to move it up and down. The adjustment is made at the back of the saw. If it is too tight, it will be hard to move the arm.

Test the arm-to-column adjustment by releasing the column clamp and then, with the motor locked in the middle of the arm, lift up and push down on the end of the arm. There should be no movement.

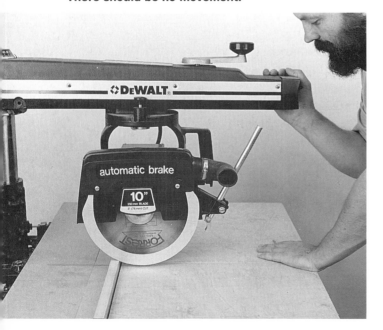

The arm-to-column clamp adjustment is made at the junction of the arm and the column. On some saws the adjustment is an Allen screw rather than a bolt.

Tighten the column-to-base adjustment from the back of the saw. On most saws the adjustment is made by forcing the split casting closer together.

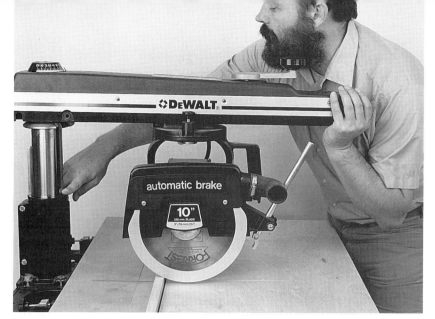

Test the column-to-base adjustment by keeping one finger on the joint between the column and the base casting and lifting up on the end of the arm. If you can feel any movement, the fit needs adjustment.

Column-to-base adjustments   The two column-to-base adjustments are both made on the base casting at the back of the saw. The base casting is a split casting with an opening in the back. The first adjustment is for the rise and fall of the column. Raise and lower the column as far as it will go in both directions. The action should be smooth; if the column binds or is jerky in operation, it probably needs further cleaning. Next, lock the motor at the midpoint on the arm and put one finger on the joint between the column and the base casting. Lift up the front of the saw and then release it to see if there is any movement between the column and the base. If there is movement, the split casting that forms the base should be tightened around the column. One set of bolts forces the two halves of the casting together.

If the connection between the column and the base is too loose, it will be easy to raise and lower the column and you may be able to feel some movement between the two parts. You may even hear a clicking sound as the column is raised or lowered. If the connection is too tight, it will be hard to move the column. The correct clamping pressure is the grey area in between: The column does not move in the base but still moves freely up and down without requiring brute force.

Adjust the column rotation by tightening the bolts on the column bar.

Check the column rotation by putting a finger on the column and base and applying pressure to the side of the arm. Movement between the column and base means that the bolts on the column bar need tightening.

Once the base has been adjusted so that the column is held securely, the second column-to-base adjustment is to make sure that the column does not rotate in the base casting. Put your finger at the corner of the column and the base and try to move the front of the arm back and forth. If you can detect any movement, the pressure against the bar on the back of the column should be increased.

Adjusting the roller bearings

There is a mechanism on all radial-arm saws for adjusting the tension of the roller bearings that ride in the track on the underside of the arm. The usual approach by the manufacturer is to make two of the bearings on one side of the track adjustable and the opposite two bearings nonadjustable.

As with all radial-arm-saw adjustments, you must achieve that subtle compromise between too tight and too loose. Before testing the tension on your rollers, make sure that both the track and the rollers are absolutely clean. Test the tension on the rollers by pulling the saw head out to the end of the arm. Place your thumb on the front roller and push the saw head backward. If you can stop the roller from rotating with the pressure from your thumb, the roller is too loose and it needs to be tightened. Next repeat this test with the back rollers. Remember to push the head away from you so you don't pinch your thumb. If the tension on the rollers is too tight, it will pull hard, so back it off. Usually the two rollers on one side are on an eccentric shaft, and the adjustment is made by rotating the shaft. Refer to your owner's manual for the specifics of adjusting the rollers.

Adjusting the clamps

There are three different clamps on the radial-arm saw that require adjustment. You must be able to tighten the clamps enough to prevent the part from moving but not so tight that it is hard on the equipment. Test the clamps by tightening them, and then see if there is any movement in the mechanism. Never lubricate the clamping mechanisms. They should, however, be cleaned occasionally with a 50:50 solution of ammonia and water.

Because each manufacturer uses a different type of clamping mechanism, you will need to refer to the owner's manual for the details of your particular saw.

Arm-to-column clamp   The arm-to-column clamp holds the arm in place when it is not held by the stops at 90° and 45°. Test the clamping pressure by clamping the arm at the middle distance between 90° and 45°. Now hold the table with one hand and try to move the clamp. If the clamp moves easily, it needs to be tightened. If you can't move the arm at all, it is too tight and needs to be loosened. The arm should move with firm pressure. Don't worry that the arm will move during the cut, because there is very little side pressure on the arm when the saw is cutting.

Yoke-clamp adjustment   The clamping mechanism between the roller head and the yoke is called the yoke clamp. It is important that the clamp hold the yoke and thus the motor secure. To test the clamp, disengage the locking pin and rotate the yoke so the blade is halfway between ripping and crosscutting and then lock the clamp. At this point when you try to rotate the motor, it shouldn't move. If it does move, tighten the yoke-clamp assembly.

Bevel-clamp adjustment   The motor/blade assembly is designed to tilt in the yoke for bevel cuts. A stop holds the motor at 45° and 90°, and a clamp holds the motor securely at the other angles. To test the clamp, tilt the motor to a position between 45° and 90° and engage the clamp. Now try to tilt the motor with your hands. It should not move. If it does, tighten the clamp. If it is hard to close the handle on the clamp, it is too tight and the adjustment should be backed off.

To test the arm clamp, engage the clamp between 45° and 90°. The arm should move with moderate pressure.

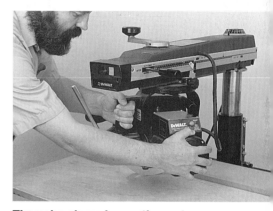

The yoke clamp keeps the motor from rotating. To test the clamp, lock it between the rip and crosscut position. You should not be able to change the position of the motor.

Test the bevel clamp by locking between the 45° and 90° positions. Tighten the clamp if you can move the motor.

Once the saw has been lubricated and all the clamps have been tightened, you are ready to make the adjustments so that the saw cuts accurately. There are two kinds of adjustment, one for squareness and another for alignment.

It is important to make these adjustments in the correct sequence, because the accuracy of one adjustment is usually dependent on the accuracy of the previous adjustment. It is best if you alternate the adjustments for squaring and alignment. The table top is first aligned parallel with the arm, then the blade is squared vertically and to the fence. These adjustments should be tested first with a static test, using a square against the nonmoving blade. Then, in an operation that may seem redundant, the saw should be aligned horizontally and vertically and checked with a dynamic test. The dynamic test is an evaluation of the saw's squareness during operation. Trust me, you need to make both tests to get a sweet-running saw.

Aligning the table top and the arm

The table is the foundation of the radial-arm saw, and, therefore, should be adjusted first. The table may be plywood or particleboard and is meant to be easily replaced. The table-top surface must be parallel with the horizontal plane of the arm tracks at both the 45° and 90° positions. Because the arm is fixed, the adjustment is made on the table frame under the table top. Remove the blade and the guard, and rotate the motor so that the arbor points downward. If possible, release the arm lock on your saw so that it will be easy to swing the arm to various points on the table.

Position the arbor so that it touches the highest point on the table. Alternately, stick a piece of plywood between the table and the arbor like a thick feeler gauge. Rotate the arbor to an adjacent corner and raise the table up to the arbor and tighten it. Repeat this procedure on the other corners. Then check to make sure that all four corners have the same setting.

Also, don't forget to check the middle of the table, especially near the blade. Most saws have a mechanism for raising or lowering the table in the middle. It is imperative that the saw table be flat. If it is not, you may have to remove some material with a belt sander or orbital sander, but be careful not to remove too much. One option is to put a sanding disc on the end of the arbor and sand the table flat.

Once the table is flat, cover it with an auxiliary surface made of high-quality ¼-in. plywood. Leave a ⅛-in. gap between the fence and this auxiliary table to capture sawdust and chips, which are a common source of inaccuracy. The gap allows them to drop out of the way.

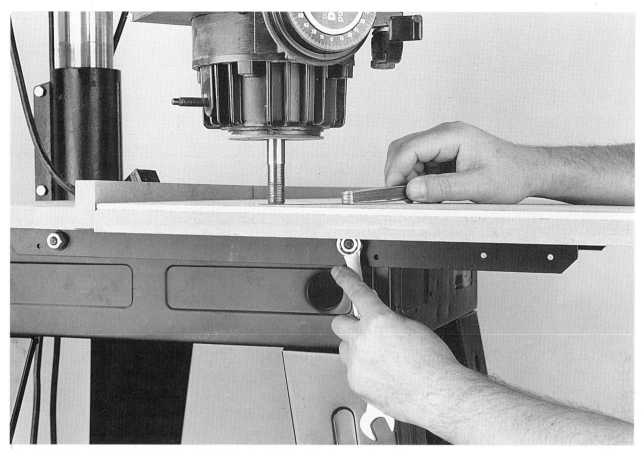

The table should be adjusted so that it is parallel to the saw arm. Remove the blade and guard and rotate the arbor toward the table. Adjust the four corners of the table to the end of the arbor.

A ¼-in. plywood auxiliary table is easily replaced when the surface becomes worn. Leave a small gap between the fence and the plywood to capture the sawdust.

Use a framing square for the preliminary squaring of the blade to the table.

Attach the auxiliary table to the base table with small brass nails spaced about 4 in. apart. (Brass won't damage the blade.) Apply a layer of rubber cement to hold the edges down so that sawdust does not get under the table cover. Also lay a strip of rubber cement where the blade travels so that sawdust doesn't creep under the table cover if you saw through the top. Don't confuse rubber cement with contact cement. Contact cement will prevent you from removing the top when it needs replacement. You may want to cement paper shims under the auxiliary table to make slight adjustments. I'd use rubber cement for this, too.

Preliminary squaring of the blade to the table

The goal of squaring the blade is to get the saw as accurate as possible before adjusting the saw for proper alignment. Make sure that the arm clamp, yoke clamp and carriage clamp are locked. UNPLUG THE SAW. Now release the bevel clamp and wiggle the motor up and down to make sure that the indexing pin is engaged all the way at the 90° setting. This ensures that the saw motor is as rigid as possible.

To square the blade to the table, slide a square against the blade, as shown in the photo above. Place the blade of the square as close as possible to the middle of the sawblade and in between the teeth. A large framing square usually works well for this purpose. If the blade is not square, refer to your owner's manual for adjustments. The usual technique is to loosen two bolts and reposition the motor so that the blade is square to the table, and then retighten the bolts.

Preliminary squaring of the arm to the fence

The next step is to square the arm to the fence. First, check for squareness. Make sure that the arm-to-column clamp mechanism is secure. Wiggle the arm back and forth to make sure that the indexing pin is engaged. Place the square on the table with one leg against the fence and the other against the blade. Raise the blade so that the bottom of the tooth is even with the bottom of the square. Mark one tooth and use that as your reference point. Move the sawblade forward so that the tooth touches the corner of the square. Now slowly pull the blade further toward you, paying attention to the contact between the blade and the square. If the tooth contacts the square evenly as you pull the carriage forward, the arm is square to the fence and you do not have to make any adjustments (see the drawing below). If the tooth stops touching the square, the angle is more than 90° and the arm needs to be adjusted to the left. If the tooth binds against the saw, it means that the angle is less than 90° and the arm needs to be adjusted to the right.

Check the squareness of the arm to the fence with a square. Keep one tooth in contact with the square as you pull the saw forward.

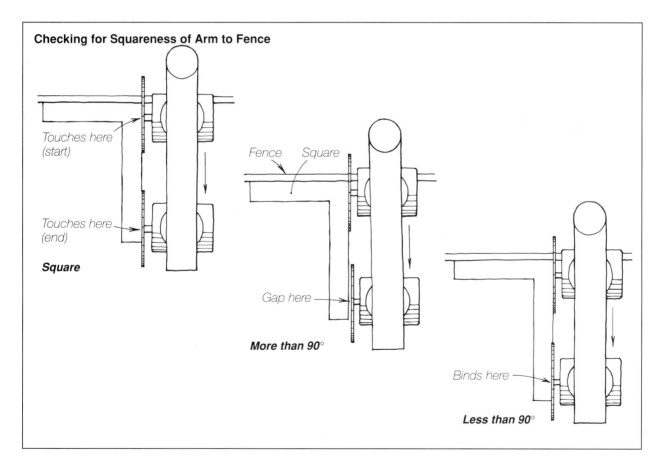

Checking for Squareness of Arm to Fence

Touches here (start)

Touches here (end)

Square

Fence *Square*

Gap here

More than 90°

Binds here

Less than 90°

If the arm is not square to the fence, you have two options. You can either move the arm or the table slightly until the fence is square to the table. Most people agree that it is easier to move the table, especially if the saw is freestanding.

To adjust the table, loosen the screws that hold it to the metal base. Keep one corner tight to serve as a rotation point for the whole table surface. Move the table slightly with a light tap from a rubber mallet, then tighten the opposite corner and recheck the blade and fence for squareness. You may have to repeat this procedure several times. When the table is square, tighten all of the screws.

If the saw is built into a large table, you will find it easier to adjust the arm. If you decide to move the arm, follow the instructions in the owner's manual. On Sears and DeWalt saws, the column remains stationary and the arm is rotated. On Delta (Rockwell) saws, the column is rotated and it in turn moves the arm.

There is one type of saw on which the arm is never rotated. This saw has a guide wire on each side attached between the table and the user's end of the arm. A turnbuckle allows the end to be held securely, and it also functions as another means of adjusting the arm.

Checking the alignment of the blade

After you have squared the arm to the table and fence, you are ready to check the alignment of the blade. It is fairly obvious that for a square cut the sawblade must be at 90° relative to both the fence and the table. What is not so obvious is that the blade may be perfectly square yet not cut precisely because the yoke or blade is misaligned or slightly rotated. This alignment problem is called "heeling." Heeling occurs when the blade goes through the cut at a slight angle. The leading edge of the blade (the toe) and the trailing edge (the heel) are not perfectly lined up with the travel of the blade. The heel rubs against the kerf causing a double cut, which in turn causes splintering, burning and binding. Heeling is dangerous when ripping and is one of the chief causes of kickback.

To eliminate one source of the problem of heeling, the motor must be rotated slightly so that the blade is aligned with the travel of the head. Because the sawblade cuts in both the vertical and the horizontal plane, the blade must be aligned in both planes. Horizontal alignment is usually ignored in the owner's manuals. However, both horizontal and vertical alignment are critical when the motor is tilted for making angled cuts.

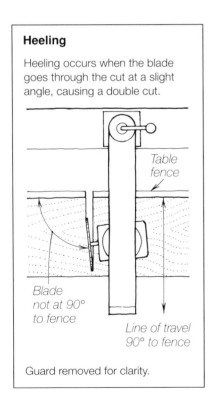

Heeling

Heeling occurs when the blade goes through the cut at a slight angle, causing a double cut.

Table fence

Blade not at 90° to fence

Line of travel 90° to fence

Guard removed for clarity.

Vertical Alignment

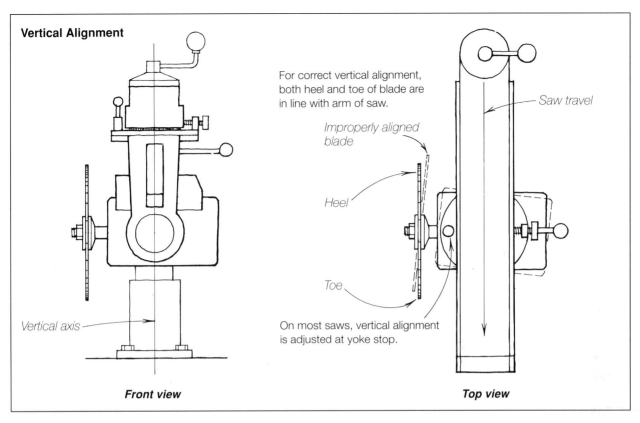

For correct vertical alignment, both heel and toe of blade are in line with arm of saw.

Improperly aligned blade

Heel

Saw travel

Toe

On most saws, vertical alignment is adjusted at yoke stop.

Vertical axis

Front view

Top view

Horizontal Alignment

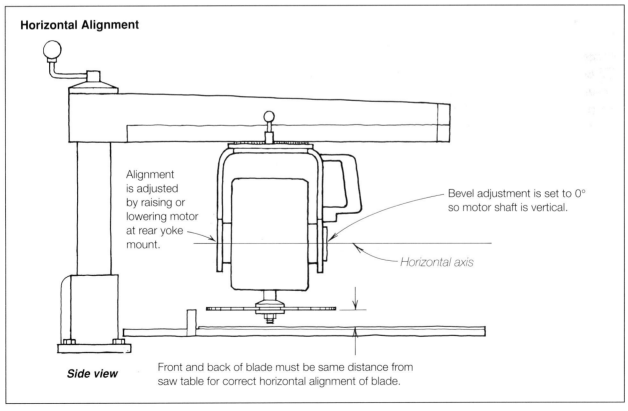

Alignment is adjusted by raising or lowering motor at rear yoke mount.

Bevel adjustment is set to 0° so motor shaft is vertical.

Horizontal axis

Side view

Front and back of blade must be same distance from saw table for correct horizontal alignment of blade.

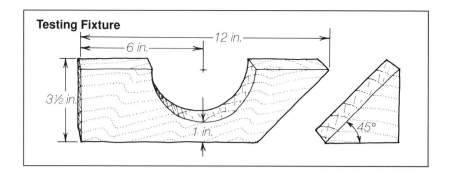

Testing Fixture

After years of following the owner's manuals with mixed results, I decided to design a fixture that would accurately test for heeling in both planes, as described below in the sections on horizontal and vertical alignment. This fixture is not affected by blade runout, which is the downfall of most of the other methods.

The fixture is a piece of plywood about 12 in. long. The width of the board is ⅛ in. less than the distance between the table and the bottom of the saw flange. On a 10-in. saw this distance is usually about 3½ in. There are two saw cuts made on the board. A 45° cut descends from one corner. (Keep the triangular cut-off, too.) A semicircular cut is made in the center of the board on the same side as the point so that the fixture can be clamped to the fence.

Horizontal alignment Horizontal alignment is often ignored in owner's manuals, because it is relatively unimportant for the vertical cuts that constitute 99% of the radial-arm saw's work. However, proper horizontal alignment is required to make safe, accurate bevel cuts without heeling. The blade's dragging heel can hurl the cut-off scrap, especially if it is small. It is important to adjust the horizontal alignment before the vertical alignment. If you adjust the vertical before the horizontal, the vertical may no longer be square, whereas adjusting the vertical after the horizontal won't affect the horizontal alignment.

To check for horizontal alignment, rotate the blade so that it is in the horizontal position. Make sure that the yoke pin is tight in its hole. Loosen the yoke clamp and wiggle the motor to make sure that the pin is engaged completely, then retighten the clamp. Repeat the procedure for the motor-tilt mechanism.

Clamp the test fixture flat on the table against the fence, with the cut-off triangle standing on edge. The point of the triangle should be near but not touching the washer nut. Slide the head backward and lock it so that the tips of the teeth are above the point, as shown in the top photo on the facing page. Slowly rotate the blade as you slowly lower the head until you hear the blade touch the point. It will touch at one or more teeth. Mark the point of contact. I make an X with a felt-tipped marker.

Next move the head forward until the tips of the teeth are over the point and lock the head, as shown in the bottom photo below. Rotate the blade to see if it touches the point. If the saw is aligned, the marked teeth will touch the point. If more teeth touch the point or if no teeth

Check horizontal alignment by lowering the blade until it touches the point of the cut-off triangle. Mark the tooth that contacts the point.

Move the head forward and rotate the blade so that the marked tooth is over the point. If the saw is aligned horizontally, the tooth will contact the point and make the same sound as in the first test.

contact the point, the saw is misaligned and needs adjustment. The adjustments on most saws are at the back of the saw where the motor rotates in the yoke. Check your owner's manual for the details of the adjustment. After adjusting the saw, check it again.

Vertical alignment Vertical alignment guarantees that the body of the blade is parallel to its path of travel. The properly aligned blade is straight in the cut rather than slightly twisted. The usual method of checking vertical alignment is to place a large square against the fence and against the body of the blade, as shown in the drawing on the facing page. The drawback of this test is that it doesn't account for any runout in the blade.

I make a more accurate test with the same fixture I used to check horizontal alignment. Clamp the fixture to the fence as shown in the photo on the facing page. Make sure that the blade does not contact the table. Rotate the blade and tap the end of the fixture lightly until there is contact between its point and a tooth on the front of the blade. Mark the tooth that touches the point. Next pull the head forward and rotate the blade so that the marked tooth, now at the back of the blade, is in contact with the point. If you hear the same sound you heard when testing horizontal alignment, the saw is vertically aligned. If you hear more sound or no sound, adjustment is needed. Adjustments for vertical alignment are made at the top of the yoke where the motor/blade assembly pivots for ripping. Once again consult the owner's manual for explicit adjustment instructions for your saw.

Measuring runout You can also check for blade runout with this fixture. First check the flange for runout with a dial indicator, if you have one. If there is more than 0.003 in. runout at the flange, or if you don't have a dial indicator, you need to test for runout on the blade. The set-up is the same as when testing vertical alignment. Clamp the fixture to the fence so that the point just touches one tooth. But this time, rotate the blade backward by hand and listen for the loudest sound. Mark the loudest tooth with a felt-tipped pen. Move the carriage forward until the rear of the sawblade is even with the point of the fixture. Rotate the blade backward until the marked tooth sounds against the point. You quickly develop an ear for very precise measurement, and you can also measure the runout with a feeler gauge.

Radial-arm saws generally have more runout than table saws. If the runout exceeds 0.020 in. at the edge of the blade, check for flange and blade problems as described in Chapter 1. Minimize runout by rotating the blade to various positions on the arbor, also as described in Chapter 1.

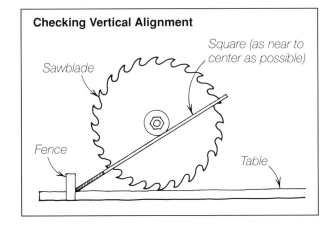

Checking Vertical Alignment

Sawblade

Square (as near to center as possible)

Fence

Table

To test for vertical alignment, rotate the blade as you move the head so the same tooth contacts the point of the fixture.

Testing for Squareness

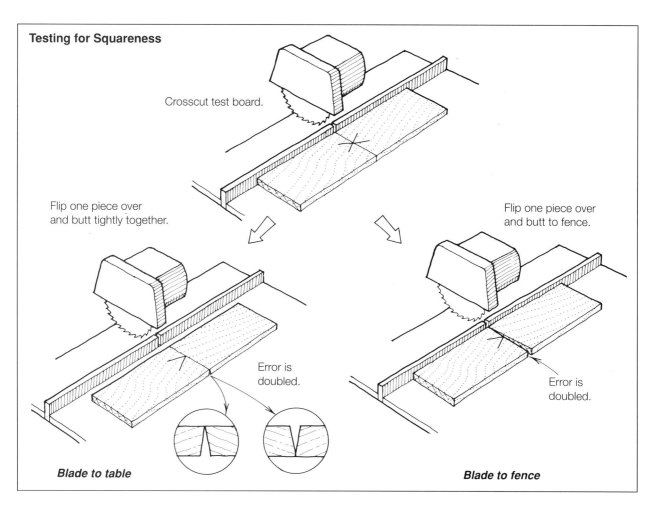

Crosscut test board.

Flip one piece over and butt tightly together.

Flip one piece over and butt to fence.

Error is doubled.

Error is doubled.

Blade to table

Blade to fence

Shimming a Table

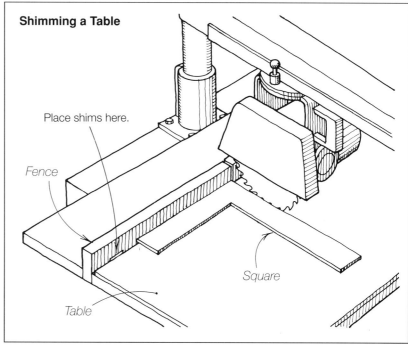

Place shims here.

Fence

Square

Table

Feedback from the workpiece

Thus far we have discussed static testing, but the real test is the dynamic test that you get from a saw cut. Feedback from the work-piece lets you know if the saw is accurate, and tells you how much and in which direction any adjustment should be made.

Choose a piece of wood that is flat and dimensionally stable (such as plywood). It is very important for this test that the edges are parallel. Machine a piece ¾ in. thick by 8 in. wide by 30 in. long, and put a big X in the middle of the board, as shown in the top drawing on the facing page. Crosscut the board right through the marked X. To check for squareness of the blade and table, flip one half over and slide the pieces back together. Any error will be doubled. Next flip both boards over and check again. To check for squareness of the blade and fence, keep one half of the board flipped over and place the pieces firmly against the fence, or stand them up on edge. The cut ends should fit tightly together. If they don't, the widest part of the gap is double the error between the blade and the fence. In both these tests, the work-piece shows the direction in which you need to make the adjustment, as well as how much of an adjustment you need to make.

Fine-tuning the radial-arm saw

The biggest problem with the radial-arm saw is that the adjustments are not gradual or progressive. Very accurate final adjustments of the saw are tedious and frustrating. After the machine has been used for a while the setup nightmare must be repeated if accuracy is a must.

However, there is one simple way of making gradual adjustments that makes fine-tuning easy and predictable. Use standard adjustments to get as close as possible, then insert paper shims for the final adjustment. If the fence and the blade are not quite square, slide one or several paper shims between the fence and the table. When the saw is accurate, the last step is to adjust the pointers on the angle scales.

Using the radial-arm saw

There are two approaches to using the radial-arm saw. According to one school of thought, the radial-arm saw should be used for all the functions it is capable of performing, such as ripping, crosscutting and mitering. If you do not have any other tools available or if you are a contractor who only wants one tool to haul around and set up for the job, using the radial-arm saw in this way is the logical approach.

The other approach is to use the saw exclusively for crosscutting. The table saw is then used for ripping, and a miter saw is used for angled cuts. In the extreme case, a guide wire is attached to each side of the arm so the arm cannot be angled. If an angled cut is made, a jig or fixture is used to hold the workpiece at an angle. This fixed-arm concept is used in some European saw designs that have a rotating table. The environment that you work in usually determines which approach you will use.

Safety is also a consideration. Basically, if you keep one hand on the handle and the other on the workpiece, out of the way of the sawblade, you'll be safe. But the radial-arm saw has been much promoted as a universal machine. I have a book on the radial-arm saw that was published in 1956, which was probably the heyday of the one-machine shop idea. There's not enough money in the world to get me to do some of the things recommended in that book. Can you cut circles on the radial-arm saw? Sure. Would I? Nope. Use good sense when it comes to exotic applications. Remember that the radial-arm saw is designed primarily for crosscutting. Any deviation from this single purpose compromises its engineering and, very probably, your safety. There's an old Wisconsin saying: You can teach a pig to sing, but it wastes your time and it makes the pigs irritable. Cutting circles on the radial-arm saw falls in the same category, and, in addition, it endangers appendages.

Other potentially dangerous procedures on the radial-arm saw include making coves, cutting tapers and shaping with a molding cutter. These procedures are better done with a router table or miter saw. In recent years sales of radial-arm saws have decreased to the point that Black & Decker no longer makes the DeWalt, which many woodworkers believe was the best radial-arm saw made. The radial-arm saw is losing ground to new technologies such as the telescoping compound angle-miter saws, which are lightweight, very accurate and half the price of a good radial saw.

Crosscutting

The 90° angled and compound-angled crosscut is the forte of the radial-arm saw. The accuracy of the cut is maximized if you use an adjustable drafting square for setup and a stop for stability and repeatability during the saw cuts. The hinged stop block shown in the top photo and drawing on the facing page allows you to establish a squared end on a long board, with the hinged stop up, then quickly crosscut any number of pieces to the same length after you flip the hinged stop down.

When cutting miters, angle the arm to the right (if right-handed) because the wood can easily be controlled with the left hand. If you are cutting a molding to make a continuous frame, you have to angle the arm in both directions. Accurate angles are easily adjusted if you use a magnetic fence on the blade and an adjustable drafting triangle or fixed-angle setup fixture.

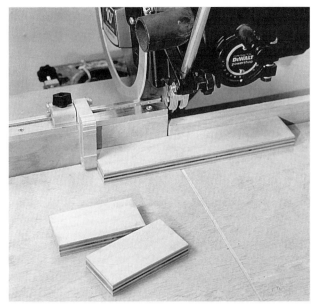

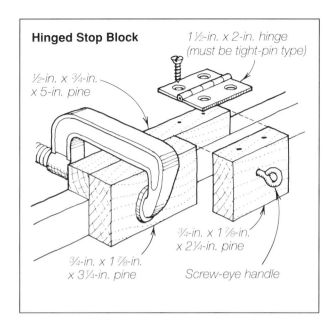

Hinged Stop Block

1½-in. x 2-in. hinge (must be tight-pin type)

½-in. x ¾-in. x 5-in. pine

¾-in. x 1⅞-in. x 2¼-in. pine

¾-in. x 1⅞-in. x 3¼-in. pine

Screw-eye handle

To set up the saw for crosscutting, fix the distance between the end of the board and the sawblade with a stop block. A hinged stop is handy for making a rough and finish cut.

A magnetic fence and an adjustable drafting triangle make accurate blade-angle adjustment easy. Two magnets hold the straightedge to the blade.

Commercially available setup fixtures like this angle gauge allow precise, quick arm-angle adjustments for frames with six or eight sides.

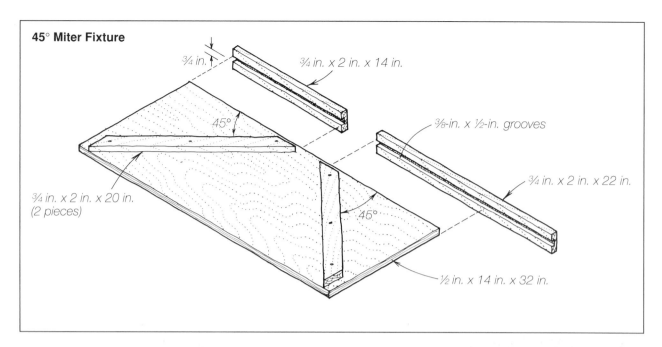

45° Miter Fixture

¾ in.

¾ in. x 2 in. x 14 in.

45°

⅜-in. x ½-in. grooves

¾ in. x 2 in. x 20 in.
(2 pieces)

45°

¾ in. x 2 in. x 22 in.

½ in. x 14 in. x 32 in.

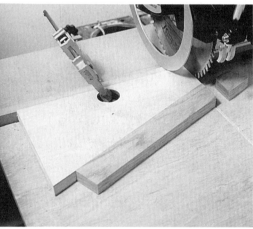

For production work, an angle jig makes fast and accurate setup possible.

The most accurate miter fixture points to the operator. Clamp a stop block to keep the pieces from sliding during the saw cut.

Miter fixtures

A better option for miter cuts is to make a fixture to hold the wood on an angle so that the arm does not have to be angled. If the fixture is accurate, the result will be an accurate cut with minimal setup. Although fixtures can be attached directly to the table, it is best to make them with a plywood base roughly the size of the table (see the drawing on the facing page). A strip of plywood attached to the back of the fixture replaces the fence, making setup and removal painless. The angle can point toward the fence or away from it. If the pieces are long, the end of the workpiece can be supported if the angle points toward the fence.

It is also handy to have a fixture with an adjustable fence. If you cut a lot of miters on moldings, make a fixture that will hold the molding on an angle (see the drawing below).

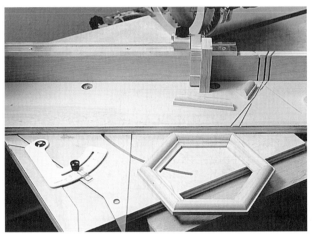

This adjustable miter fixture allows any angle between 45° and 90° to be cut.

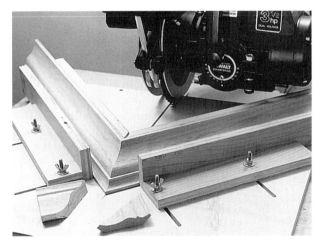

This fixture holds the molding on its edge to make accurate miters while the blade and table remain fixed at 90°.

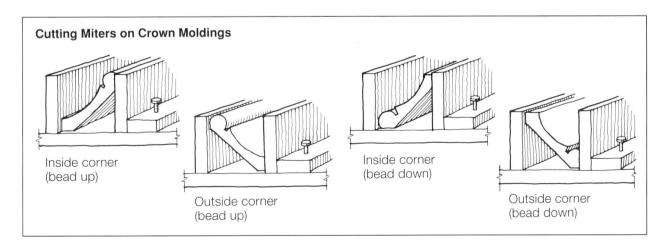

Cutting Miters on Crown Moldings

Inside corner
(bead up)

Outside corner
(bead up)

Inside corner
(bead down)

Outside corner
(bead down)

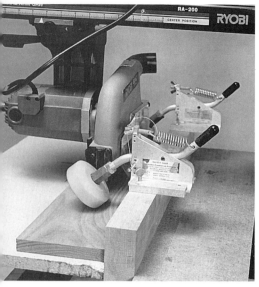

Spring-loaded wheels prevent kickbacks while ripping by keeping the wood against the fence and secure on the table.

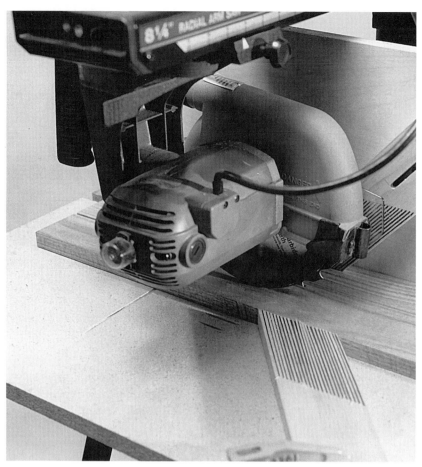

Shopmade featherboards serve the same purpose as the commercially available hold-down jigs.

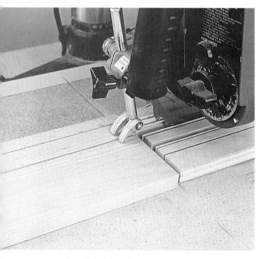

Antikickback pawls prevent the wood from coming backward at the operator. The spreader prevents the wood from closing after the cut, which minimizes the likelihood of kickback.

Ripping

The radial-arm saw is dangerous in the rip position because you feed into the teeth of the blade as they're coming up from the table. The blade is applying an upward force, which greatly increases the potential for kickback. Make sure you adjust the antikickback pawls and clamp on wheel hold-downs or featherboards. A standard-sized push stick can cause the workpiece to rotate and catch at the back of the blade; for that reason a wide pusher should be used to move the wood safely past the back of the blade. The most dangerous situations arise when the wood is captured between the blade and the fence, resulting in a kickback. When bevel ripping, avoid capturing the wood under the blade, as shown in the bottom drawing on the facing page.

A wide push stick prevents the workpiece from rotating at the end of the cut.

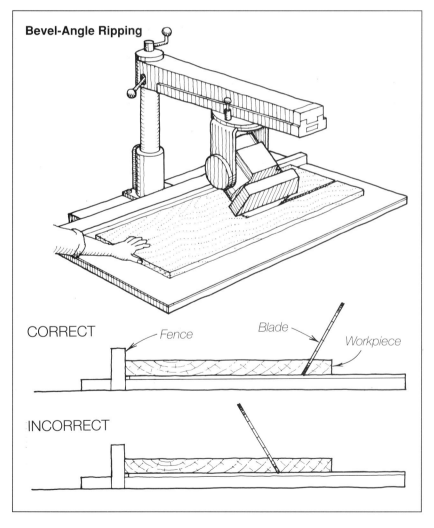

Bevel-Angle Ripping

CORRECT

Fence *Blade* *Workpiece*

INCORRECT

Alternatives to the radial-arm saw

During the 1970s and 1980s manufacturers introduced a number of portable saws that have proved to be popular alternatives to the radial-arm saw. These include the electric miter saw and the sliding compound-miter saw.

Electric miter saw

The electric miter saw is a portable circular saw on a hinge. The blade is lowered into the work, and a rotation mechanism angles the saw in relation to the fence. The simple design was an instant hit because the saw was dependable and accurate. The miter saw is very popular with contractors because it can be moved from site to site with no loss of accuracy. Some manufacturers developed a tilt mechanism to allow the saw to make compound-angle cuts. The only drawback was that the saw did not cut wider than 4 in., but larger saws are now available.

The miter saw is very easy to adjust. The fence is usually solid, and the angle is adjusted by loosening the fence and placing a square between the fence and the blade. The blade is squared to the table with a simple single-bolt mechanism. In contrast to the radial-arm saw, the miter saw can be accurately readjusted in less than five minutes.

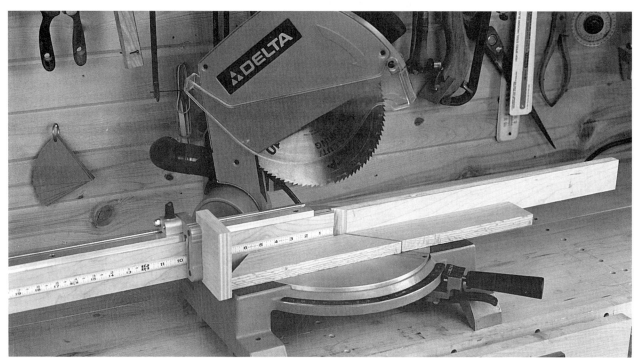

The electric miter saw is a saw mounted on a hinge, with a sawblade that is lowered into the workpiece. The saw rotates for miter cuts.

The sliding compound-miter saw

Creativity is often a matter of mixing two seemingly unrelated objects into a totally new object. The sliding miter saw is a blend of the radial-arm saw and the miter saw. It has the pivoting feature of the miter saw and the width capacity and compound-angle cutting ability of the radial-arm saw. Yet it comes in a compact design that makes the saw easy to carry. The saw also stays accurate for a long period of time and is easy to adjust.

The beauty of the sliding compound-miter saw is that it offers the option of three different sawing techniques. Like the miter saw, the blade can be lowered through the work. As with the radial-arm saw, the blade can be pulled through the work. It also allows the third option of pushing the saw through the work, which is a European concept. When using the sliding saw on wide stock, the saw is first lowered onto the work and pushed forward through the remaining material. The chop-and-push technique is possible because the motor and hinge are supported by a sliding arm that allows the saw to move in and out. The mechanism is squared in a similar fashion as the miter saw; the only additional adjustment is a means of tightening the slop in the slide tube.

It may take some time to get used to the push technique, but once you do it will seem very natural. When you think about it, pushing is the logical way to cut. No one would ever consider pulling a portable circular saw backward when cutting a sheet of plywood, yet that is exactly what you are doing when you pull a radial-arm saw through a piece of wood. Pushing allows you the option of feeding the blade a manageable amount of material. When the blade is pulled into the wood, it has a tendency to feed itself and can take too much material at once. This creates the familiar radial-arm saw phenomenon of the saw bogging down, which in turn causes a rough cut.

Like the radial-arm saw, the sliding saw can also be used to cut a compound angle. This is accomplished by a simple design that allows the whole motor mechanism to rotate at an angle. The mechanism is easily readjusted, and the scale is easy to reset.

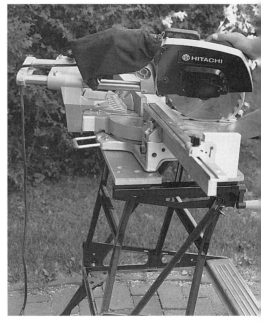

The sliding compound-miter saw crosscuts and compound-miters wide boards. The motor slides back and forth on round tubes. The blade cuts with the push or pull stroke and can also be lowered into the wood.

CHAPTER 3
The Bandsaw

The bandsaw is named for its blade, a thin band of steel with teeth on one side that is welded together to form a loop. The blade is suspended over either two or three wheels. As the wheels rotate, the blade also rotates, creating a continuous cutting action. Because the blade is narrow, you can turn the workpiece while cutting to make curves.

A bandsaw cuts curves better than just about any other machine in the shop, but it can also make straight cuts effectively. The blade is so thin that it cuts stock with a minimum of effort and waste. This attribute is particularly important when resawing an expensive exotic or a nicely figured domestic wood. The bandsaw is also the tool of choice when cutting through thick wood. Nothing hogs its way through a 12/4 burl of elm or hard maple like a bandsaw with a hook-tooth blade. As an additional advantage, the bandsaw is one of the safest machines in the shop—its teeth cut downward and there's no danger of kickback, as with a circular saw.

However, the bandsaw does have a reputation as a troublesome tool. Unlike the radial-arm saw or table saw, where you simply install the blade and you're ready to cut, each blade has to be individually adjusted on the bandsaw. Other factors that affect bandsaw performance include the condition of the tires and the alignment of the wheels. If the tool is properly adjusted, its behavior is very predictable. The problem with the bandsaw is that most people either don't know how to adjust the machine correctly or lack the patience to learn. Once you learn, however, adjustment takes only a minute or two.

The 14-in. Bandsaw

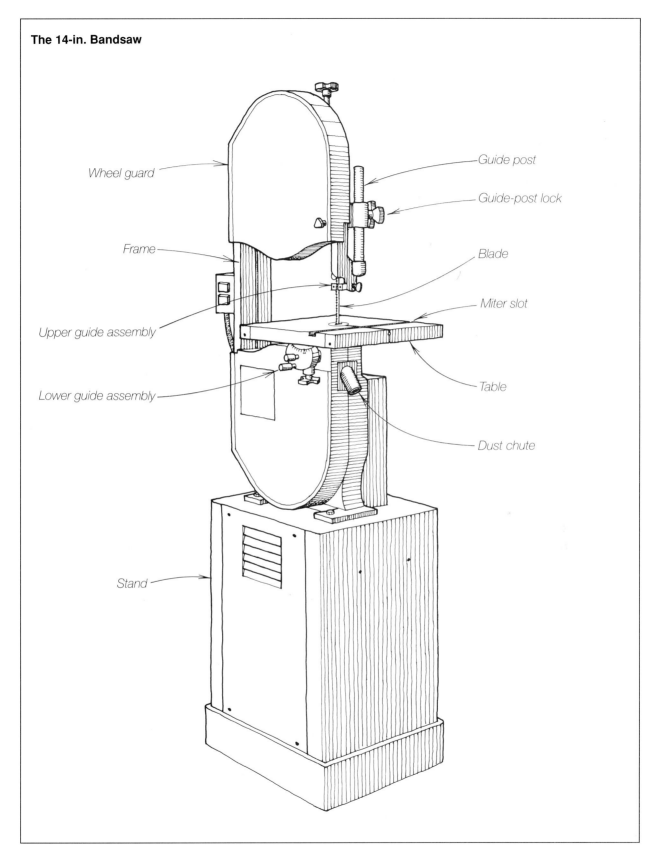

Wheel guard

Guide post

Guide-post lock

Frame

Blade

Miter slot

Upper guide assembly

Table

Lower guide assembly

Dust chute

Stand

A bandsaw mill allows you to harvest wood where you find it. The log remains stationary while the saw rides horizontally along a small track.

Bandsaw design

Bandsaws for woodworking are available in a variety of vertical and horizontal designs and range from small portable units to large industrial heavyweights. The most common design is exemplified by the two-wheel Delta 14-in. bandsaw, as shown in the drawing on p. 79. There are three basic styles of bandsaws: floor models, stand-mounted models and bench-top models. In addition to woodworking bandsaws, there are also a number of different bandsaws for use in metalworking and the plastics industry, in butcher, upholstery and print shops and in a host of other work settings.

Bandsaws are categorized by wheel size, number of wheels, throat size and maximum blade width. In the past, saw size was determined by the diameter of the saw wheel, but today it is more commonly ex-

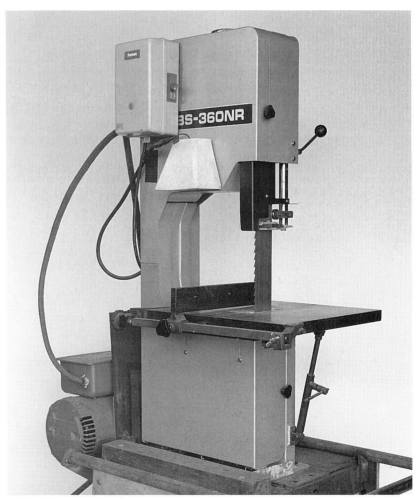

A bandsaw designed for resawing has a greater throat depth than the common 14-in. bandsaw and can handle a 3-in. wide blade.

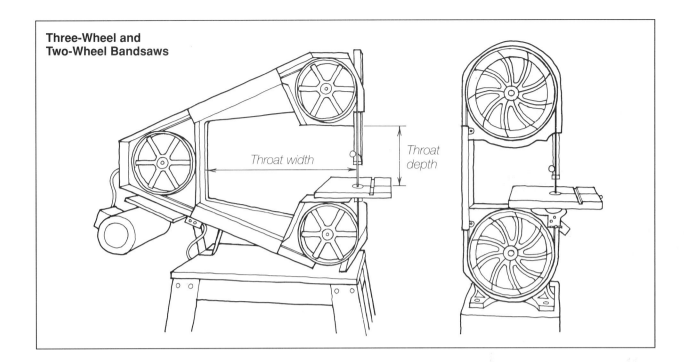

**Three-Wheel and
Two-Wheel Bandsaws**

Throat width

Throat depth

pressed as throat width. A three-wheel bandsaw usually offers the widest throat in the least amount of space, and it is usually a less expensive machine than the two-wheel saw. However, the three-wheel design has a number of drawbacks: It is more difficult to track and more difficult to align the wheels, and some users report premature blade wear. Throat depth determines the maximum thickness you can saw. A typical 14-in. bandsaw can saw a 6-in. thick piece of wood.

The typical consumer-grade bandsaw comes with a ½-hp motor as standard equipment. This size motor is adequate unless you plan to re-saw thick work, in which case a ¾-hp motor is a minimum requirement. On some cast-iron bandsaws you can purchase a height extender that raises the top wheel 6 in. This extender doubles the thickness of the wood that can be cut.

On most bandsaws the table tilts to allow angled cuts. Most saws have a slot milled in the table top for a miter guide. Recently Sears has revived an old idea: One of their machines has a stationary table and a tilting head. This design was more common in the past, particularly in the boatbuilding industry.

More than any other woodworking tool, you get what you pay for with a bandsaw. Although two bandsaws may look the same, the more expensive one will probably have bearings that last longer and wheels that are balanced.

The tilted table allows the operator to make a variety of angled or beveled cuts.

Bandsaw anatomy

The bandsaw is a much simpler machine than either the table saw or the radial-arm saw. The two or three wheels that carry the blade are attached to a frame, which can be cast iron, steel or cast aluminum. On some cheaper, smaller saws much of the frame is plastic.

The bottom wheel is either driven by a direct-drive motor or is connected to the motor via pulleys and a belt. The top wheel is attached to the frame and adjusts up and down, its upward adjustment creating the tension on the blade. The top wheel also has a tilt mechanism that can tilt forward or backward and is used to steer or track the blade.

Two guide mechanisms above and below the table prevent the blade from deflecting sideways or moving backward off the saw (see the drawing on p. 97). Either bearings or solid guide blocks on the side of the blade prevent it from deflecting sideways. A bearing directly behind the blade prevents backward deflection. The top guide mechanism is attached to a post that moves up and down and is adjustable for the height of the wood.

Bandsaw blades

Each bandsaw blade is a continuous metal band with teeth stamped or cut along one edge. The blade rides on the rims of either two or three metal wheels. There are a number of different styles of blade suitable for different operations, such as cutting curves, resawing or ripping. Although a coarse blade cuts like a chainsaw and a fine $\frac{1}{16}$-in. blade like an expensive scrollsaw, the design of bandsaw blades is the same across different widths. Blade width determines how tight a curve the saw cuts. Blade pitch, tooth form and tooth set determine how the blade cuts. To stretch your bandsaw to its fullest potential, you must select the appropriate blade for the task.

Blade width   Blades are most commonly described by blade width, or the distance from the back of the blade to the front of the teeth. The narrower the blade, the tighter the turn the blade can make. The wider the blade, the more likely it is to resist deflection. Wider blades are preferred for straight cuts.

The largest practical blade on a consumer-grade bandsaw is the $\frac{1}{2}$-in. blade. Some owner's manuals inflate their saw's capacity, but blades wider than $\frac{1}{2}$ in. need wheels 18 in. or larger in diameter. I think a $\frac{1}{4}$-in. blade is the most useful general-purpose blade. For years the smallest blade available was the $\frac{1}{8}$-in. blade, which makes a turn about the size

A direct-drive bandsaw.

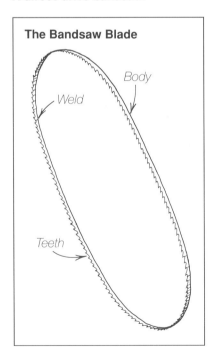

The Bandsaw Blade

Body

Weld

Teeth

of a pencil eraser. The latest development, however, is a ¹⁄₁₆-in. blade that makes extremely tight turns similar to those made by a scrollsaw. This very small blade requires the use of special nonmetal guide blocks called Cool Blocks® (see p. 101).

Pitch The pitch of a blade determines how fast and how smooth the blade cuts. Pitch is usually expressed as the number of teeth in 1 in. of blade (written "teeth per inch" or "TPI"). "Coarse," "medium" and "fine" also describe the number of teeth in a blade, but these terms are less precise than TPI. The coarser the blade, the faster and rougher the cut.

At least three teeth must be in the material at any given time during the saw cut. More teeth create a smoother cut, but too many teeth will overheat and cut slowly. Overheated teeth soften and dull quickly. Heat also shortens the life of the band itself. Too few teeth produce extremely rough cuts, stalled cuts and blade breaks.

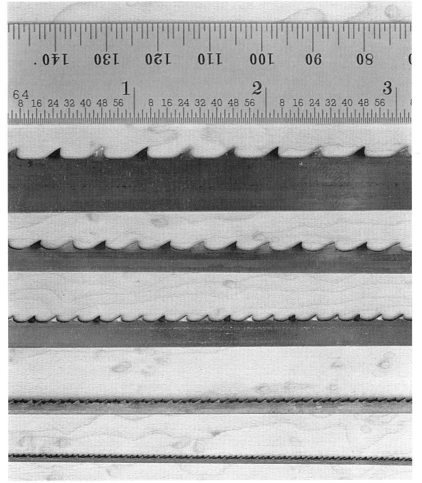

Wide blades typically have fewer teeth per inch than narrow blades.

Pitch Selection

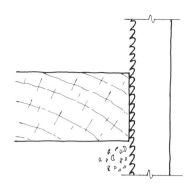

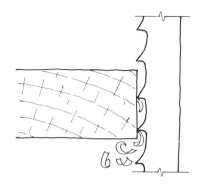

Correct Pitch

1. Fast cutting
2. Minimal heat
3. Minimal feed pressure required
4. Minimal horsepower required
5. Best blade life

Pitch Too Fine

1. Slow cutting
2. Excessive heat, causing premature blade breakage
3. Unnecessarily high feed pressure
4. Unnecessarily high horsepower
5. Excessive tool wear

Pitch Too Coarse

1. Excessive tooth wear
2. Vibration
3. Short blade life

Rake Angles

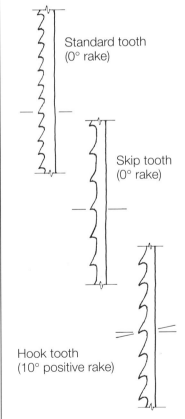

Standard tooth
(0° rake)

Skip tooth
(0° rake)

Hook tooth
(10° positive rake)

Generally, the harder the material the finer the pitch should be. For example, extremely hard woods such as ebony and rosewood require a finer pitch than oak or maple. Soft woods such as pine and poplar are best cut with a fairly coarse blade. In pitchy woods such as pine or cherry, a fine blade will soon load with pitch and overheat.

Tooth form   There are two tooth shapes. The tooth face is either 90° to the body of the blade, which is called a 0° rake, or it has a slight positive (forward) angle of around 10°, which is called a hook tooth. The 0° rake is found on standard and skip-tooth blades (see the facing page). It cuts with a scraping action, which produces a smooth cut but increased heat. The hook tooth cuts more aggressively, leaving a rougher cut, but it generates less heat and prolongs blade life.

Standard teeth are closely spaced and cut smoothly. A standard-toothed blade is the best choice when smoothness is a consideration, as when cutting fine details. It's also good for cutting across the grain because it doesn't tear the wood as it cuts. A slow feed rate is important when cutting thick stock.

A skip-tooth blade has a 0° rake like the standard configuration, but every other tooth is removed. The coarse cut from the skip tooth is much faster, particularly when cutting with the grain. Although it doesn't cut across the grain as well as the standard rake or hook tooth, the skip tooth is the most widely used blade.

The combination of the positive rake angle and fewer teeth make the hook tooth the most aggressive blade. It is particularly efficient at cutting thick stock with the grain. This makes it the best choice for ripping and resawing.

Tooth set The teeth on a bandsaw blade are "set," or bent sideways. The saw kerf is therefore wider than the body of the blade. The wider kerf allows you to rotate the workpiece around the blade when cutting a curve. The side clearance of the blade created by the set of the teeth also decreases friction between the blade and the workpiece. There are three basic set styles: alternate, raker and wavy.

The teeth on alternate-set blades are set so that every other tooth is bent in the same direction. This configuration gives the most cuts per inch and the smoothest cut. The alternate-set style, which is well suited to crosscutting, is commonly found on standard-tooth blades.

Raker-set blades are similar to the alternate-set style except that every third tooth, called a raker, is not set. Raker teeth clean out the middle of the cut like the chippers in a dado set. You find blades with a raker set most often on skip-tooth and hook blades. A raker set increases the efficiency of the cutting action but decreases the smoothness of the cut because fewer teeth are cutting the side of the kerf.

On a blade with a wavy set, groups of teeth are alternately set in opposite directions. This configuration is most commonly used for cutting metal, as in a hacksaw blade.

A 3-TPI pitch is best for cutting thick stock. Here, a 3-TPI hook-tooth blade cuts red oak.

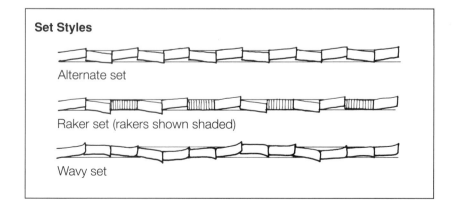

Set Styles

Alternate set

Raker set (rakers shown shaded)

Wavy set

Blade Groups			
	Small	Medium	Large
Width	1/16 in. to 1/8 in.	3/16 in. to 3/8 in.	1/2 in. and above
Pitch	14 to 32 TPI (fine)	4 to 12 TPI	2 to 4 TPI (coarse)
Tooth form	standard	standard/skip	hook
Tooth set	alternate	raker	raker

Blade groups Bandsaw blades are sometimes classified as small, medium or large. This classification refers to more than just blade width. Width, pitch, tooth form and tooth set vary within each blade group, giving rise to distinct cutting characteristics. Small blades usually have a standard tooth form and a fine pitch. Medium blades usually have a skip tooth with a raker set and a medium to coarse pitch. Large blades often have a hook tooth with a raker set and a coarse pitch. You will be prepared for most cutting if you have at least one blade from each of these groups.

Choosing a blade When you are deciding which blade to put on your saw, there are two primary considerations: the tightness of the curves you want to cut and the grain of the workpiece. The blade width determines how tight a turn you can make. Until you know your saw well it is best to look at a contour chart (see the top drawing on the facing page) to determine which size blade to use for a specific application.

Everyday items such as a coin or pencil can help to choose the correct blade width for the job. For example, a quarter corresponds to the tightest cut that can be made with a 1/4-in. blade. The arc of a dime is the tightest curve that can be cut with a 3/16-in. blade, and a pencil eraser is the size of the tightest turn that you can make with a 1/8-in. blade.

When making crosscuts, diagonal cuts or multigrain cuts, the standard-tooth blade is the best choice. The skip tooth works well for cutting gentle curves with the grain and can also be used when making multigrain cuts. For me, the best general-purpose blade is a 1/4-in. wide 4-TPI to 6-TPI skip-tooth blade. The hook-tooth blade is also good at cutting gentle curves with the grain, but its forte is ripping or resawing straight cuts.

Contour Chart: Blade Width and Cutting Radius

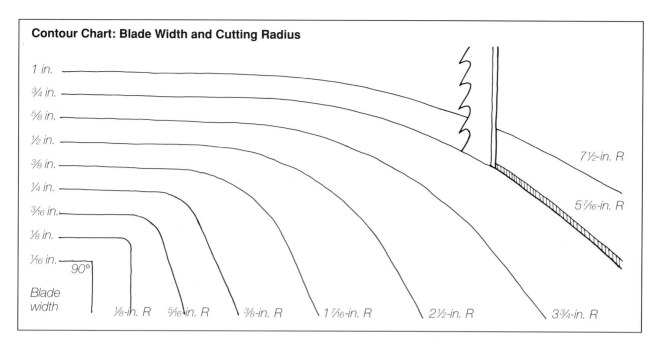

1 in.
¾ in.
⅝ in.
½ in.
⅜ in.
¼ in.
3/16 in.
⅛ in.
1/16 in.
90°

Blade
width

7½-in. R

5 7/16-in. R

⅛-in. R   5/16-in. R   ⅜-in. R   1 7/16-in. R   2½-in. R   3¾-in. R

Tooth Forms

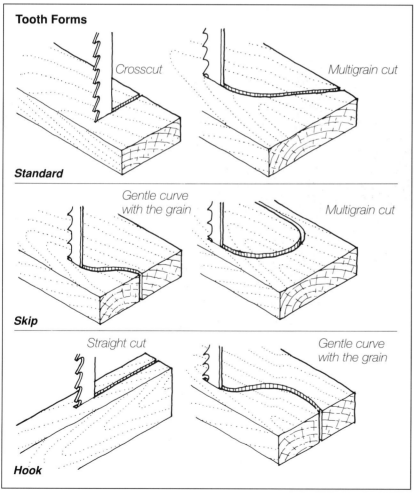

Standard

Crosscut

Multigrain cut

Skip

Gentle curve
with the grain

Multigrain cut

Hook

Straight cut

Gentle curve
with the grain

There are a number of specialized blades, such as a knife blade for cutting leather and cloth and a spiral blade for cutting continuous curves. In recent years several manufacturers and vendors have tried, with mixed results, to market metalworking blades to the wood industry. These bimetal blades are of two different metals, with a tip made from high-speed steel or carbide. Some users report good results, but many are disappointed by excessive blade breaking caused by metal fatigue. The body of a metalworking blade is usually very stiff and designed to run at low speeds with wheels that are at least 20 in. in diameter.

Blades that are sold through catalogs or local dealers are usually of high quality. They will outlast the blade that came with your saw by a considerable margin.

Blade maintenance   In the past, bandsaw blades were soft and easy to refile. Modern blades are harder and do not hand-file easily, although it can be done. Having the blade professionally sharpened will cost more than buying a new blade. Choosing the correct blade for the task and adjusting it properly on the saw will extend the life of the blade.

Blades can take a lot of use but not much abuse. When the blade becomes dull it will not cut as straight as when it was sharp. However, a blade that is too dull for good resawing may still have many hours of life for cutting curves in 1-in. stock and cutting scrap and firewood. If a dull blade breaks, it is usually not worth fixing because it will break again shortly, but it is worth fixing a broken new blade. Blade repair is a job for a professional welder.

The blade on a woodworking bandsaw travels at between 2,400 ft. and 3,200 ft. per minute. Although metalworking bandsaws need different speeds for different metals, woodworking bandsaws are single-speed machines, and justly so. One speed is fine for woodworking.

Tuning the bandsaw

Just like any other woodworking machine, the bandsaw must be tuned for performance. A poorly adjusted bandsaw vibrates, wanders, overheats, stalls and breaks blades. To get the maximum performance, you have to be able to pick the appropriate blade and know how to change and track it. It's always been a mystery to me why many people go to great lengths to avoid changing bandsaw blades. Tuning is an easy habit that can be developed quickly. Life's too short to spend cursing your bandsaw, so get good at changing blades and adjusting it, and be faithful about tweaking it into good condition.

Tuning theory

Running a well-tuned bandsaw is a beautiful experience. The blade is tracked, tensioned and square to the table. You've selected the right blade for the material and process, and the back of the blade is rounded for easy curves. The guides and bearings are perfectly adjusted and, as you negotiate a sharp corner, there's not even a whisper of protest. This dreamscape is possible only if you are well grounded in theory and adept at application.

"Tracking" is positioning or balancing the bandsaw blade on the wheels. This operation is essential because only a tracked blade stays on the saw. The blade stays on the wheels because of three factors: the shape of the rim of the wheel, the angle of the top wheel and the tension on the blade.

Rim shape   A bandsaw wheel is either crowned or flat. A crowned wheel enables you to center-track a blade. A flat wheel allows you to track the blade either in the middle of the wheel or toward its front edge. When blades are manufactured, the teeth are first ground, then hardened by heat treatment, which causes the front of the blade to shrink relative to the back. This shrinkage is most pronounced in small blades. Thus, crowned wheels work best on blades less than ¼ in. in width, whereas flat wheels are best for wider blades.

The outside rim of a bandsaw wheel is covered with a piece of rubber, called the tire, which is between ⅛ in. and ¼ in. thick. The tire acts as a cushion and shock absorber, and keeps the blade's teeth from dulling against the metal wheel.

The chief disadvantage of the crowned wheel is that the back of the blade tracks on the tire, while the front of the blade is just slightly in contact with it. Larger blades, which are the best for straight cuts and resawing, are therefore more difficult to track. Wheel alignment is

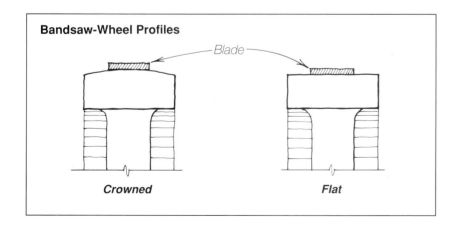

Bandsaw-Wheel Profiles

Blade

Crowned   *Flat*

more critical with the crowned wheel, too. If the wheels are not perfectly lined up, the crowns on each wheel compete for control of the blade, and the misalignment causes vibration and shortens blade life.

When tracking large blades, you want the blade to run as flat as possible on the wheels. That's why a flat wheel is preferable to a crowned wheel for big blades. Although they take more care to track, flat wheels allow you to track blades in various positions on the wheel. Large blades track best toward the front of the tire on a flat wheel. Small blades are best tracked toward the middle. Flat wheels are even more prone than crowned wheels to ruts in the tire. Ruts cut by one blade make it harder to track other blades.

Wheel angle The angle of the top wheel steers the blade in the direction of the tilt, thereby affecting the tracking of the blade. The usual approach recommended in the owner's manual is to tilt the top wheel backward until the blade tracks in the center of the top wheel. This technique is known as center tracking. Center tracking works well with blades less than ¼ in. wide. These blades are more flexible, and the misalignment of the wheel doesn't harm the performance or the life expectancy of the blades.

Larger blades are stiffer and best tracked with the wheels aligned with each other. This technique is known as coplanar tracking, because the rims of the wheels lie in the same plane and the axes are parallel. If the wheels are coplanar, the blade will quickly find equilibrium and track itself, even with a crowned wheel.

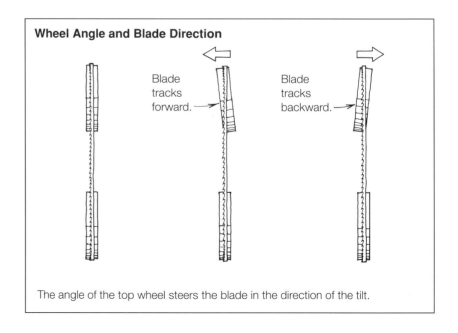

Wheel Angle and Blade Direction

Blade tracks forward.

Blade tracks backward.

The angle of the top wheel steers the blade in the direction of the tilt.

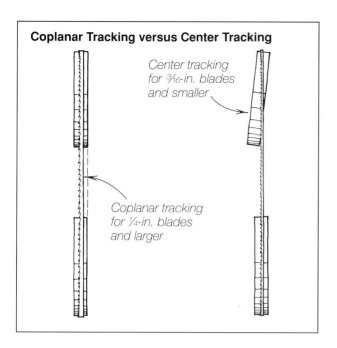

Coplanar Tracking versus Center Tracking

Center tracking for ³⁄₁₆-in. blades and smaller

Coplanar tracking for ¼-in. blades and larger

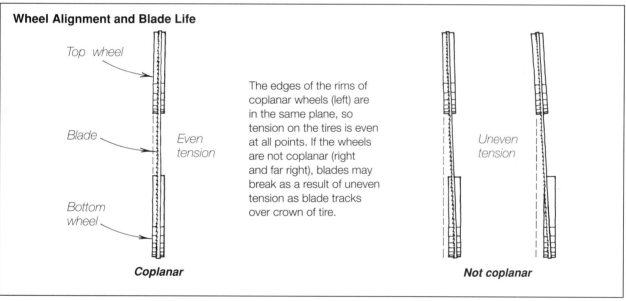

Wheel Alignment and Blade Life

Top wheel

Blade

Even tension

Bottom wheel

The edges of the rims of coplanar wheels (left) are in the same plane, so tension on the tires is even at all points. If the wheels are not coplanar (right and far right), blades may break as a result of uneven tension as blade tracks over crown of tire.

Uneven tension

Coplanar

Not coplanar

With coplanar tracking, the blade exerts the same amount of tension on the tires at all points of contact. There is no binding as with center tracking. On some saws, the wheels will not be coplanar as they come from the factory (see the drawing above). Blades on these saws may break because of the uneven tension. Bandsaw blades, particularly wide bandsaw blades, last longer, cut straighter and require less tension when coplanar-tracked. With coplanar tracking, the blade has a tendency to track toward the front of the wheels because the front of the blade is shorter than the back of the blade.

Two Ways to Fold a Blade

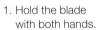

1. Hold the blade with both hands.

2. Create two loops.

3. Twist the blade again.

4. The additional twist creates a third loop.

1. Step on blade.

2. Create two loops.

3. Twist the blade again.

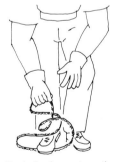

4. Push the loops together.

5. You now have three loops.

Adjusting the blade

Regardless of wheel shape, the first step in adjusting your bandsaw is to make the wheels coplanar. This adjustment should be made with a blade in place. Before we discuss the correct way to install and track a blade, let's begin by removing a blade.

Removing a blade Unplug the saw and remove the mechanism for aligning the table halves, if there is one. It is usually a pin, bolt or a front rail. Unscrew the blade guard and remove the throat plate. Release the tension by lowering the top wheel. Open or remove the covers. Take the blade off the wheels with both hands, and carefully slide it out of the table slot. Be careful. Wide blades are particularly mean-spirited, and you may want to wear gloves. It's always a good idea to wear safety glasses when removing the blade. Fold the blade (see the drawing on the facing page). Retract the thrust bearings above and below the table. Loosen the guides on the side of the blade and retract them, too, to make it easier to install the next blade.

Installing a blade Unplug the machine. Put on a pair of gloves and uncoil the blade. Wipe off any oil or dirt with a rag or a paper towel. Pull the blade through the rag backwards so that the teeth don't hook. Inspect the teeth. If they are pointed in the wrong direction, you will have to turn the blade inside out (see the drawing below).

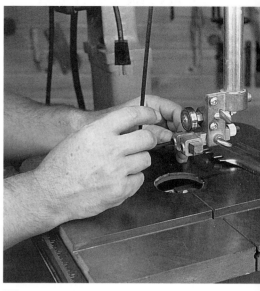

When removing the blade, retract the guides and the thrust bearing above and below the table.

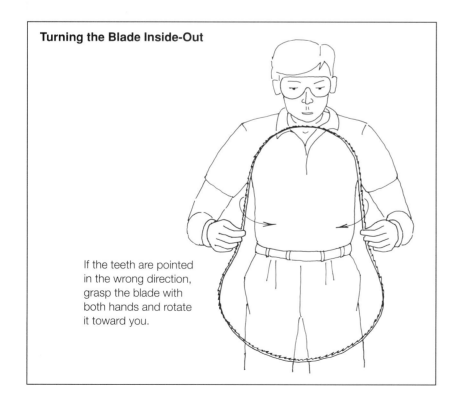

Turning the Blade Inside-Out

If the teeth are pointed in the wrong direction, grasp the blade with both hands and rotate it toward you.

Check the tension on the gauge on the inside cover or on the back of the bandsaw and make final tension adjustments.

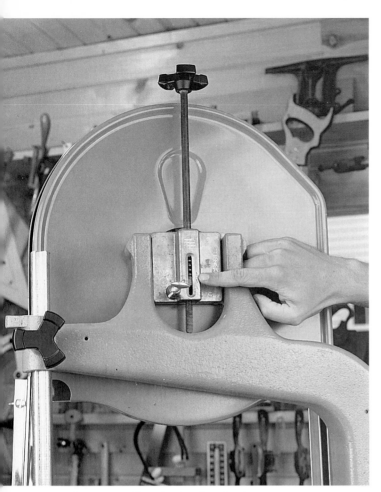

After installing the blade, slowly raise the top wheel with the tension knob.

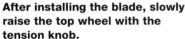

Hold the blade with both hands with the teeth edges toward you. Slide it through the table slot and place it on the wheels. Slowly raise the top wheel with the tension knob. As you rotate the blade with one hand, increase the tension with the other. Most bandsaws have a tension scale to give a general idea of how much pressure the wheels apply on the blade. For straight cuts with dull blades, higher tension and a slower feed rate are needed. If your saw is old, the tension spring may be weak and you may want to tension your saw to the next higher setting. For example, tension a ⅜-in. blade at the ½-in. setting. You can also order a new spring from the manufacturer. On the other hand, never apply so much pressure that you completely compress the tension spring, which has a secondary role as a shock absorber. Continue to tighten until you have adequate tension. A blade cannot be correctly tracked until it is at the appropriate tension.

Checking wheel alignment Next check the alignment of the wheels with a straightedge. On Sears and INCA saws the adjustment is made by changing the position of the bottom wheel. On Delta and imported clones the adjustment is made by removing or adding washers behind the top wheel. Once the wheels are in the same plane (coplanar), you are ready to track the blade.

Check coplanar wheels with a straightedge.

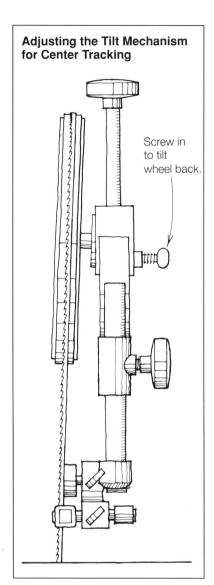

Screw in to tilt wheel back.

Tracking the blade If you want the blade to center-track, rotate the wheel by hand and tilt the top wheel until the blade rides in the middle of the top wheel. If the blade moves forward, tilt the top of the wheel back. If the blade moves backward, angle the top of the wheel forward. Make slight adjustments. Rotate the wheel through several revolutions to make sure that the blade stays in the same place on the wheels. Lock the tilt knob. Center tracking works best on blades that are 3⁄16 in. wide and smaller.

If you want coplanar tracking, align the wheels with a straightedge. Turn the wheel through several revolutions so that you know that the blade stays in the same place. The blade may or may not track in the center of the top wheel; it will usually track toward the front of the wheels. Lock the tilt knob. Tilt the top wheel slightly backward if the blade starts to move forward or comes off the front of the saw. Coplanar tracking works best with blades that are ¼ in. wide and larger.

Never tension or track the blade with the saw running. After the blade has been tracked, replace the cover and the blade guard and plug in the electrical cord. Turn the saw on for a second, and then turn it off again. Observe how the saw runs. If the blade still seems to track well, run it under full power. If not, unplug the saw and retrack the blade.

After tensioning and tracking the blade, square it to the table.

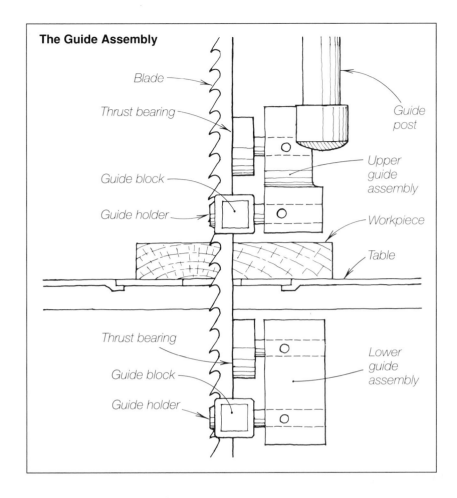

The Guide Assembly

Blade

Thrust bearing

Guide block

Guide holder

Guide post

Upper guide assembly

Workpiece

Table

Thrust bearing

Guide block

Guide holder

Lower guide assembly

Squaring the blade to the table   After tensioning and tracking the blade, check for squareness of the blade and table. Check squareness frequently and adjust the 90° stop as needed.

Adjusting the guides

Guides prevent the blade from deflecting or falling backward off the wheel. Two sets of guides are located above and below the table. Each set of guides is a two-part system of support for the blade. One part, the thrust bearing, supports the back of the blade as you cut and prevents the blade from being shoved off the back of the wheels as wood is fed into the blade.

The other components of the guide system, the guide blocks or guide bearings, prevent side deflection or rotation of the blade. Guide blocks or bearings, held in place by a guide holder, are located on either side of the blade. Both the thrust bearing and the guide blocks or bearings are held in place by a cast piece of metal, called a guide assembly.

Adjusting the guide post The top guide assembly is attached to a movable post that is raised or lowered to accommodate different thicknesses of wood. Adjust the post so that there is ¼ in. of clearance between the bottom of the post and the top of the workpiece.

Adjusting the thrust bearings The two thrust bearings must be aligned with each other so that the blade is supported equally above and below the table. Find the blade weld, which is a different color from the rest of the blade, and position it by the guides. The back of the blade serves as a straightedge for the thrust bearings, and the weld may not be perfectly straight. The two thrust bearings should be positioned about ¹⁄₆₄ in. (0.016 in.) behind the blade. When the cut begins, the blade moves backward and contacts the thrust bearings. When the cutting stops, the blade moves forward again and the thrust bearings stop rotating. Insert a feeler gauge or a dollar bill folded twice behind the blade to get the correct spacing.

Adjusting the guide blocks Guide blocks are held in place by guide holders above and below the table. Some manufacturers use bearings instead of solid metal guide blocks. Either kind of guides should be

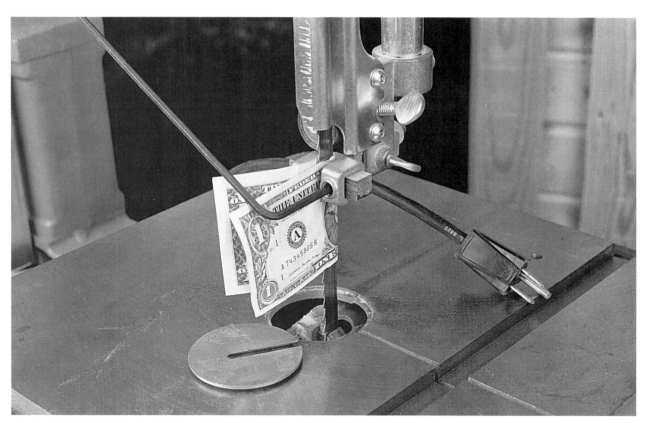

Adjust the guides with a flat feeler gauge or a dollar bill.

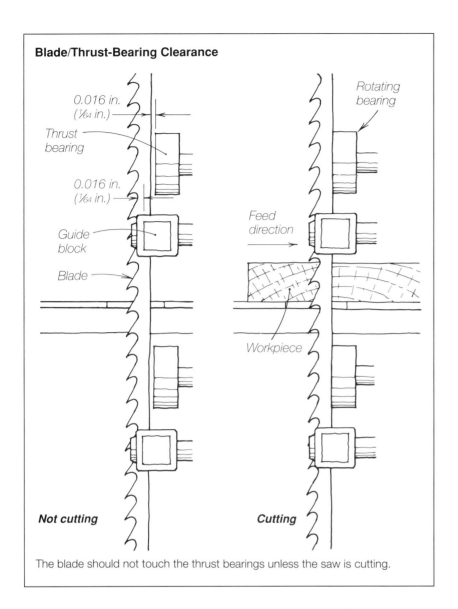

Blade/Thrust-Bearing Clearance

0.016 in.
(1/64 in.)

Thrust
bearing

0.016 in.
(1/64 in.)

Guide
block

Blade

Rotating
bearing

Feed
direction

Workpiece

Not cutting

Cutting

The blade should not touch the thrust bearings unless the saw is cutting.

placed about 0.004 in. from the blade. This is the thickness of a piece of typing paper or a dollar bill. Be careful to maintain a 1/64-in. distance between the gullet and the front of the guide block, because the blade flexes backward during the cut.

The top thrust bearing and the top guide blocks should be rechecked for alignment each time the guide post is raised or lowered.

Rounding the blade back

Blade performance and blade life are improved if the back of the blade is rounded with a stone. A round blade back creates smooth interaction between the bearing and the blade. If the blade rotates slightly, no

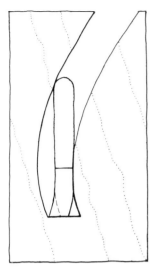

The round blade back has a smooth interaction with the edge of the saw kerf.

Rounding the Blade Back

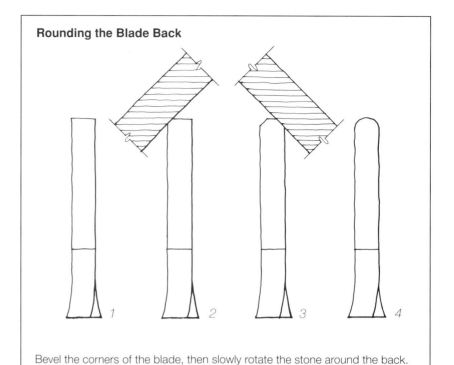

Bevel the corners of the blade, then slowly rotate the stone around the back.

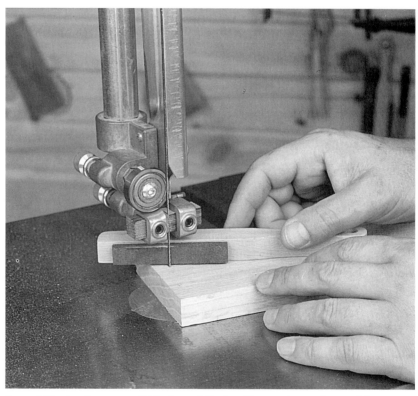

Round the back on small blades while feeding a piece of wood from the front.

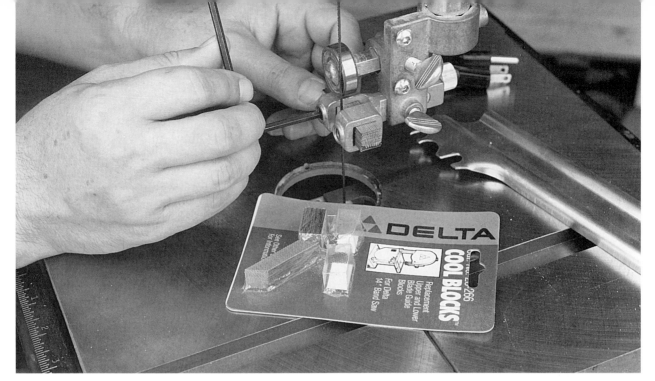

Install Cool Blocks® when you mount a ⅟₁₆-in. blade.

sharp blade corner digs into the thrust bearing, and rounding smooths the weld, too. A round blade back improves performance when making right-angled turns, because the round back has smooth contact with the saw kerf.

To round the blade back, hold a coarse stone against the corner of the blade for about a minute (after the guides have been adjusted). Repeat on the opposite corner, then slowly move the stone to round the back. The more pressure you put on the back, the faster you will remove the metal. Before you begin, check that the inside of the machine is free from sawdust, because the sparks could start a fire.

When rounding small blades, the pressure on the back of the blade may push the blade off the front of the wheels. To prevent this, I feed wood into the blade during the rounding process.

Adjustments for small blades

To run ⅟₁₆-in. and ⅛-in. blades, you must replace the metal guide blocks with Cool Blocks®. These nonmetal guide blocks are made of a compressed fibrous material that has been impregnated with a dry lubricant. Cool Blocks® decrease friction and heat, thereby increasing blade life. Place the blocks just behind the blade's gullets, directly in contact with the blade. This decreases twist and deflection and improves the accuracy of the bandsaw cut.

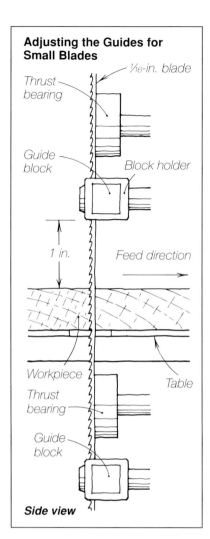

Adjusting the Guides for Small Blades

Thrust bearing

¹⁄₁₆-in. blade

Guide block

Block holder

1 in.

Feed direction

Workpiece

Table

Thrust bearing

Guide block

Side view

Center-track small blades and keep the top guide assembly about 1 in. above the work. Smaller blades flex a lot more than wider ones. The blades last much longer when the guide is raised, but beware of the extra inch of blade exposure.

For added support, the thrust bearing should be resting against the back of the blade with no space between the bearing and the blade.

Maintenance

Guides and wheel tires require regular maintenance. The tires are rubber and, just like a car's, they wear in the middle. This is especially true of tires that are mounted on flat wheels. It's hard to track the blade on a saw with worn tires. Restore the original shape by sanding the tire with 100-grit sandpaper. Remove the blade and sand the bottom tire with the saw running. Get a helper to spin the top wheel with a hand drill and a 1½-in. dia. sanding drum. If the tire needs a lot of reshaping, sand with the paper attached to a stick or block.

Clean the tires occasionally with 100-grit sandpaper while the saw is running without the blade.

Get a helper to drive the upper wheel with a 1¼-in. sanding drum in a drill.

You can restore the original shape to the wheels by removing the blade and sanding with 100-grit paper mounted on a stick or block.

Diagnosing Bandsaw Problems	
Broken Blades	Crooked Cuts
1. Excessively high feed rate.	1. Guides and bearings poorly adjusted.
2. Guides or bearings poorly adjusted.	2. Blade tension too low.
3. Blade tension too high.	3. Dull blade.
4. Blade too thick in relationship to the diameter of the wheels and sawing speed.	4. Pitch too fine.
5. Poor weld.	5. Damaged teeth.
6. Material too coarse or too thin.	6. Fence poorly aligned.

Thrust bearings can wear or become scarred. Some bearings can be removed from the shaft and reversed to provide a new surface. If your bearings are scarred and cannot be reversed, replace them. Also check the rotation of the bearings frequently. If the bearings do not rotate easily, they should be replaced. Order new bearings from your dealer or the manufacturer.

Guide blocks wear and become rounded, fiber blocks slightly faster than metal guides. Resurface both types with a file or a power disc or belt sander as needed.

Using the bandsaw

The operation that makes the bandsaw essential in the workshop is cutting curves. As a process, cutting curves is a combination of cross-cutting and ripping. Feed rate and how the blade tracks will vary from piece to piece. You should be prepared to speed up, slow down or alter the feed direction slightly as you're cutting each piece. Blade width determines the tightest diameter curve that can be cut. A secondary consideration is the pitch and tooth form. Changes in species and grain direction force changes in pitch and tooth-form selection.

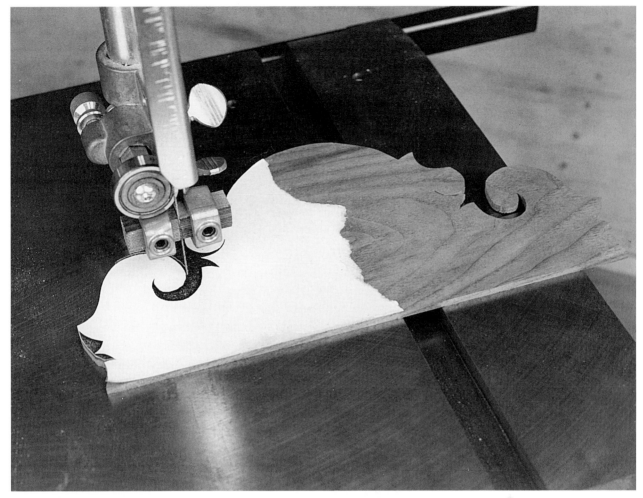

A ¹⁄₁₆-in. bandsaw blade cuts curves much faster than a scrollsaw, particularly in hardwood.

Although most woodworkers think of the bandsaw as a tool for cutting curves, a well-tuned bandsaw with a ½-in., 3-TPI blade can produce very accurate straight cuts, too. One advantage of the bandsaw for straight cuts is that it's safer than either the table saw or radial-arm saw because it can't kick back.

Ripping

When you are ripping on the bandsaw, the blade tends to cut at a slight angle, which is termed "lead." Rather than fighting blade lead, learn to compensate by feeding the wood into the blade at a slight angle. A single vertical edge provides a better guide for this than a long straight fence. If you are ripping a lot of wood, however, change the rip fence to match the cutting angle of the blade.

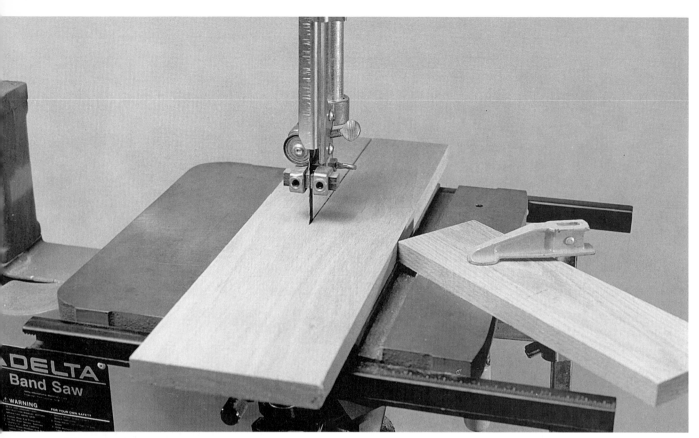

When ripping on the bandsaw, use a single-point fence to compensate for lead.

Determining the correct fence angle is not difficult. First, scribe a line parallel to the edge of a straight board (a marking gauge works well, or snap a line with a chalkline). If the line is difficult to see, darken it with a pencil. Make the test cut by feeding the work into the blade as you cut down one side of the line. You may have to angle the board slightly to make a straight cut. Stop cutting halfway through the board. Mark the angle at which the saw is cutting on the table with a pencil.

Adjust the angle of the fence to correspond to the angle of the workpiece. At this angle, the saw should cut straight without the workpiece pulling to one side or the other. Start the saw and finish the second half of the cut. At the end of the cut, the workpiece should just touch both the blade and rip fence. If the cut follows the pencil mark, the rip fence is parallel with the cut.

Repeat the test with a fresh edge riding against the fence. Stop halfway through the cut. If the cut has veered toward the fence, the blade will spring the wood back to its normal position and pull the workpiece away from the fence. Moving the end of the fence slightly toward the blade will correct this problem.

If the cut has veered away from the fence, you will cut a taper that's wider at the end of the cut. This deflects the blade and forces the workpiece against the rip fence, making it hard to move. Fix this problem by moving the end of the fence slightly away from the blade.

It may take some experimentation to get the correct fence angle. I use paper shims such as playing cards, dollar bills and typing paper to make slight fence adjustments.

To determine the correct fence angle, stop cutting midway along a line scribed parallel to a straight edge (left). Pencil a line on the table along the edge and adjust the fence so that it's parallel to the line. Make a test cut for final adjustments (below). If the wood springs away from the fence after you release it, adjust the end of the fence toward the blade; if you cut a taper, move the end of the fence slightly away from the blade.

Resawing

Resawing is the process of cutting a board in half through its thickness. The halves will be mirror images of each other, and when the two halves are edge-glued together the resulting board is said to be "bookmatched." Resawing is also the efficient way to cut veneer or remove waste from a thick plank that must be planed thin.

Resawing is similar to ripping, except that the workpiece is thicker. You have to deal with the same problem of blade lead. Test the setup with a piece of scrap first. Because the board is on its edge, support the piece well so that it doesn't tip.

As when ripping, a single-point jig works well for resawing one or two boards, but if you have a number of boards to resaw, it's best to use the rip fence. It is imperative that the piece of wood be flat and square. Stock preparation is covered at length in Chapter 7. When cutting wide stock, extend the height of the fence with a board to provide extra support. Make sure that the table is square to the blade, and then square the fence to the table. Insert paper shims between the fence and the extension board for any final adjustments.

Resawing is cutting a board in half through its thickness.

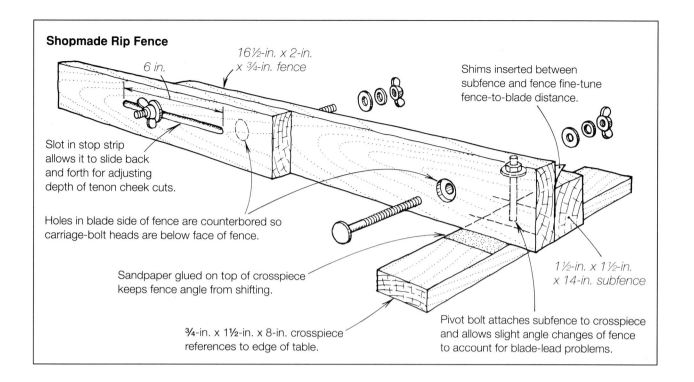

Shopmade Rip Fence

6 in.

16½-in. x 2-in. x ¾-in. fence

Shims inserted between subfence and fence fine-tune fence-to-blade distance.

Slot in stop strip allows it to slide back and forth for adjusting depth of tenon cheek cuts.

Holes in blade side of fence are counterbored so carriage-bolt heads are below face of fence.

Sandpaper glued on top of crosspiece keeps fence angle from shifting.

¾-in. x 1½-in. x 8-in. crosspiece references to edge of table.

1½-in. x 1½-in. x 14-in. subfence

Pivot bolt attaches subfence to crosspiece and allows slight angle changes of fence to account for blade-lead problems.

If your saw doesn't have a rip fence, you can make one from wood scraps and carriage bolts, as shown in the drawing above. The face of this fence bolts to a subfence with wing nuts, which allows you to insert paper shims for fine-tuning the fence-to-blade distance. The subfence is bolted to a crosspiece that references to the edge of the bandsaw table and is attached to the table with a clamp. The crosspiece allows the angle of the fence to be fine-tuned for accommodating the tendency of the blade to pull slightly one way or another during the cut. The adjustable stop, bolted to the fence through a slotted hole, allows you to set the depth of the cut and is removed when resawing.

Feed rate is very important when you are resawing. A sharp blade is a must. The blade should be kept busy, but not too busy. The motor should never bog down or lose speed. Experienced users saw much more slowly than beginners.

Crosscutting

Like the table saw, most bandsaw tables have a slot milled in the table top and many also come with a miter gauge. I have never found the miter gauge to be particularly effective for crosscutting, however, because after the first few cuts with a new blade, the cut tends to drift to the right or left.

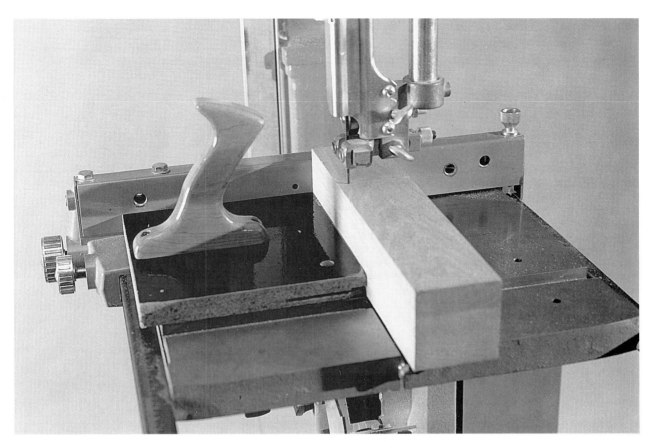

Use a push block to complete the cut when crosscutting on the bandsaw.

On the other hand, with a sharp blade, freehand crosscutting to a squared line can be quite accurate. I like to crosscut a test piece first so that I can anticipate the lead of the blade, and then use a slow feed rate while the blade cuts just to the waste side of the scribed line.

I use one of the new $\frac{1}{16}$-in. or $\frac{1}{8}$-in. blades for crosscutting. These small blades are much less apt to lead, but breakage is a problem. Try to keep the upper guide assembly adjusted about 1 in. above the work so that the blade can flex backward without stress. Take extra care with the additional length of exposed blade.

If you have a fence adjusted to the lead of the blade, you can crosscut to the fence as shown in the photo above (use a push block to complete the cut). Of course, this limits the length of the crosscut piece to the throat size minus whatever space the rip fence occupies.

Just about any bandsaw can rip or crosscut 6-in. stock, but not if the workpiece is unsupported, weighs 200 lb. and is 14 in. wide and 8 ft. long. The capacity of your saw is really determined by your capacity to guide the work through the saw in an unstressed fashion. With large stock you really have to plan out how you're going to manipulate the workpiece. Outfeed and infeed support are essential, and a helper is invaluable. Auxiliary tables such as the one shown in the top drawing at right are also invaluable. Remember to slow down your feed rate when cutting large work.

Thin stock requires a fine blade and some kind of support under the work. Cut veneers and laminates on a scrap of cardboard, fiberboard or plywood.

The bandsaw is much less likely than the table saw to drag your hands or fingers into the sawblade, as long as your work is flat on the table. However, because they feel safer working on the bandsaw, many users try to cut stock that's really too small. Use a handscrew as a gripper for small stock or fasten the piece to a larger scrap with Superglue®.

Ripping or crosscutting round or roughly cylindrical stock is impossible without a V-block or a custom fixture to hold the workpiece. Make V-blocks to size as needed (see the middle drawing at right). I rip mine in two cuts on the table saw, with the blade angled to 45°.

Resawing logs   The real joy of owning a bandsaw is that you can salvage found wood from the firewood pile or from your neighbor's lilac prunings, and build up small stockpiles of exotic hardwoods at virtually no cost and with little guilt over the state of the rain forest.

The drawback to working with irregular stock is that it's not safe to cut anything on the bandsaw that doesn't ride steadily on the table. However, there are a couple of things you can do if your found wood has no flat surface. If the wood is a log, you can split it with wedges and a sledgehammer or you can make the fixture shown in the bottom drawing at right to secure your work to an auxiliary table that slides on the bandsaw table. Some users have even fixed up a sliding jig that lets you surface a face on the log with the router. Regardless of the manner in which you solve this bandsaw problem, remember that the work must be flat to the table.

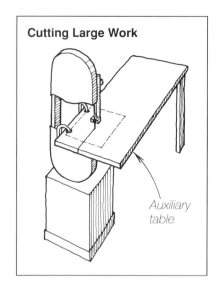

Cutting Large Work

Auxiliary table

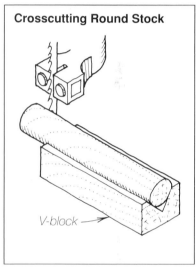

Crosscutting Round Stock

V-block

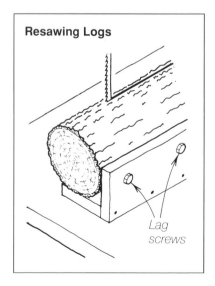

Resawing Logs

Lag screws

CHAPTER 4
The Jointer and the Planer

A piece of wood that has been accurately prepared should have three pairs of smooth, parallel surfaces. Each pair of surfaces is perpendicular to the other two, and any subsequent shaping or cutting of the workpiece at least has the potential for perfection. Any error in stock preparation, however, will compound exponentially as the wood is processed.

For precise woodworking, most machines need at least two adjacent, perpendicular planes. Joint cutting, which is the final step in machine woodworking, is particularly dependent on the initial accuracy of the wood. The first square edge, therefore, is just as critical as the last dovetail and requires the same attention to detail.

Stock preparation requires two machines: the jointer and the planer. The jointer establishes a flat face and perpendicular edge. The planer creates a second face parallel to the first. Subsequent passes plane the workpiece to the appropriate thickness. Consequently, the planer is also called a thickness planer or surfacer. Since a similar cutterhead is central to both machines, some manufacturers make a dual-purpose machine called the jointer-planer.

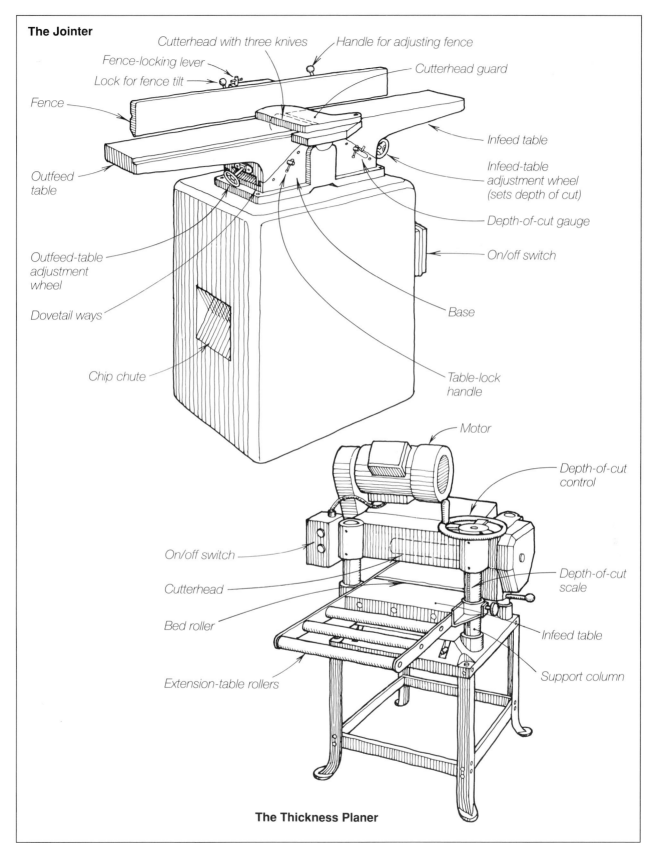

The Jointer

Cutterhead with three knives

Handle for adjusting fence

Fence-locking lever

Lock for fence tilt

Cutterhead guard

Fence

Infeed table

Outfeed table

Infeed-table adjustment wheel (sets depth of cut)

Depth-of-cut gauge

On/off switch

Outfeed-table adjustment wheel

Base

Dovetail ways

Chip chute

Table-lock handle

Motor

Depth-of-cut control

On/off switch

Depth-of-cut scale

Cutterhead

Bed roller

Infeed table

Extension-table rollers

Support column

The Thickness Planer

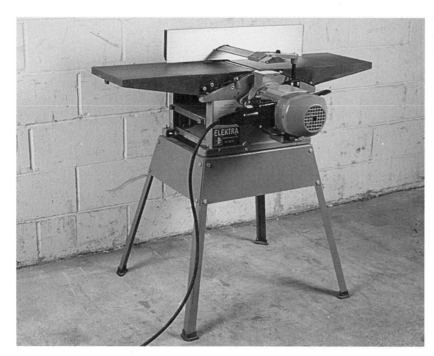

The combination jointer-planer is a space saver for small workshops. (Photo by Gary Weisenburger.)

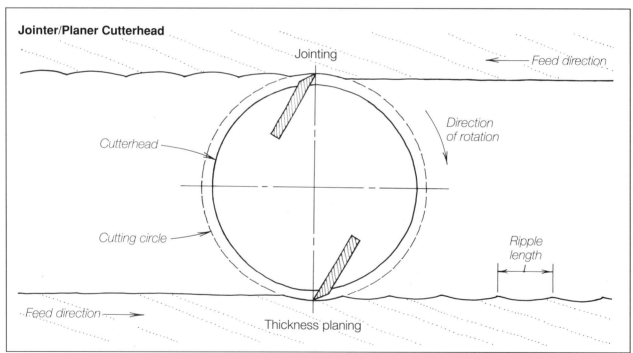

Jointer/Planer Cutterhead

Jointing

Feed direction

Cutterhead

Direction of rotation

Cutting circle

Ripple length

Feed direction

Thickness planing

The cutterhead on both the jointer and the planer removes short, arc-shaped lengths of wood from the workpiece. Consequently, close examination of machine-jointed and machine-planed surfaces reveals a slightly rippled surface, a series of minute hollows and ridges.

Jointers are distinguished from planers in that the workpiece is typically hand-fed into the jointer and power-fed into the planer. Also, the cutting action of jointing takes place over the cutterhead, whereas planing occurs below.

Jointer design

The jointer consists of two parallel tables with a revolving cutterhead between them. The outfeed table and the knives in the cutterhead are adjusted to precisely the same height. The infeed table is adjustable for the depth of cut and is positioned lower than the outfeed table by the desired amount of the cut, usually 1/16 in. to 1/8 in. An adjustable fence slides across the cutter for wider or narrower stock.

There are two basic jointer designs. On industrial designs, both the infeed and the outfeed tables are adjustable. The chief advantage of an adjustable outfeed table is that the height of the table can be changed to create concave, convex, tapered or decorative cuts. An adjustable outfeed table also enables you to sharpen the knives in the cutterhead and then adjust the outfeed table to match the height of the knives.

The width of the jointer knives determines the largest possible width of the cut. Knives range in width from 4 in. to 36 in. I'd recommend 6 in. as a bare minimum if you intend to dress rough lumber. Narrower jointers are useful only for squaring the edge of a board. Another important consideration is the length of the tables. Longer tables make it easier to joint long boards, but they are more expensive and more prone to warping, twisting and alignment problems.

On a jointer with a fixed outfeed table, the knives must be removed from the cutterhead for each grinding and then accurately adjusted to the height of the outfeed table. Because this design is simpler, it costs less. On some of these jointers the outfeed table and the machine base are one casting, which means that there is no easy way to adjust the outfeed table. If the tables should warp or become misaligned, repair is expensive.

Traditionally, the infeed table or both tables mate to the base with interlocking dovetail ways. On most machines, you can adjust the fit tighter or looser. Delta has developed an adjustable parallelogram system to raise and lower the tables. Refer to the owner's manual if you have one of these jointers.

In the typical jointing sequence, the wood rests on the infeed table and is fed into the cutterhead (see the photo on the facing page). A thin layer of material is removed, and the newly jointed surface is supported by the outfeed table. This process is repeated until the face of the board is straight and true. The flat face is then held firmly against the fence, and an adjacent edge is jointed until it too is straight and true and at 90° to the flat face. The operator usually scribes a faint line across each square and true surface with a pencil so that the prepared surfaces are readily apparent.

Tuning the jointer

If you were to adjust the jointer every day, you would soon get into the habit and tuning would be easy. Few users do, however, and the subtleties of tweaking your jointer to that extra level of precision are often forgotten. It's a good idea to keep a notebook on your machine to record the step-by-step sequences of adjustment. You'll also need a straightedge as long as your jointer, several open-end or box wrenches and an assortment of hex wrenches. Always unplug the machine before you do any adjusting. The consequences of accidentally turning the machine on are too grave to risk.

Consult your owner's manual before adjusting your jointer. If you don't have a manual and the manufacturer is still in business, send for one. If no manual is available, take the jointer off its stand and turn it upside down to see what is inside the base. On some older models with fixed outfeed tables, the outfeed table is held in place by bolts that are tightened from the inside.

Adjusting jointer tables

Jointer tables are typically formed from cast iron, a die-cast alloy or sheet metal. Woodworkers tend to think that metal is impervious to degradation, but, unfortunately, this isn't the case. For example, cast iron warps, although not in the same manner as wood. Warping is particularly problematic in machines on which the casting was improperly or inadequately aged before machining. Die-cast alloys and sheet metal have similar weaknesses. You should never place anything on a jointer table that doesn't belong there, nor use your jointer as a sawhorse when painting the house. A shop-teacher friend of mine tells of the time that someone left a box of textbooks on the end of the outfeed table of the school's new jointer. When he came back to school at the end of the summer, the outfeed table had sagged ¼ in.

Checking jointer tables The first step is to check the jointer tables for flatness, using a long straightedge. Raise the infeed table until it is level with the outfeed table. Check the individual tables first, longitudinally

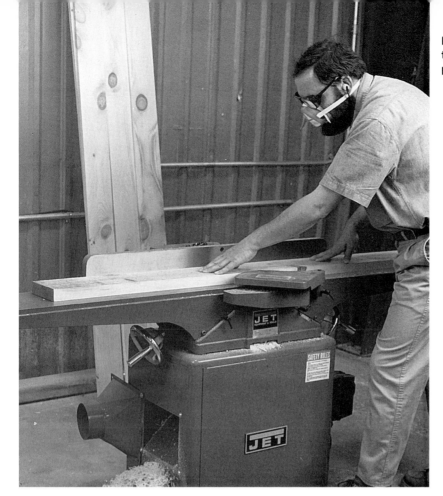

Face jointing — jointing one face of the board — is the first step in preparing rough lumber.

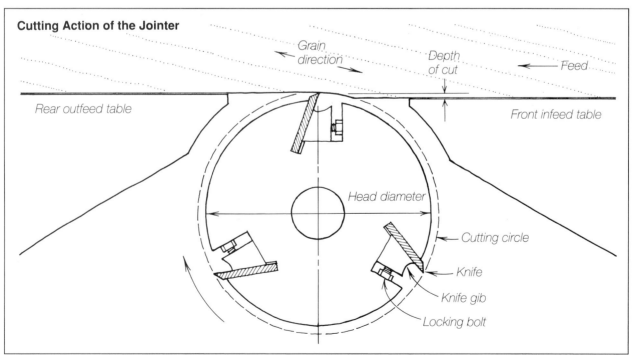

Cutting Action of the Jointer

Grain direction

Depth of cut

Feed

Rear outfeed table

Front infeed table

Head diameter

Cutting circle

Knife

Knife gib

Locking bolt

for parallelism and then diagonally for flatness. Measure any space under the straightedge with a flat-blade, automotive-type feeler gauge—any gap should be less than 0.010 in. The table castings may sag a couple of thousandths of an inch in the middle, but that's to be expected. Next, check both tables as a unit. Check next to the fence and on the opposite side, then check the diagonals for twist. Ideally the jointer should be less than 0.010 in. out of parallel end-to-end. If the misalignment is greater, you have some work to do.

The measurements you make when checking the jointer tables tell you one of four things: The tables are flat and parallel to each another; the tables are not in the same plane; there is twist across both tables as a unit; or the individual tables exhibit twist, cup or bow.

With luck, your tables are flat and you're reading this section of the book for its Wisconsin wit and wisdom. If not, the second and third scenarios are the next most preferable, since manufacturers design jointers so that they can be adjusted to remedy tables that are out of plane or twisted as a unit. You will not be able to adjust the machine to

Check table alignment with a straightedge. Measure any space under the straightedge with a feeler gauge.

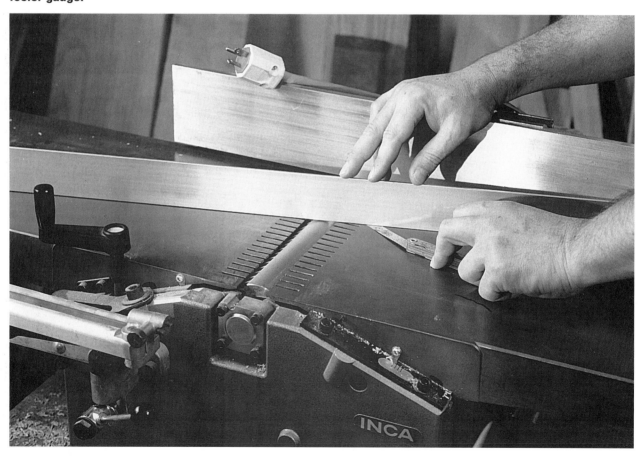

Table Alignment

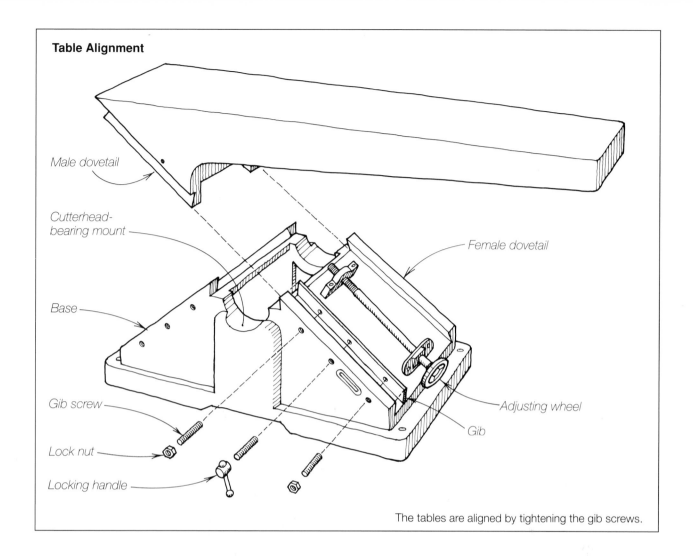

Male dovetail

Cutterhead-
bearing mount

Female dovetail

Base

Gib screw

Lock nut

Locking handle

Adjusting wheel

Gib

The tables are aligned by tightening the gib screws.

remedy casting flaws in the infeed and outfeed tables, though you can grind the tables to correct warped and deformed castings, as explained on p. 121.

In brief, table adjustment involves tightening or loosening the fit between the tables and the base. The sliding dovetail ways of the tables and base are designed so that you can reduce the play in the table caused by wear. The most common table problem is that the table droops downward on the end. Tightening the setscrews on the table's gibs usually brings the drooping end back up into alignment with the other table. Gibs are pieces of flat bar stock that are located between the mating surfaces of the ways of many machine tools. The adjustment screws are called gib screws, and on the jointer they are either on the side of the base casting or inside the machine.

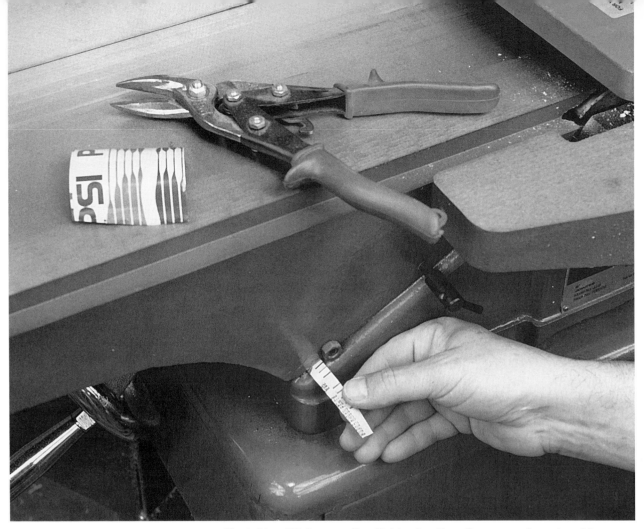

If a table still droops after tightening the gib screws, insert a shim between the base and table casting.

Use an appropriately sized hex wrench to tighten the gib screws until the tables align and then tighten the lock nuts on the screws. Ideally, the tables will be in alignment and will still move up and down. If not, back off the gib screws slightly until the table moves up and down with moderate effort and still doesn't sag at the tail end.

If tightening the gib screws does not align the tables, take the machine apart, clean all surfaces and lubricate it with a light lithium grease. Sometimes dirt between the parts can build up and cause alignment problems. When you reassemble the machine, you should also check the height of the jointer knives. They will probably need to be readjusted in relation to the outfeed table.

Shimming jointer tables Occasionally you will find that a table still droops even after you've cranked the gib screws down as far as they'll go. Before you make an appointment to have your tables ground, try shimming between the base and table casting, as shown in the photo on the facing page. Brass or sheet-steel shim stock is the best choice, but cut-up soda cans and tin foil also work.

If you have an adjustable outfeed table or if your outfeed table is fixed but not the same casting as the base, shim the outfeed table so that it is aligned with the infeed table at its highest point. Obviously, this adjustment negates your ability to raise or lower the outfeed table, but that is no great loss.

When the outfeed table and the base are one casting and the infeed table sags severely, one option is to shim the infeed table permanently for a light cut and not move it up or down, or glue the shim in place so that it cannot move. Because this remedy sacrifices some of the machine's utility, I recommend that you send your jointer to a machine shop for resurfacing.

Warped or bent tables are often the result of neglected maintenance and excessive wear. The dust and vibration from surfacing miles of hard maple or pitch-filled pine loosen adjustments and make sliding parts sticky. A sloppy fit hammers adjoining precision surfaces, and poorly lubricated mating surfaces wear quickly. Other trauma can permanently pull tables out of alignment, too. Avoid moving your machines cross-country, and don't carry your jointer to a new location in the shop while lifting it by the tables. This is the machinery equivalent of carrying your beagle by the ears.

Grinding jointer tables If shimming doesn't solve the misalignment problem, you still have a couple of options you can do yourself. You can scrape or grind the table's high spots with a machinist's scraper or sanding equipment. You can also fill the low spots with epoxy paint and then smooth the paint (when it has dried to some extent) with a sheet of plate glass. After the paint has completely dried, flatten the paint with carborundum paste or liquefied powder and a sheet of plate glass. I also know of people who have trued both tables by rubbing them against each other with water and carborundum grit between them.

If all else fails, have the tables ground flat at a machine shop. Some manufacturers offer this service for their machines. The jointer is placed on a frame that supports the end of the tables so the tables don't deflect during the grinding process. If you have the tables ground, it is important that the entire top be ground as a unit and that the table ends be supported.

Cutterhead adjustments

In the jointer's most pristine, precise state of tune, its honed knives spin even with the surface of the outfeed table just at the highest point in their rotation. Like most things, this blissful state doesn't last forever, and you'll soon find that you need to have the knives sharpened and the knife gibs adjusted.

Changing knives When the edges of your jointer knives are visible, they need to be sharpened. Manufacturers don't recommend that you take all the knives out of the cutterhead at one time because it stresses and could possibly distort the cutterhead. For this reason, remove one knife at a time.

Each knife is held in place in a milled slot in the cutterhead by a knife gib and locking screw or bolt. On each knife, loosen each screw slightly before backing them off all the way. The idea is to equalize pressure to prevent distortion. If you have an adjustable outfeed table, scribe a mark on the machine base and the outfeed table before you remove the knives so that you can easily realign these two parts after you replace the knives.

It doesn't take many knife changes to make you want a longer life span for your knives. Dirt and sand quickly dull knives. To extend the life of your knives, inspect your wood before jointing and remove any debris with a wire brush. Some exotic species such as teak and purpleheart are abrasive and quickly dull steel knives. In industrial applications the problem is solved by using carbide knives, or jointers with knife-grinding attachments. Carbide knives are very expensive and never give as good a finish as steel. I think steel is more appropriate for home shops and small professional shops, unless you are milling exotic woods and don't want the expense of a knife-grinding attachment.

I don't sharpen my knives myself even though I have the Japanese waterstone grinding apparatus specifically for knife grinding. For me, it's just not time- or cost-effective. I have three sets of knives and whenever I install the third set, the other two go to the sharpener. I hone my knives frequently with a small diamond hone (see p. 133).

After the knives have been sharpened, replace one knife at a time. The trick is to tighten the gib against the knife slowly until the knife barely moves. Tighten the locking screws moderately, working alternately from each end toward the middle.

Adjusting jointer knives Before you torque down the gib screws, you must align the knives with either the outfeed table or the cutterhead. It doesn't make any difference which point of reference you use, as long as the cutterhead and the tables are aligned with each other. If the cutterhead is not perfectly aligned with the tables, the knives should be adjusted to the outfeed table. Check that the cutterhead is parallel to the table by lowering either table (if possible, the outfeed table) and then placing a straightedge across the table so that it touches the cutterhead on each end. If the straightedge touches at both ends, the cutterhead is parallel to the table.

Every manufacturer has slightly different techniques for adjusting the knives. Some use a special clip or locking device that aligns the knife automatically with no adjustment on the part of the user. Others have disposable knives that can be changed in a matter of seconds.

On the commonest cutterhead—with only milled slots, knife gibs and locking screws—there's no easy way to adjust knife height. This antiquated design is frequently found on older or less expensive machines. A more sophisticated cutterhead design employs springs or lifting (jack) screws to raise the blade into position. A number of techniques have been developed to make knife adjustment easier. The best approach is to use strong magnets to hold the blade in position as it is tightened, as described on p. 125.

Regardless of the cutterhead design of your jointer, to align the knives you will need to find what I call "top dead center" (TDC). At this point the knife edge should be at the apex of the arc in its rotation and simultaneously even with the outfeed table.

To find top dead center (TDC), lower the infeed table until a straightedge touches the cutterhead.

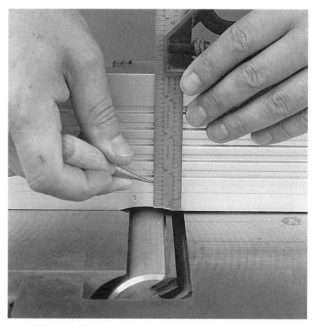

After you have located TDC, scribe a vertical line on the fence so you'll be able to find it easily for future knife alignment.

To find TDC, place a 12-in. rule or straightedge on the infeed table and lower the table until the rule touches the cutterhead. The point where it touches is TDC. By checking both sides of the cutterhead you can see whether the cutterhead is aligned to the infeed table. After you have located TDC, scribe its location with a scratch awl on the fence.

If your cutterhead has spring-loaded knives, press them into the cutterhead with a flat piece of plywood resting on the outfeed table. Align the edge of the knife with the TDC mark on the fence and then tighten the knife in place. Some manufacturers offer a fixture that presses the spring-loaded knife into position.

A cutterhead with jack screws should be tightened so the knife has no play but is still movable with the screws. Align the knife edge with the TDC mark. Rest a flat piece of wood about 1 ft. long on the outfeed table. Mark the board about 4 in. from the end with two marks 1/8 in. apart. Align the first mark with the outfeed table. Raise the knife until

A magnetic jig can be used to align the knives and the outfeed table if your cutterhead doesn't have springs or lifting screws.

A piece of wood with two marks 1/8 in. apart makes an effective knife-height gauge. Raise the knife until it moves the stick about 1/8 in. when the cutterhead is rotated.

Measure any error between the knife edge and the outfeed table with a feeler gauge placed under the jig at the edge of the table.

it moves the stick about ⅛ in. when the cutterhead is rotated. This indicates that the knife is the desired height of 0.001 in. to 0.002 in. higher than the outfeed table. Test both sides and then tighten the knife.

If your cutterhead has neither springs nor jack screws, use a jig to align the knives in the cutterhead. The best jig has two strong bar magnets (see the photo at right on the facing page). Hold the knife at approximately the correct height while you tighten the locking screws until the knife barely moves. Lay the bar magnets on the outfeed table and let the magnets pull the knife to the right height. Align one magnet at the edge of the knife next to the fence at the TDC mark.

Gradually tighten the screws that hold the knife in place. To prevent the knife from moving higher in the cutterhead, hold the jig down firmly with one hand as you alternately tighten the middle screws. Holding the jig down reduces the annoying tendency of the knife to squirm upward, but even with pressure the knife can still move up.

Error can be measured with a flat board and a feeler gauge at the edge of the outfeed table. Knives set as much as 0.002 in. above the outfeed table are acceptable.

Rough-ground gibs seem to have the worst blade-lift problems. I rework the gib surface on a piece of wet or dry sandpaper laid on a flat surface such as a piece of plate glass. Jointer knives must also be smooth, so hone them in the same way if they are rough. A friend of mine coats the knives with a thin film of mineral spirits before he puts them in the cutterhead. He claims it acts as a lubricant and prevents the knives from moving upward as the gib is tightened. The mineral spirits evaporate in a minute or so.

The tendency for the knife to move up as it is tightened can be an advantage if the increased knife height is consistent and not excessive. If the knives are set about 0.002 in. higher than the outfeed table, they will be just about perfect after planing a plank or two. If one knife is high, you'll get a distinct wave on the surface of the wood.

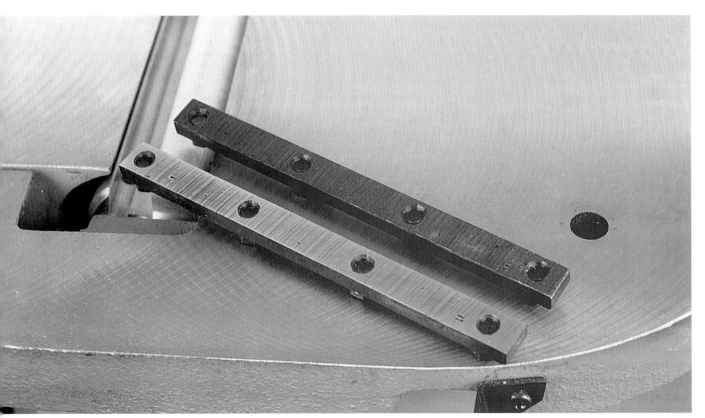

The surface of the gib should be smooth and flat with no rough areas. The gib on the left was reworked on a piece of wet or dry sandpaper laid on a flat surface.

Adjusting the fence

The jointer fence supports the workpiece at the proper angle relative to the table and the cutterhead. Many jointer fences are adjustable for any angle between 45° and 90°, and there are stops for 45° and 90°. Double-check the fence with a square before making a series of cuts.

Check the fence for twist and cup. If you do not get the same reading with a square at the front and back of the fence as you do at the cutterhead, the fence is warped. If your jointer is still under warranty, consult with the manufacturer. Otherwise, you can have the fence machined flat. A less expensive option is to bolt a length of plywood to the fence and shim it with paper or shim stock.

Adjusting the guards

The jointer can be an extremely dangerous machine if it is used incorrectly. Some machines require you to remove the guard in order to execute special techniques such as rabbeting and tapering. I deal with either problem by using another machine, such as a router table, shaper or table saw. Never operate the jointer without a guard. Use push sticks, and don't joint boards that are less than 12 in. long.

Most guards are spring-loaded, and the tension of the spring is adjustable. There should be enough tension to pull the guard up to the fence but not so much that the guard slams against the fence after the wood is jointed.

Lubrication

The bearings on most jointers are sealed and don't require lubrication. If there is a grease fitting or if the machine has poured babbitt bearings, lubricate with lithium grease, which is specifically made for fast-running machinery. If your babbitt-bearing machine doesn't have a fitting for continuous lubrication, you may want to drill and tap a hole for an oil well in each bearing housing. Babbitt bearings are really outdated technology because they periodically need to be repoured. It's best to convert babbitt bearings to ball bearings, if possible. Consult a bearing house or a machine shop to explore alternatives.

The jointer's dovetail ways are frequently neglected, which can cause difficulty in making adjustments. A quick fix is to pour light machine oil at the union of the two surfaces and let the oil run down the seam. The best solution, however, is to take the machine apart, clean it and lubricate with lithium grease.

Feedback from the workpiece

Any adjustment problems with the jointer will show on the workpiece. If the outfeed table and cutterhead are out of alignment, the resulting cuts will not be straight. If the outfeed table is too low or the knives are too high, there will be a snipe, or gouge, on the end of the board. If the outfeed table is too high or the knives are too low, the cutters will remove more material at the end of the cut, producing a taper.

If the surface of the workpiece is not smooth or has ripples, it indicates a misalignment of the knives. If one knife is too high, you get a more pronounced ripple effect that you can either see or feel with your fingers.

Planer design

The planer makes the faces of a piece of wood parallel and a specified thickness. In the past, planers were giant machines, and it was quite common for a professional shop not to own one. As planers have evolved they have became smaller and cheaper. In recent years, portable models that weigh less than 60 lb. have been introduced.

All planers function on similar principles, but some designs are more complicated than others. The basic design comprises a cutterhead, a table and a motor supported by a frame. The planing process is relatively simple. The wood lies on the table, and two rollers push or pull it under the rotating cutterhead. The adjustable distance between the table and the cutterhead determines the thickness of the stock.

Tuning the planer

The planer is a precision machine and must be tweaked into prime condition more often than the jointer. Large, older planers require more care than newer designs. Adjustments must be made to the feed system, the table system and the cutterhead system. Some planers have other features that require adjustment and maintenance, including bed rollers, chip breakers and pressure bars.

Antikickback pawls, sharp fingers located between the cutterhead and the infeed roller, are a feature of some machines. The pressure of the infeed roller also helps as an antikickback mechanism. Even with these safety features, however, you should never stand directly behind a planer that is running. Always unplug the planer before you clean or adjust it.

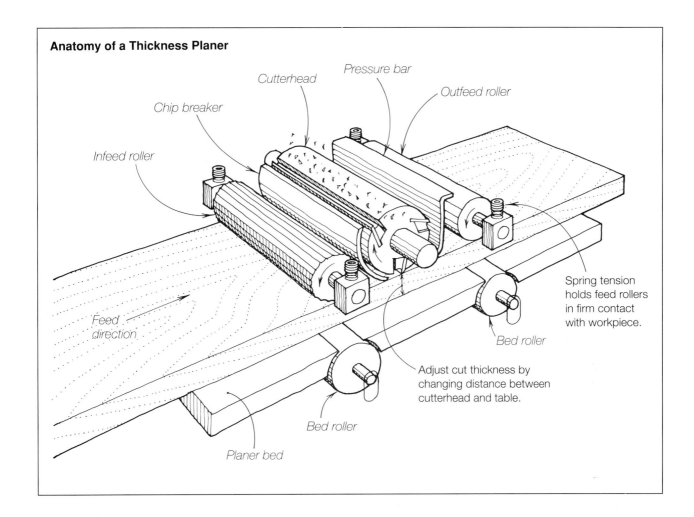

Anatomy of a Thickness Planer

Infeed roller

Chip breaker

Cutterhead

Pressure bar

Outfeed roller

Feed direction

Spring tension holds feed rollers in firm contact with workpiece.

Bed roller

Adjust cut thickness by changing distance between cutterhead and table.

Bed roller

Planer bed

Adjusting the feed system

Feed rollers at the front and rear of the cutterhead push and pull the wood through the rotating planer knives. The infeed roller is located at the front of the cutterhead and is made of either serrated metal or rubber. A metal infeed roller actually embosses the wood as it is forced under the cutterhead, but the roller marks are removed by the rotating planer knives. At the rear of the cutterhead is a smooth metal or rubber outfeed roller.

Both rollers are powered by chain or belt through a gear-reduction mechanism. On some planers the feed-roller speed is adjustable. Rollers are spring-loaded to accommodate variations in wood thickness; some roller springs are adjustable so that the pressure on the wood can be varied.

Lubricate the gear-reduction system periodically. Oil the chain frequently with light machine oil, and apply belt dressing to the belts.

Adjusting the feed-roller pressure may require some experimentation. If the pressure is too light, the rollers may slip and not feed the wood through the cutterhead. If the pressure is too great on the serrated metal infeed roller, the serrations may be deeper than the cutterhead can plane off, especially on thin soft stock. In such cases the pressure should be reduced. Rollers don't require a lot of pressure for light cuts. If you plan to take deep cuts, you'll have to increase the pressure. If increased spring pressure does not propel the wood through the cutterhead, the rollers need cleaning, the table bed rollers need adjusting or the tables need to be waxed.

Rollers are particularly hard to keep clean when planing pitchy woods such as pine. Use solvents and a fine wire brush to clean metal rollers. Rubber rollers should be cleaned by scraping with a cabinet scraper, since solvents can degrade the rubber.

The gear-reduction system needs periodic lubrication, perhaps as often as every two hours under heavy use. The chain that drives the rollers should also be oiled frequently with a light machine oil. If the rollers are belt-driven, apply a small amount of belt dressing from time to time. Even though planers seem well shielded from dust, they are inevitably dirty machines and critical parts must be cleaned often. Graphite or a dry lubricant may prove more effective than oil in high-dust situations.

Adjusting the table system

The planer table should have a slight amount of play — it should move just a hair when you wiggle one end. If the table is too tight, it will bind and be hard to crank up and down. If it is too loose, it can vibrate or chatter, and a visible ripple will appear on the stock. There are two table designs, a smooth table without rollers or a table with rollers.

The smooth table will require occasional waxing, but that is the extent of its maintenance. Tables with rollers ("bed rollers") require more attention. Bed rollers reduce contact (and thus friction) between the work and the table. They are adjustable for the type of work being planed. The rougher the lumber, the higher the bed rollers should be. On roughsawn lumber, adjust rollers to 0.010 in. to 0.020 in. above the table. Once the rough surface has been planed off, adjust rollers to 0.005 in. above the table. If the bed rollers are too high, wood vibrates and the surface is rippled. Vibration is more of a problem with thin stock, which should be planed with bed rollers set just 0.002 in. above the table.

Adjust the bed rollers by measuring the gap between a straightedge spanning the two rollers and the table surfaces with a feeler gauge as you manipulate the adjustment mechanism. On some planers adjustment is simply made with a lever, on others it requires turning a screw at the end of each roller. If a roller is bent, vibration problems multiply. Bent rollers are easy to detect. If your board advances in a stop-and-go fashion, check the rollers. Unplug the machine and rotate each roller by hand while checking it with a dial indicator. It's easiest if you unhook the feed chain or belt first. On some machines, the rollers are easily removed; in this case, roll the roller on a flat surface to see if it is bent. If it is, replace it.

Check for parallel tables by running two boards of the same thickness through opposite sides of the planer. Compare the thickness of the boards by laying them next to each other for direct comparison. If they're substantially different (more than 0.005 in.), you need to adjust the tables. Most tables have an adjustment for maintaining parallelism with the cutterhead. The owner's manual should contain detailed information about adjusting for parallel. If you don't have a manual, adjustment is usually made from the bottom of the table. Alternatively, some machines have adjustable cutterheads that you can tweak into parallel. Another alternative is to set the knives farther down on the high end.

The table raising-and-lowering mechanism (depth-of-cut control) should be well lubricated. If exposed threads raise and lower the table, wax rather than an oil-based lubricant should be applied.

For planing thin stock or making finish cuts, it is a good idea to make an auxiliary table with a smooth plastic laminate top, as shown in the photos below. The table can be a straight piece of plywood with a cleat on each end. Wax the laminate surface often with a non-silicon wax. The auxiliary table lets you keep the bed rollers at one higher setting and obviates the need to readjust them. It is also useful when planing wood on edge.

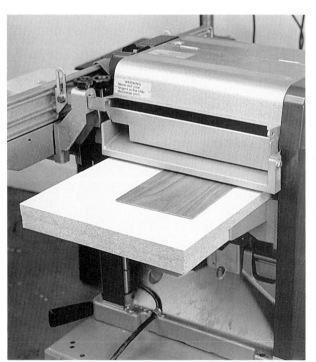
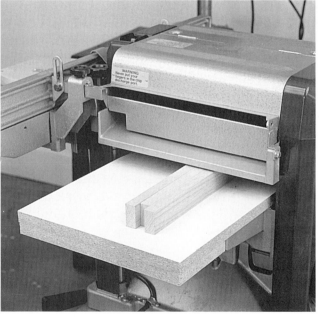

An auxiliary table allows you to plane thin stock (left) and is also useful for planing stock on edge (above).

Hone the knives every month with a stone or a diamond hone to extend the period between sharpenings.

Adjusting the cutterhead system

The smoothness of surfaced stock depends on the condition of the cutterhead bearings and on how well the knives are sharpened, installed and adjusted. Large industrial machines have knife-grinding attachments so that the knives can be reground in the cutterhead. Without such a device the knives must be removed, sharpened and replaced. Most woodworkers do not have the knife-sharpening equipment (or know-how) and send their knives out to be sharpened.

Sharpening knives   Planer knives should be removed and sharpened when they are dull or chipped (you can see the edge of a dull knife). The knives are removed from the cutterhead in the same fashion as jointer knives (see p. 122). You can extend the time between sharpenings by honing the blades periodically with a stone or a diamond hone. Keep the stone flat on the bevel of the knife (see the photo above).

When you have the knives ground, maintain the angle that the manufacturer recommends. That angle is generally appropriate for both hardwood and softwood. If you are going to be planing thousands of board feet of a particular species, you may want to have your knives ground to the angle appropriate for that particular species. Some woods, such as bird's-eye maple and a number of exotic species, chip out easily. These woods respond better to a scraping action rather

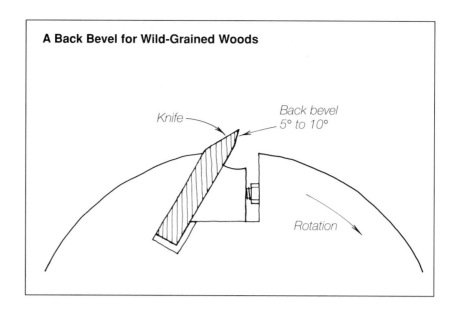

A Back Bevel for Wild-Grained Woods

Knife

Back bevel
5° to 10°

Rotation

than a cutting action. A 5° to 10° back bevel will make the knives more effective for scraping. When using knives that have a back bevel, take extremely light passes and use a slow feed rate.

Installing knives   Before you install your newly sharpened knives, clean the groove and the gib. I use a stick and a piece of paper towel or dry cloth. (Once the knife is installed, waxing the knife between the edge and the gib prevents a buildup of pitch and resins.) Check to make sure that the knives are straight before you install them. As with jointer knives, if a gib or a knife has a burr on the edge, remove it by honing on wet-and-dry silicon carbide abrasive paper on a flat surface.

Installing the planer knives in the cutterhead is similar to installing jointer knives, except that the edge of the knife is always referenced to the cutterhead. If your machine comes with a jig for installing knives, it is advisable to use it. Some machines have clips or spring-loaded installation devices. A simple, but effective device is the three-foot saddle (see the top photo on the facing page). Another option, if your planer has lifting screws, is to use a dial indicator with three feet to span the cutterhead. If your planer is the most primitive design and has no lifting screws or springs, the best way to align the knives is to use a magnetic jig to hold the cutter in place as you tighten the gib. As with the jointer, slightly tighten the end screws first and work slowly toward the middle. Check the knife height and retighten the screws again in the same sequence.

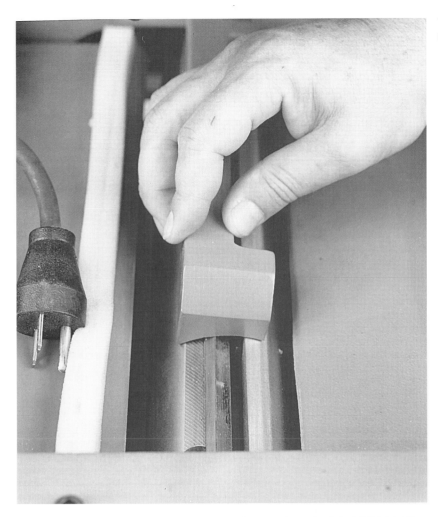

The three-foot saddle is a simple device for checking knife height.

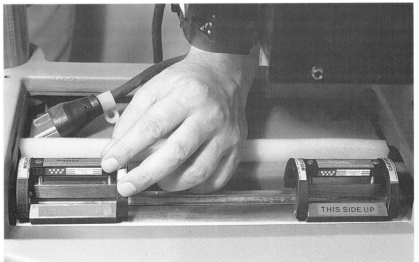

Use a magnetic jig to hold the knife in place as you tighten the gib, if your planer's cutterhead has the simplest design with no lifting screws or springs.

The chip breaker and the pressure bar   As the knife exits the wood the upward thrust can chip out, tear or splinter the wood. To prevent this problem, a chip breaker is often fitted in front of the cutterhead, usually resting on the workpiece. When making a deep cut on a large planer, the knife lifts the material and the chip breaker snaps it off. You can actually hear the wood snapping. The chip breaker is usually curved and is designed to deflect the chips. On some of the newer planers the chip breaker does not contact the wood. On these machines there is a short distance between the knife edge and the gib, which creates a smaller curl and less tear out.

The pressure bar is a piece of metal located between the cutterhead and the outfeed roller. Its purpose is to hold the wood down on the table to decrease vibration, thereby giving the spring-loaded outfeed roller some extra help. If the pressure bar is adjusted too high, it does not hold the wood down and the wood can bounce and be gouged by the cutterhead. If it is too low, it will rub on the new surface or even hinder the wood from exiting the planer.

On some very old machines the chip breaker is adjusted with a weight. The chip breaker and the pressure bar should be adjusted so that their lower edge is just even with a line to the bottom of the cut-

Cutting Action of the Planer

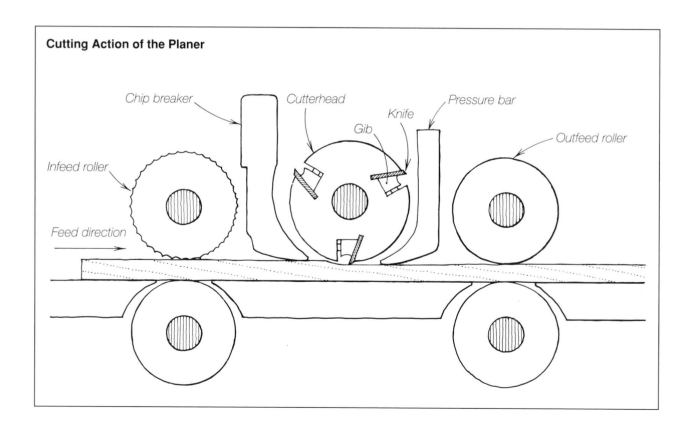

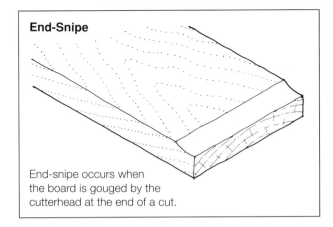

End-Snipe

End-snipe occurs when the board is gouged by the cutterhead at the end of a cut.

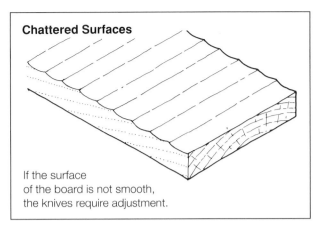

Chattered Surfaces

If the surface of the board is not smooth, the knives require adjustment.

ting circle. However, the height of the bed rollers may also affect this adjustment. Here again, experimentation is in order. You may find that a higher pressure bar (adjusted 0.001 in. to 0.010 in. higher) works best on your machine.

Feedback from the workpiece

As with the jointer, any incorrect adjustment of the planer will show on the surface of the workpiece. End-snipe occurs at the end of a cut when the board is no longer held down against the table by the infeed roller. The end of the board can spring up and be gouged by the cutterhead. Bed rollers aggravate the situation, particularly if they are set high. End-snipe, which is usually more of a problem with long boards, can be decreased by using an auxiliary table and by lifting up the board at the end of the cut.

If you notice wide wave marks on the workpiece, one knife is set too high. Check the knife settings if the surface is not smooth.

A chipped knife is the curse of the planer because it leaves an unplaned line on your otherwise smooth surface. To remedy this problem, loosen one knife just enough so you can nudge it slightly to the left or right—1/32 in. should be plenty. Tighten the knife, replane the workpiece and the line will disappear.

CHAPTER 5
The Drill Press

The drill press is one of those machines you can survive without for years, then when you finally get one, you wonder how you ever managed before. It was originally designed as a machine for drilling holes in metal, but most woodworkers today find many more uses for this versatile tool. I sand, mortise and tenon, dovetail and even plane on my old-time model. Because of its flexibility, I think the drill press should be the second woodworking machine to buy after you've made that initial investment in a table saw, radial-arm saw or bandsaw.

Drill-press design

There are two styles of drill press found in woodworking shops: bench models, which mount to a stand or bench, and floor models, which have a longer column so that the base rests on the floor. A bench drill press obviously has less space under the chuck than a floor model.

In addition to the basic models, there are a number of industrial-grade special-purpose drilling machines: multiple-spindle drill presses, power-feed and speed machines, and numerically controlled radial machines that drill an array of holes to different depths and in constantly changing patterns. You can often pick up a used industrial-grade drill press cheaply at an auction or bankruptcy sale. Although these heavyweights are often superb machines, they are better suited to metalworking and I don't find them particularly useful in a woodshop.

The Drill Press

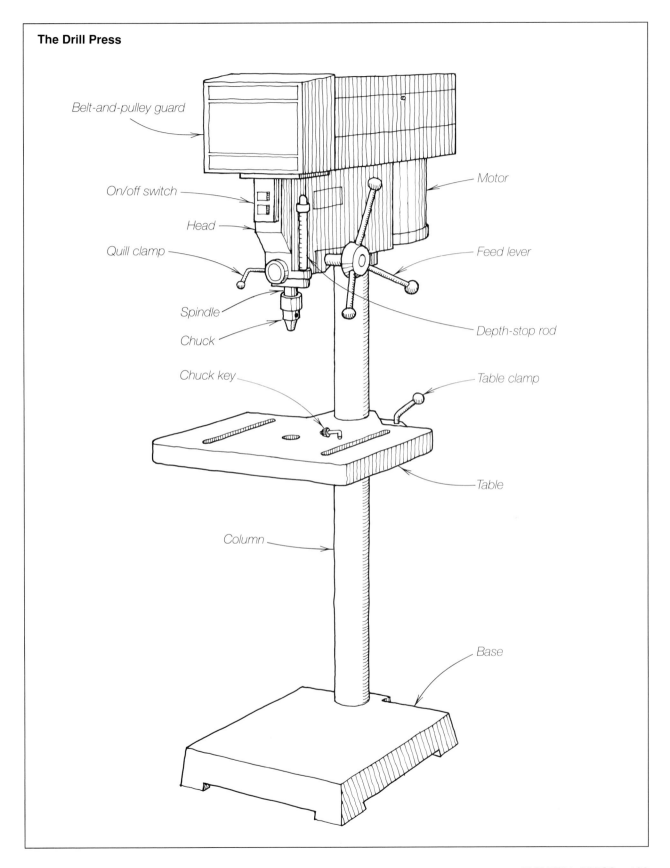

Belt-and-pulley guard

On/off switch

Head

Quill clamp

Spindle

Chuck

Chuck key

Column

Motor

Feed lever

Depth-stop rod

Table clamp

Table

Base

The primary consideration when choosing a drill press is throat size — the distance between the chuck and the column. Most machines are in the 14-in. to 17-in. range.

Chuck size is also an important consideration. Most machines are equipped with ½-in. chucks that allow you to insert any bit with a ½-in. or smaller shank. You can get ⅝-in. and ¾-in. chucks, but twist bits above ¾-in. diameter typically have tapered shanks and are seldom used in woodworking. Almost all large-diameter woodworking bits have ½-in. or smaller shanks. Some drill presses have ⅜-in. or even smaller chucks. I recommend that you avoid these, unless you're a miniaturist or someone who likes a challenge.

The number of steps on the pulleys determines how many speeds the machine has, but this isn't a major consideration when choosing a drill press. Correct speed is important when drilling, but you should be able to change pulley cones if your machine doesn't have a lot of speed options.

Drill-press anatomy

The drill press consists of a base, column, table and head. The base supports the column on which the head is mounted. The table slides up and down the column, allowing adjustment of the space between the table and the drill bit.

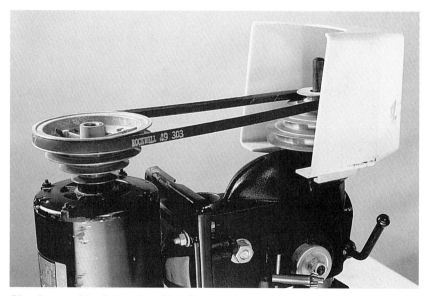

Chuck speed is determined by the position of the belt on the cone pulleys.

Suggested Spindle Speeds (rpm)

Hole Size *	Softwoods	Hardwoods	Plastics	Aluminum	Brass	Cast Iron	Mild Steel
¹⁄₁₆ in.	4,700	4,700	4,700	4,700	4,700	4,700	2,400
⅛ in.	4,700	4,700	4,700	4,700	4,700	2,400	1,250
³⁄₁₆ in.	4,700	2,400	2,400	4,700	2,400	2,400	1,250
¼ in.	2,400	2,400	2,400	4,700	2,400	1,250	700
⁵⁄₁₆ in.	2,400	1,250	1,250	2,400	1,250	1,250	700
⅜ in.	2,400	1,250	1,250	2,400	1,250	700	700
⁷⁄₁₆ in.	2,400	1,250	1,250	1,250	1,250	700	
½ in.	1,250	1,250	1,250	1,250	700	700	
⅝ in.	1,250	700	700	700			
¾ in.	1,250	700	700	700			
⅞ in.	1,250	700					
1 in.	700	700					
1¼ in.	700	700					
1½ in.	700	700					
2 in.	700	700					

* For intermediate sizes, use speed suggested for next larger hole.
Use slower speeds for deep holes or if drill bit burns.

The motor mounts on the back of the head, and a series of stepped cone pulleys change the rotating speed of the chuck. A guard covers the front of the pulleys. The pulley system usually allows a choice of speeds from 700 rpm to 4,700 rpm. The rule of thumb is, the larger the bit diameter and the harder the material, the slower the spindle speed. The chart above should help you select the appropriate speed.

The head is the cast piece that houses the quill, which is a machined tube fitted with ball bearings at each end in which the spindle rotates. The chuck that holds the drill bit or accessory is connected to the end of the spindle. The feed lever lowers the quill and thus the bit into the workpiece. A quill clamp locks the quill when sanding or routing.

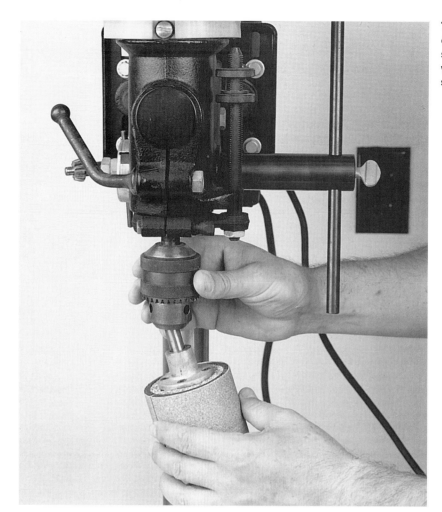

The three-jaw chuck, or Jacobs chuck, holds hex-shaped or round shanked bits and accessories. It won't hold tapered or square shanks.

The tool holder for the drill press is a small three-jaw chuck. It is commonly referred to as a "Jacobs chuck." Most drill-press accessories have straight mounting shafts that fit directly into the chuck.

The chuck key is spring-loaded to minimize the possibility that you'll start the machine with the key still in the chuck. In spite of this precaution, several people are wounded every year by forgotten chuck keys. Never remove your hand from the chuck key as long as the key is in the chuck. As a last precaution, tie the key to the column with a short piece of nylon string.

Drill bits

The earliest drill bits were probably slivers of bone lashed in an incision in a wood shaft and spun with a bow. We've added a few twists (literally and figuratively) to this technology, but the big picture is still much the same.

Twist bits   The ubiquitous twist bit is what most people have in mind when they think of drill bits. It is a cheap, multipurpose bit that can make adequate holes in almost any material, though it is truly effective only in mild steel.

Brad-point bits   The brad-point bit is a twist bit that has been modified to cut wood. The lip or cutting edge of the twist bit is cut back so that the tip of the bit forms a point and the edge of each land, or margin, serves as a perimeter knife or spur.

Spade bits   The spade bit is a flattened rectangular spade of steel on the end of a 4-in. long shank. A triangular pilot juts out of the spade. The width of the spade determines the diameter of the hole.

Forstner bits   The Forstner bit is the bit to use for boring a segment of a hole at the edge of a board or a flat-bottomed hole. The Forstner is a round slug of steel at the end of a ⅜-in. or ½-in. shank. The perimeter of the circle is a honed knife edge. Two chisel edges eject chips from the circle defined by the knife edge. The multispur bit, a variant of the Forstner bit, has sawteeth on the perimeter edge and is used chiefly for large-diameter holes. Both these bits should be used only in the drill press.

The only drill bits that should not be used in the drill press are bits that have screw points (see the drawing below). The screw point is designed for slow hand-fed drilling, in which the screw pulls the bit into the wood. If a screw point is used on the drill press, it pulls the bit into

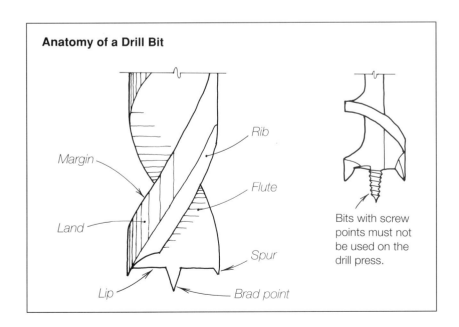

Anatomy of a Drill Bit

Rib

Margin

Flute

Land

Spur

Lip

Brad point

Bits with screw points must not be used on the drill press.

Drill Bits

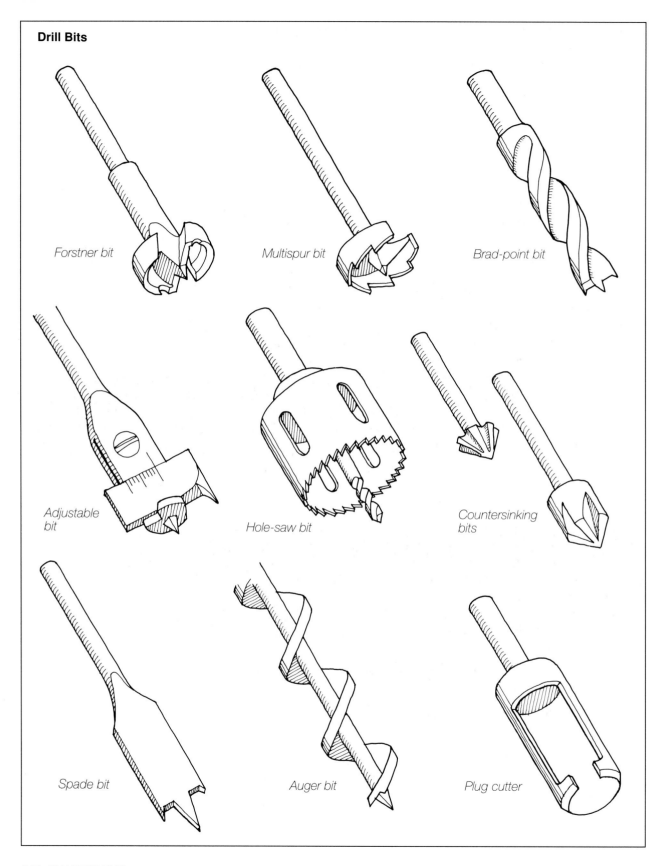

Forstner bit

Multispur bit

Brad-point bit

Adjustable bit

Hole-saw bit

Countersinking bits

Spade bit

Auger bit

Plug cutter

the wood very quickly and can possibly tear up the work. A potentially dangerous side effect is that the screw point can pull the workpiece off the drill-press table and cause it to rotate if it is not clamped down.

Other types of metalcutting and woodcutting drill bits, such as those shown in the drawing on the facing page, work well in the drill press. You may want to experiment with the type of wood, speed and depth of cut. If you are drilling a deep hole, it is best to retract the drill bit occasionally to remove the waste.

Safety considerations

The drill press seems like a fairly benign machine until the bit seizes in an unsupported piece of metal or wood. Then, the mechanical advantage of even a small electric motor rapidly becomes apparent. I've survived one or two painful encounters and know of some folks who haven't been so lucky. When using the drill press, clamp ALL metal pieces and small wood pieces to the table or hold them in a vise. Clamp small and odd-shaped pieces in a fixture or make sure they're held securely by a jig. A good fence is adequate support for many drilling operations when working with larger pieces.

Dangling shirt sleeves, necklaces or wisps of beard or ponytail are all too easily caught by the revolving chuck. Once you're tangled up in the machine, you won't be able to stop it, so take appropriate precautions before you begin. As when using any woodworking machine, wear eye protection.

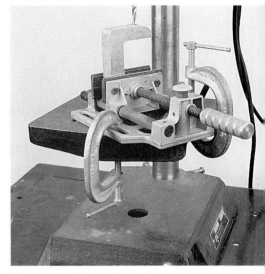

Clamp workpieces less than 12 in. long to the table or in a drill-press vise.

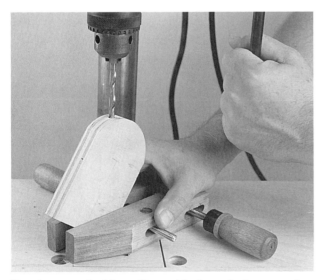

Hand screws hold small or odd-shaped pieces and can easily be clamped to the drill-press table.

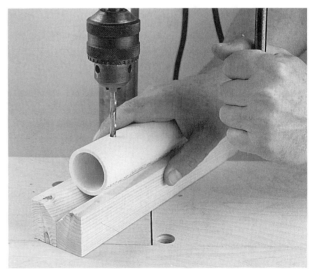

Support round stock in a V-jig. Drill at the top dead center of the workpiece.

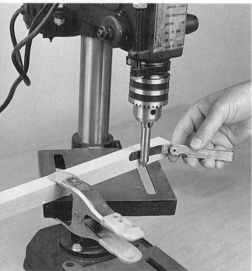

Use a dial indicator to check for runout in the chuck. You can also check for runout using a stick clamped to the table and a feeler gauge.

Tuning the drill press

Drill presses are fairly simple machines. As long as the spindle turns true and the chuck is concentric with the spindle, you should be able to drill straight holes. There are few adjustable parts, and accuracy depends on runout at the chuck. If your drill press is not running true, first polish and lubricate the table and column. Then check for endplay and sideplay of the spindle by locking the quill and shaking the chuck side to side and up and down. The cause of any movement should be isolated and repaired before testing runout.

Checking for runout

Runout in the drill press is usually caused by one of three things: the chuck is untrue, the spindle is bent or the chuck is improperly mounted on the spindle. Check for runout at the chuck by mounting a "know bit," a precision metal dowel pin, in the chuck and measuring the amount of deviation with a dial indicator. Position the plunger of the dial indicator against the know bit, and rotate the chuck with the belt. Measure runout as the bit rotates. Alternatively, clamp a piece of wood next to the bit and measure runout with a feeler gauge. Clamp the stick with a spring clamp so that one end is free to move slightly. Rotate the spindle with the belt so that you don't deflect the chuck or the spindle and so that the bit touches the wood at some point of the rotation. Measure the runout with a feeler gauge between the bit and the piece of wood. Runout will be most pronounced 180° from the point where the bit touches the wood. If you get more than 0.010 in. runout at a point 2 in. below the chuck, your spindle or chuck is not running true.

After you've checked for runout at the chuck, remove the chuck and check the spindle for runout. Depending on the age and design of your machine, removing the chuck can be easy or difficult. One type of chuck threads onto the spindle, the other mounts to the spindle with a taper fit. If there is a ring around the top of the chuck and the ring has holes in it, the chuck is probably threaded onto the spindle. To remove this type of chuck, wrap a shop cloth around the spindle and clamp it in a vise. Try to unscrew the chuck. If it doesn't unscrew easily, try heating the chuck with a torch to break the bond.

If you have a chuck that mounts to the spindle with a taper fit, the chuck can often be removed without removing the spindle from the machine. You may have to remove the depth-gauge mechanism from the machine to get good access to the top of the chuck. Lower the quill and lock it in place, exposing the top of the chuck. Take an open-end wrench that fits over the spindle between the chuck and the quill. Give the wrench a sharp upward blow and the chuck should fall off. If it doesn't, rotate the spindle 90° and try again.

To remove the chuck from a tapered spindle, insert an open-end wrench around the spindle and give the end of the wrench a sharp upward blow.

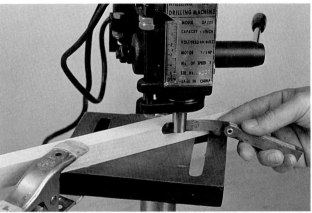

After removing the chuck, check the spindle for runout with a dial indicator (above left). Measure runout from the end of the taper. You can also use the movable-stick method to check the runout of the spindle (above right).

If the chuck still won't budge, pour a light-viscosity penetrating fluid, such as Liquid Wrench®, on the spindle above the chuck and let it sink in overnight. Another option is to heat the chuck with a torch in an attempt to break the bond of the two tapered surfaces. (Caution: Many penetrating oils are flammable, so don't try these two methods together.) If all your efforts fail to persuade the chuck to abandon its grasp of the spindle, your only alternative is to take the spindle to a machine shop or service center. To remove the spindle from the drill press, take the pulley off the spindle and unscrew the knurled knob that's opposite the feed lever. This knob adjusts the return spring tension for the feed lever and keeps the feed-lever gear meshed with the rack cut into the side of the quill. Once you've removed the feed lever, the quill should just slip down from the head of the drill press.

Assuming you are successful at removing the chuck, check the runout of the taper at the bottom of the spindle with a dial indicator or use the movable-stick method. If runout is more than 0.004 in., either order a new spindle or, if the spindle is straight, take it to a machine shop and have a new taper cut.

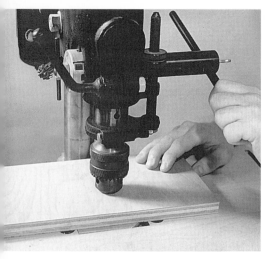

To mount the chuck on the spindle, gently lower the chuck onto a clamped piece of plywood with the feed lever. Turn the machine on low speed and slowly increase the pressure on the feed lever.

To determine whether the spindle is straight, remove it from the drill press and roll it on a flat surface. Any deviation will be apparent, and you can measure the amount of bend with a feeler gauge. If the spindle is bent more than 0.004 in., have the taper recut.

A bent spindle wobbles more than a cornered congressman. If the spindle rolls true, the problem is probably in the chuck. It may simply be that the chuck was incorrectly mounted on the spindle. While you've got the chuck off, give it a thorough examination. If the parts seem loose or worn or if the chuck tightens erratically, replace it.

To mount the chuck on the tapered spindle, clean both surfaces with a dry rag. Pressure-fit the chuck on the spindle. The best way to seat the chuck on the spindle is to apply even pressure on the bottom of the chuck. Retract the jaws and place the chuck just a hair above a piece of plywood on the drill-press table. Start the drill press at low speed and slowly press the chuck against the plywood. If the spindle and the chuck are true, this mounting technique should yield a drill press that runs true. If the spindle is true and the machine is still giving an eccentric result, replace the chuck.

A last desperate measure is to bend the spindle. Experienced machine restorers can work wonders with this technique, but it takes considerable skill and a fair share of good luck to pull it off. To bend the spindle, tighten a metal rod in the chuck and determine which way the runout is the most severe. Take a hammer and pound the rod in the opposite direction. Be advised that you are running a real risk of damaging both the chuck and the spindle beyond repair.

Using the drill press

The utility of the drill press can be greatly enhanced by employing various fences, jigs and fixtures. In addition, there are a number of accessories that allow you to use the drill press for much more than just drilling holes.

Drill-press fences

A fence stabilizes work and aligns an edge of the workpiece with the drill bit, which is important when making holes parallel to the edge. The simplest fence is a board clamped to the table, but I find this option a little clumsy. Most woodworkers develop a more substantial fence. There are two styles of fences. One mounts on the side of the table and remains perpendicular to the edge of the table. The other mounts at one point of the table and swings through an arc. The movable side of the fence either clamps to the table or is secured with a bolt. Both designs are enhanced by the use of a stop system.

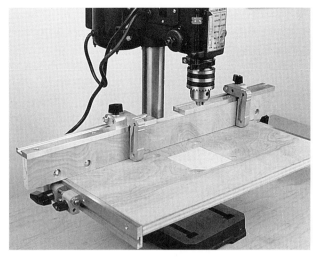

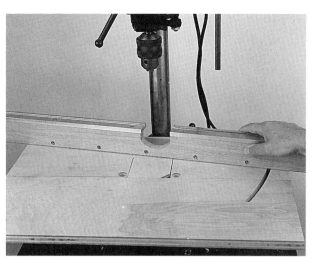

This drill-press fence is designed to stay perpendicular to the edge of the table. It has an optional micro-adjuster and flip stops for repeatable drilling operations.

This fence has one fixed end and one end that pivots through an arc. The adjustable end is secured to the table with a clamp or a routed slot.

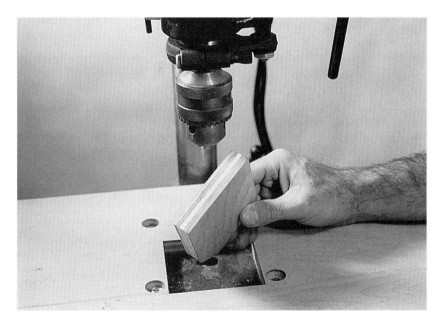

Using a replaceable insert in the auxiliary table saves having to replace the entire table top as it wears.

Auxiliary tables

Although the metal table that comes with the drill press is ideal for drilling metal, it's best to use an auxiliary wooden table for woodworking. The best auxiliary table I've seen on a drill press is a wooden table with a square hole for a replaceable insert. The insert can be flipped and rotated up to eight times before it's so full of holes that you must discard it.

Drilling angled holes

Woodworkers often need to drill holes at an angle. On some drill presses the table is designed to tilt; on the radial drill press, the head tilts rather than the table. On both these kinds of drill presses, you measure the angle of tilt with a scale found on the head or column of the machine. If the scale is missing, measure the angle with a bevel gauge. If your drill press doesn't have a tilt mechanism, make an auxiliary angle table, as shown in the drawing below. If you have to make a series of holes with the same angle, make an angled fixture, as shown in the top left photo on the facing page.

Jigs and fixtures

Although the terms are often used interchangeably, a fixture is technically a device that holds and positions the work, whereas a jig goes one step further and also serves as a tool guide. When you design a fixture or jig, try to think clearly about what it will ultimately be used for.

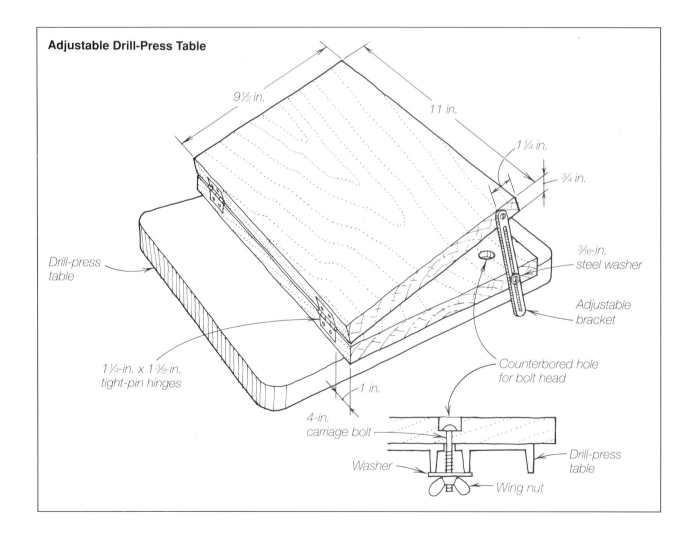

Adjustable Drill-Press Table

9½ in.

11 in.

1¼ in.

¾ in.

Drill-press table

³⁄₁₆-in. steel washer

Adjustable bracket

Counterbored hole for bolt head

1¼-in. x 1⅜-in. tight-pin hinges

1 in.

4-in. carriage bolt

Washer

Drill-press table

Wing nut

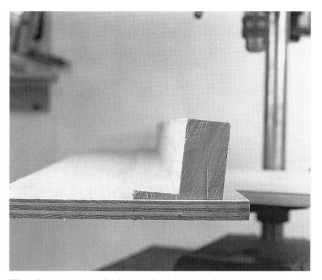

The fixed-angle jig is made from a piece of scrap plywood fastened to a 2x4 cut at a 5° angle. It is ideal for production runs.

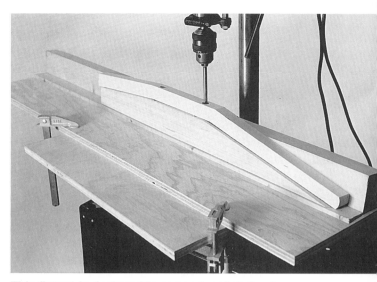

This fixture is designed to support a chair back as the side stretcher holes are drilled. It rests on a fixed-angle jig.

Creativity has been described as problem finding rather than problem solving. A good example is designing a fixture that will hold a chair back at a specific angle for drilling the stretcher holes.

The fixture must solve two distinct problems. First, it must support the chair back so that two holes for the chair stretchers can be drilled 5 in. apart. Second, it must be designed to hold the chair back at a 5° angle, but each chair has two chair backs with the holes angled in opposite directions. The photo above right shows a solution. The fixed-angle jig holds the support fixture at a 5° angle. Half of the chair backs are drilled with this setup, the other half are drilled with the support fixture reversed. A spacer block is used to position the support fixture accurately for drilling the second hole.

An elevated auxiliary table allows you to sand across the entire length of the sanding drum.

Sanding

The drill press can also be used as a spindle sanding machine. Sanding drums of various sizes are available. The industrial spindle sander is designed so that the spindle moves up and down as it rotates, making the sanding process more efficient and extending the life of the paper. This up-and-down action can be achieved on the drill press by moving the feed lever. You will be able to use the entire surface of the drum if you make an elevated auxiliary table. Make the table so that you can clamp it to your drill-press table, and cut a hole in it ⅛ in. larger than the size of your drum.

Pattern sanding

Although you'll probably use pattern sanding with a router for straight cuts, when you have complex curves to shape, pattern sanding can be a real time-saver for limited production runs. It's particularly useful for making end-grain cuts, or when cutting against the grain, where using a router might cause the surface to chip out.

If you're copying a piece and have the original part, make a pattern of the original first. Attach the part to the pattern blank with double-faced tape, hot-melt glue or brads. Masonite®, MDF® or Baltic birch plywood are good choices for patterns. Rough-cut the pattern on the bandsaw with a rub block riding against the original part (see the photo below). Leave about 1/16 in. to be removed with the sanding drum.

Rough-cut the shape of a pattern for pattern sanding using a rub block on the bandsaw. It is easier to see the saw cut if the pattern blank is on top. The original piece contacts the rub block during the saw cut and leaves about 1/16 in. of waste, which is removed with the sanding drum on the drill press (see the drawing below).

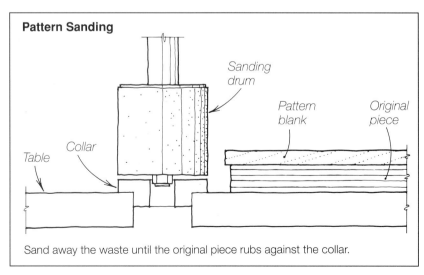

Pattern Sanding

Sanding drum

Pattern blank

Original piece

Collar

Table

Sand away the waste until the original piece rubs against the collar.

A hollow-chisel mortising attachment can be mounted on the drill press.

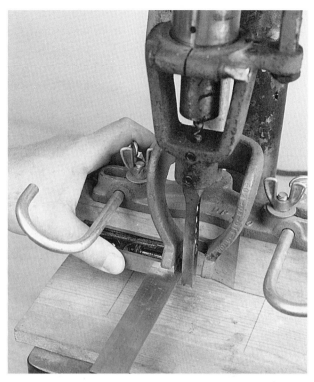

When adjusting the chisel holder on the mortising attachment, make sure that the chisel is square to the fence.

Make a circular collar the size of the drum and position it under the drum so that the edge of the collar and the drum are flush. Sand off the waste on the pattern blank, until the original part rubs against the collar, as shown in the drawing on the facing page. On completion, you'll have an exact replica of the original. It can serve as the master for you to produce 100 more.

Mortising

In industrial applications mortises are cut with a specialized machine, but you can adapt your drill press to make mortises. Many hollow-chisel mortising attachments that mimic the industrial mortiser are available. The attachments consist of a square hollow chisel with sharp corners and an auger bit that rotates inside the chisel. A bracket holds the fixture on the quill.

The mortising attachment is lowered into the wood with the feed lever. The chisel's square sharp corners compress the wood and force it into the auger bit, which removes the wood like a traditional drill bit and creates a square hole. To work efficiently the attachment must be sharp and correctly adjusted. The tip of the bit must be accurately

Mortising Sequence Using Mortising Attachment

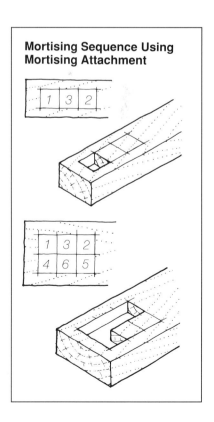

positioned relative to the chisel, with enough clearance for chips to clear. The bit should not rub the tip of the hollow chisel. Also check to make sure that the chisel is square to the fence.

Spiral-fluted router bits can also be used to cut mortises. These bits both plunge and cut sideways. Make the plunged holes first and then remove the waste by moving the workpiece back and forth. Experiment to find which speed and drilling technique work best for the type of wood that you are using. Another option is to drill the holes with a drill and then use the router bit to remove the waste. The mortise made with this technique has rounded corners. Making the tenon for this type of mortise is discussed on pp. 211-213.

Depth of cut is critical for mortising and it's important for most drilling and boring operations, too. It's a two-phase adjustment. Draw a line to the depth of cut you want on a piece of scrap that's the same thickness as your workpiece. Raise the table enough so that the bit is fairly close to the top of the workpiece. You want to be able to slip the workpiece under the bit while it's rotating without danger of it inadvertently mak-

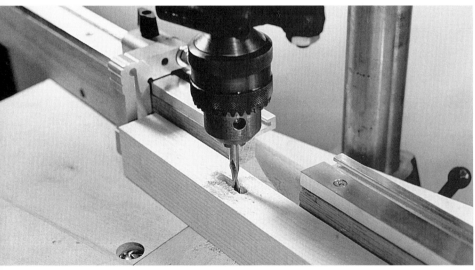

A spiral-fluted router bit mounted in the drill press can also be used to make mortises.

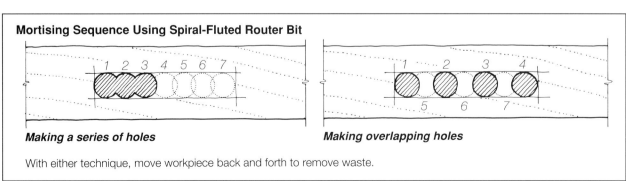

Mortising Sequence Using Spiral-Fluted Router Bit

1 2 3 4 5 6 7

Making a series of holes

1 2 3 4
5 6 7

Making overlapping holes

With either technique, move workpiece back and forth to remove waste.

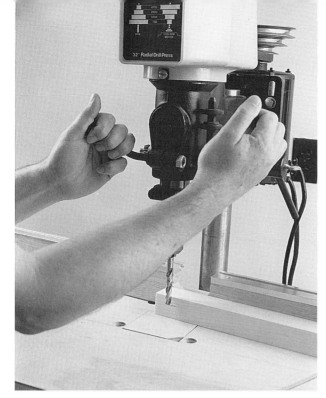

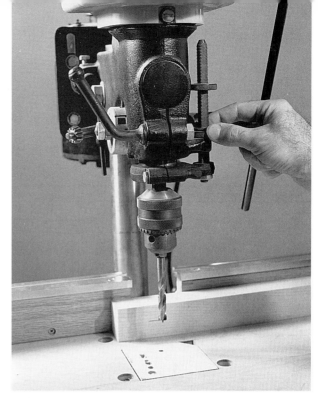

To set the depth of a drill hole, adjust the table to approximately the correct position. Mark the desired depth on the side of the board, lower the bit and lock the quill.

Make the final depth adjustment with the adjustable stop.

ing contact. Next, lower the bit so that its bottom reaches the scribed line on the piece of scrap. Lock the quill clamp at this depth and spin the nuts on the depth-lock rod down to the stop on the head casting.

Feedback from the work

Any operation that you perform on the drill press will give you feedback about the condition of the machine and the sharpness of the drill bit. If the bit burns or cuts very slowly, it is either dull or the speed is too fast.

A machine that is running true will made a clean hole with no vibration. If the drill press seems to vibrate or shake, either the machine is not running true or the drill bit is eccentric. Check the drill bit for bend by rolling it on a flat table. Vibration can also indicate trouble with the bearings. Unplug the machine, and try to shake the chuck side to side and back and forth. Any movement should be explored. It may mean that the bearings are bad or that they are simply loose in the quill. If the latter, tighten the mechanism that retains the bearings. If the former, replace the bearings.

CHAPTER 6
The Router and the Shaper

The table-mounted router and the shaper are known as "spindle machines," so-called because the cutter is mounted on a spindle or shaft that sticks up through the middle of the table. There are a number of advantages to having a cutter mounted in this position. It's easier to control the wood than the tool, particularly when working with small pieces. A number of devices, such as fences, bearings, patterns, forms, jigs or fixtures, can be attached to the table, fence, miter gauge or spindle to guide the cut. The most important advantage, however, is safety: It should be fairly obvious that you are much safer pushing a small piece of wood against a stable fence and table than hoisting a 3.5-hp motor with a bit screaming at 25,000 rpm.

The shaper is a stationary machine that includes a table, stand, motor and fence. The router table mimics the shaper. The best router tables feature a removable plate, which the router mounts to, that fits in a recess in the table. This plate allows easy removal of the router for changing bits and making adjustments.

The Shaper

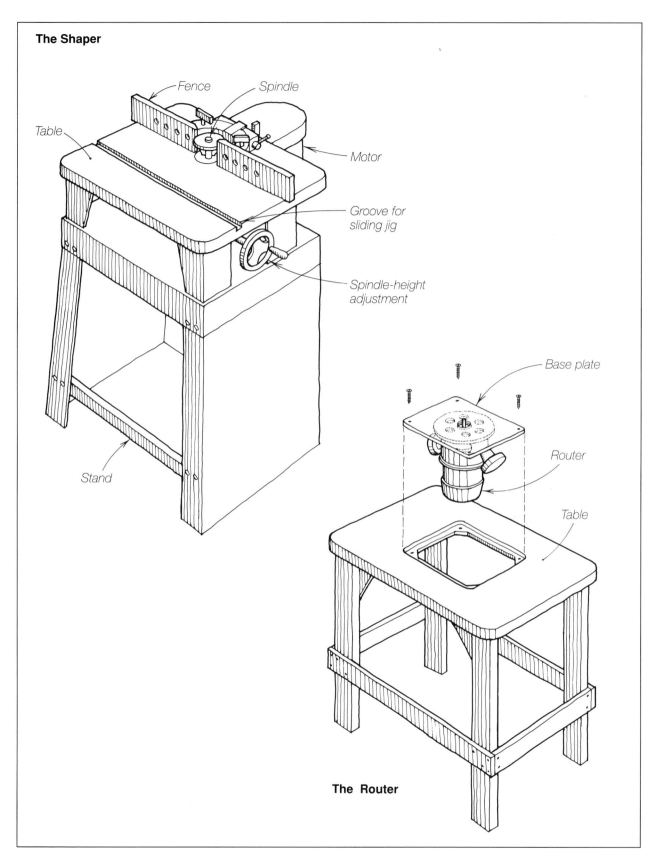

Fence

Spindle

Table

Motor

Groove for
sliding jig

Spindle-height
adjustment

Stand

Base plate

Router

Table

The Router

The shaper cutter (left) attaches to the spindle and is held in place with a nut. The standard router bit (right) consists of the shank and the cutter in a single unit.

Shaper spindles, available in ½-in., ¾-in., 1-in. and 1¼-in. sizes, are usually interchangeable. Collets that hold router bits (shown at left) are also available for some shapers.

The router and the shaper differ in the type of cutter that is used. The shank and cutter of a router bit are usually cast or machined from one piece of metal. The shaper cutter, on the other hand, is just that, and is secured to the spindle with a spindle nut. Shaper spindles are usually interchangeable and are available in ¼-in. increments from ½ in. to 1¼ in. in diameter.

Great advances have been made in router technology over the past decade or so. Prior to 1980, the router table was used exclusively for light work. Heavy work, such as processing raised panels and rail-and-stile doors, could be performed only on the shaper. With the development of large, high-powered, variable-speed routers and the introduction of mounting plates, high-quality router tables and better collets and router bits, the distinction between the two machines has become blurred. Variable-speed routers enable large cutters to spin at a safe 10,000 rpm to 12,000 rpm range. This allows the tip speed of even the largest cutter to be in the safe range of under 120 mph.

Being able to mount the router in a table or use it independently makes the router a more versatile machine than the shaper. It is also less expensive—you can buy a high-quality router table, router and tooling for less than the price of a small shaper alone.

Router design

The router is an American invention that has invaded virtually every aspect of woodworking. It can perform more woodworking tasks than any other tool and is consequently often recommended as the first power tool for a novice. It is also a workhorse for the professional. If you asked 100 woodworkers which tool they'd want if stranded on a desert island that just happened to have electrical service, 99 would probably choose the router.

Routers can be divided into two categories: standard routers and plunge routers. The difference is in how the motor is attached to the base. The standard router (see the top drawing on the facing page) has a motor that twists up and down inside a threaded round base and can usually be completely removed from the base. This feature makes it convenient to use in a router table, because you can easily separate the base from the motor when you are changing bits, and height adjustment is simpler.

The plunge router (see the bottom drawing on the facing page), which was originally a European design, has two rods, one on each side of the motor, that allow the motor to be raised and lowered at will. This design has a height-adjustment knob and a depth-stop adjust-

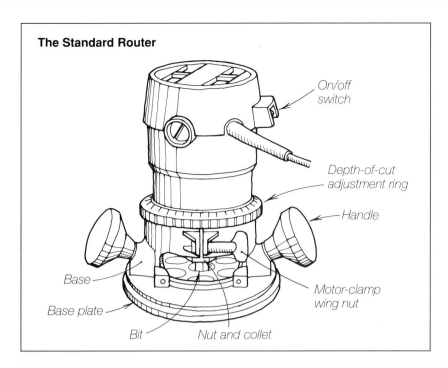

The Standard Router

On/off switch

Depth-of-cut adjustment ring

Handle

Base

Base plate

Motor-clamp wing nut

Bit

Nut and collet

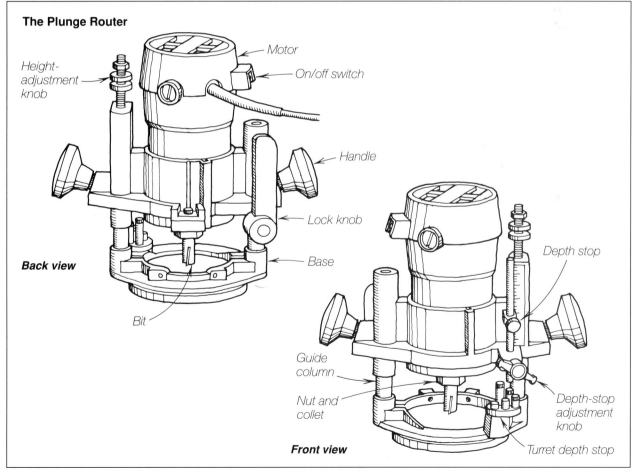

The Plunge Router

Height-adjustment knob

Motor

On/off switch

Handle

Lock knob

Base

Back view

Bit

Depth stop

Guide column

Nut and collet

Depth-stop adjustment knob

Turret depth stop

Front view

The replacement plunge base (middle) turns a standard router into a plunge router.

ment so that the amount of travel in either direction can be adjusted. A lever locks the router at the desired depth. The plunge mechanism with its multiple parts adds considerable expense to the cost of the router, but it makes a plunge-type cut, such as a mortise or stop dado, much easier to make. One disadvantage of most plunge routers is that the motor cannot easily be separated from the base.

A recent innovation (shown in the photo above) is a standard-type base that also has a plunge mechanism. The base can be used in a hand-held position or in a router table.

Router anatomy

The router is essentially a motor with a collet on one end of the motor's shaft. A slide mechanism raises and lowers the motor in relation to the base plate. The motor on the plunge router slides straight up and down, whereas the standard-router motor may slide straight up and down or spiral up and down along a large threaded mechanism.

The collet

The collet is the cone-shaped device that holds the router bit. The inside is straight to fit the bit's shaft, whereas the outside is tapered and fits into the cone at the end of the arbor shaft. As the locking nut is tightened, the collet is pushed into the arbor cone and the bit is squeezed tight. The compressive force on the outside of the collet is concentrated on the bit shaft. Unlike the drill chuck, which holds the drill with three points, the collet holds the bit with the entire inside surface.

Not all collets are created equal, and many routing problems can be traced to the design of the collet itself. A router can have a powerful motor and attractive features, but if it has an inferior collet it is still a poor machine.

To hold the bit securely, the collet must be flexible; the more flexible the better. Collet flexibility is directly related to the number of slits in the collet. The best collets have many slits and are so flexible that you can easily squeeze them together with your fingers. Conversely, poorer collets have only one slit and are very stiff and do not do a good job of transferring the compressive force to the bit. An inferior collet is one of the reasons some bits slip no matter how hard you tighten them.

Size also affects the performance of the collet. The holding power of the collet is greater the more surface shared by the collet and the bit. A ⅜-in. long collet doesn't get much grip on a shaft that is 1 in. long. A short collet usually has more runout, too.

There are four categories of collets: one-piece, two-piece, three-piece and three-piece self-releasing. The different collet designs are compromises between performance and economy.

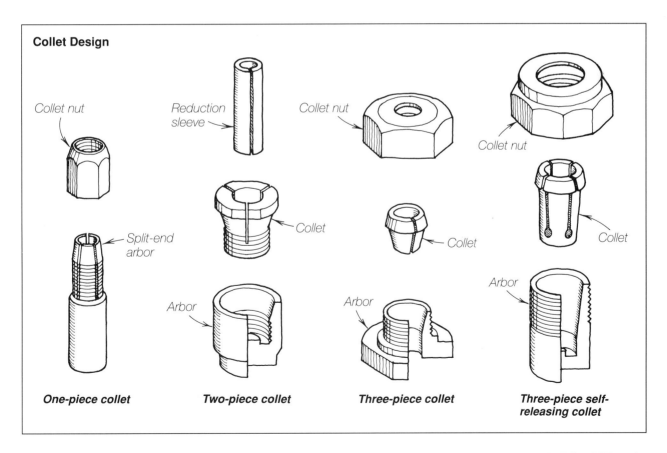

Collet Design

Collet nut

Reduction sleeve

Collet nut

Collet nut

Split-end arbor

Collet

Collet

Collet

Arbor

Arbor

Arbor

One-piece collet   **Two-piece collet**   **Three-piece collet**   **Three-piece self-releasing collet**

Router collets: from left to right, a two-piece collet, a three-piece collet and two three-piece self-releasing collets.

The one-piece collet With the simple one-piece design, which is not a collet in the true sense, the collet is machined directly onto the end of the arbor. The arbor end is hollow, with a threaded outer surface and slits in the sides. A locking nut that fits over the shaft tightens the collet around the bit. This is the type of collet used on many laminate-trimming routers and some Sears models. The problem with the one-piece design is that there is no way to replace a damaged or worn-out collet without replacing the entire arbor. If you have this type of collet on your router and it needs replacing, you may be better off buying a new router.

The two-piece collet The two-piece system, which is used on most Japanese routers and the dome-top Porter-Cable router, has a separate threaded collet that screws into the end of the arbor. As the collet's integral nut is tightened, the arbor's tapered socket compresses the collet's cone-shaped body, tightening the collet around the bit.

The advantage of the two-piece collet is that theoretically the collet cannot get stuck in the interior taper in the arbor cone and thereby freeze the bit. But there are a number of problems with this design. First, two-piece collets (even those with multiple slits) tend to be stiff and don't grab the bit very well. Second, the mating surfaces of the collet cone and the arbor socket rub against each other and can abrade and gall (see p. 164), making the collet difficult to tighten and loosen. As a result, the two-piece system is susceptible to bit slippage and/or collet freezing. If the collet freezes, it may require tremendous force to release it, which may damage the surface of the collet and the arbor cone. An additional disadvantage is that the two-piece design is often available only with a ½-in. collet; to use a ¼-in. collet you have to use a reduction sleeve, which further reduces holding power.

The three-piece collet With a three-piece collet, the arbor, collet and locking nut are separate pieces. The collet fits into the interior taper in the arbor and is tightened by the nut. The outside angle is usually quite steep so that the collet springs back out of the taper as the nut is loosened. This design releases well unless the surface of the bit, collet or cone is rough or dirty. A tap on the nut or the bit is usually enough to release the collet, or you can back the nut all the way off the arbor. The best three-piece designs are long with multiple slits.

The three-piece self-releasing collet The three-piece self-releasing collet is the most advanced collet design. The top of the collet usually has a ridge, groove or keeper ring that fits inside the nut. As the nut is loosened it pulls the collet out of the cone. Because it self-releases, the taper angle is usually 8° to 10°, compared with the 20° to 30° angle required by the regular three-piece collet.

Three-piece self-releasing collets are typically made of high-quality polished spring steel and are usually long with multiple slits. Because of their flexibility, these collets have great bit-holding power, even on shafts that are slightly undersized. This design, which is featured on routers made by Milwaukee and Elu as well as the Makita 3612 and the Ryobi 600 series, is similar in quality to the collets used on large metal-working machines.

Tuning the router

Many people mistakenly assume that a router's accuracy is automatic, and that all they have to do is install the bit and turn on the router. But in many ways, a router needs as much maintenance and care as any other woodworking machine. Tuning the router entails caring for its wearing parts, such as the collet, bearings and brushes, and knowing when these parts need to be replaced. Replacing the parts at the right time helps keep performance up and repair bills down. The collet is the Achilles' heel of the router and the part that usually requires the most attention, so we'll begin there.

Collet maintenance

Dirt, rust, sawdust and pitch decrease the ability of the collet to hold and release the bit. A number of problems can be traced directly to a poorly maintained collet, including bit slippage, bit and collet freezing, vibration, bit bending, bit breakage, and excessive runout.

To get the best performance out of your collet, keep as smooth a surface as possible on both the inside and the outside of the collet, the interior taper in the arbor and the bit shaft. The outside of the collet can be cleaned with steel wool, a nylon pad (Teflon®-safe) or a fine-bristle

Clean the inside of the collet with a fine-bristle round brass brush.

Bell Mouthing

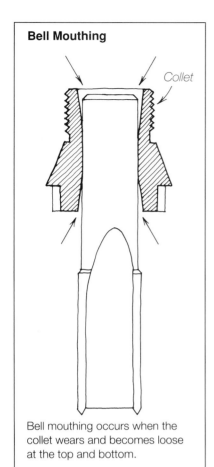

Bell mouthing occurs when the collet wears and becomes loose at the top and bottom.

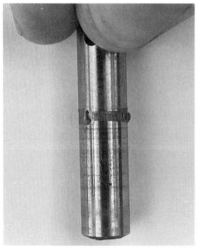

Galling occurs when a bit rotates in the collet, scraping grooves on the metal surface of the bit.

brass brush. The best tool for cleaning the inside of the collet is a fine-bristle round brass brush, as shown in the photo above. Rust is much harder to remove than pitch or dirt and may take some extra effort. No matter how badly the surface is rusted, resist the temptation to use sandpaper (even the finest grade), since the resulting scratches can decrease the collet's grip.

Likewise, liquids and oils should not be used on the collet. Some people use rubbing compound to clean the collet and bits, but that leaves a fine film that must be removed with a dry cloth. If the router is to be stored in a humid area, the collet should be removed and placed in a plastic bag to protect it from rusting. If your shop is very humid, you may want to put a fine coating of oil on the arbor cone, but make sure you wipe it off entirely before using the router.

Don't store the router with the bit in the collet. After you have finished using it, make a habit of releasing the bit and cleaning both the bit and the collet, since pitch and dirt can accelerate the rusting process.

Although proper maintenance will prolong the life of the collet, all collets eventually wear out and need to be replaced, perhaps several times over the life of the router. One of the commonest forms of collet wear is called "bell mouthing," which occurs when the collet wears more at the top and bottom than in the middle, leaving less contact area to hold the bit (see the drawing at left). Imagine drilling a hole in a piece of wood and inserting a metal rod in the hole. As you slowly rotate the rod in a circle you are bell-mouthing the hole in the wood. Eventually, only the middle is tight.

The symptoms of bell mouthing include bit slippage and bit runout. A slipping bit can cause galling on the bit shank, the inside surface of the collet or both. Galling is caused by the friction of two nonlubricated metal surfaces rubbing against each other. In the case of the router bit, it shows up as grooves or ridges on the surface of the shaft (as shown in the photo at left). If the galling is deep or extensive, the collet as well as the bit may be ruined.

If you are unsure whether your collet needs replacing, there are two ways to check for collet wear: one is to feel whether the bit moves in the collet and the other is to check for runout. Runout increases as the collet wears. I suggest you make both tests and if either is positive, replace the collet. First, take a new long bit and hand-tighten it in the router. Throw a shop rag over the sharp edges of the bit and try to wiggle the end. If you can detect movement, replace the collet.

Next, check the collet for runout by tightening an accurate rod, such as a precision drill rod or a "know bit," in the router. A know bit is a very accurately machined rod with a point on the end for setting up equipment. If you have a dial indicator, check for runout by measuring 1 in. up from the collet. If the runout is more than 0.005 in., replace the collet. You can also use the dial indicator to check for runout in the tapered collet socket in the arbor; it should have less than 0.001 in. of runout.

If you don't have a dial indicator, a low-tech method for testing runout is to clamp a narrow bar of wood to the router base with the edge pressing lightly against the bit about 1 in. up from the collet. Rotate the arbor; if there is runout, the bit will push the bar away. Measure the amount of runout with a feeler gauge inserted between the bit and the bar. As with the previous method, if runout exceeds 0.005 in., replace the collet. Even if your collet passes both these tests, replace it if the bit slips.

There are situations where bit slippage is not the fault of the collet but rather of the way the bit was installed. Straight bits should be inserted until about ⅛ in. of space is left between the end of the shaft and the bottom of the collet. As the collet tightens, it pulls the bit down into the taper. If you insert the bit too far into the collet, the bit can't move downward with it, and the inside surface of the collet rubs against the bit shaft. This friction can damage both surfaces.

Other kinds of bits (i.e., bits that do not have straight cutters) should be mounted with the cutter about ⅛ in. above the collet. This prevents the collet from tightening the bit on the fillet (the curve between the shaft and the rest of the bit). If the bit is too deep, the collet pinches the fillet rather than the shaft and the bit loosens very quickly.

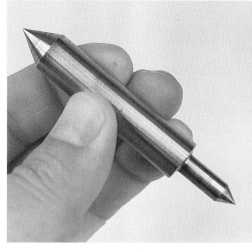

A know bit is a precision machined rod designed for testing runout and for accurately setting up the router.

Runout can be measured by inserting a feeler gauge between the know bit and a narrow piece of scrap clamped to the base.

Bearings

Bearings require occasional maintenance and replacement. Because they rotate at high speed, router bearings wear much faster than most other motor bearings. Fortunately, there are a number of things you can do to prolong bearing life.

The worst thing that you can do for your router is to let the motor run when it is not cutting. This is called "run on," and during this process those smooth little bearings pound themselves into a mess. This can happen very quickly—in a couple of days in a production shop. The problem is particularly common with a table-mounted router. When a router is hand-held, you turn it on when you use it and turn it off when you are done. With a router mounted in a table, there's a tendency to leave it on constantly. When you are not actually using the router, the bearings spin at as much as 29,000 rpm, and overheat rapidly. The heat causes the lubricant to fail, and the bearings fail shortly thereafter. The best solution I've found is to use a foot switch that is activated only when you stand on it; when you walk away from the table the motor turns off. A friend of mine who runs a production shop extended the life of his router bearings from two weeks to four months just by installing a foot switch on his router tables. The "soft start" feature available on some routers can also prolong the life of bearings by not exposing them to sudden start-up torque.

Eventually, router bearings will need to be replaced. You can hear the bearings howl when they are ruined, but don't wait for a loud noise before replacing them. If you do, you run the risk of ruining other key components, such as the arbor, that are more expensive to replace. Heat is a good indicator of bearing wear: The router should never get so hot that you can't touch the bearings. You can also feel if the bearings are worn by rotating the arbor by hand. It should feel consistently smooth; if it seems to bind or if there is a rough spot, bearing damage is likely. Also try to move the arbor back and forth and up and down. If you can detect any movement in the arbor, it's probably time to replace the bearings.

When it's time for replacement of the bearings, have the manufacturer's service center do it for you. Otherwise, a good bearing house can do the job. Make sure you get the best grade of bearings. I had a router that went through a number of bearings from the manufacturer. When I installed a better grade of bearings, they lasted about three or four times longer than the originals.

Other router parts that need occasional replacement are the motor brushes, which are found under the small removable caps on either side of the motor housing. Brushes should be replaced about every 50 hours of use, or sooner if you notice that they arc across.

Router bits

Router bits need care and maintenance for best performance and prolonged life. Like every other tool, router bits run the gamut from poor to excellent. Good bits are sharper, last longer and work better, but most important, their shafts are more consistent in size. The shaft on a high-quality router bit usually varies by only plus or minus 0.002 in., whereas a cheap bit may be as much as 0.005 in. over- or undersize.

Oversize shanks are preferable to undersize shanks. I once bought a bargain bit that was 0.005 in. undersize, and it would slip in every router that I have except the Elu. When I finally measured it and discovered how far it was off, I threw it away. It's probably a good idea to measure the shafts of new bits when you get them and send them back if they're too far off. The best way to measure the bit is with an inexpensive micrometer from the local hardware store.

Clean the bit with steel wool or a Teflon®-safe nylon pad after every routing job before putting it away. The surface of the shaft should be as clean and smooth as a new bit. If the shaft is tarnished or rusty, clean it with steel wool or a nylon pad, and then buff it with a metal polish, such as Simichrome Polish®. Another option is to buff the shaft with rouge on a buffing wheel. The buffing wheel may be the last hope for a bit that is badly rusted or tarnished. If the rust is too bad, replace the bit.

Also check the bit's shaft for galling each time you remove it from the collet. If the galling isn't too deep, you can usually clean it up with a small file. If a bit continues to gall and is your only bit that consistently slips in the router, throw it away. One of the easiest ways to ruin a collet is to use a damaged bit.

Another key to router performance is to keep the bit's cutting edges clean and sharp. Clean the edges with pitch-and-gum remover (available at hardware stores), oven cleaner or ammonia. The cutting edge of the bit is either steel or carbide. Sharpen the edges of steel bits on Japanese waterstones, Arkansas stones or aluminum-oxide or silicon-carbide stones. Carbide-tipped router bits require the use of diamond abrasives. Both types of bit can be sharpened by hand.

Sharpen only the flat inside surface of each flute. Never try to sharpen the shaped edge because you can easily destroy its profile or change its balance. Always clean the bit before sharpening. At high speed, a dull edge deteriorates rapidly, so I hone every bit by hand with a diamond hone before I put it in the router. Because I systematically maintain a sharp edge, dullness never gets a foothold in my shop.

Pitch or baked-on residue prevents the chip from exiting the cut, which increases the deterioration of the cutting edge. If you use wood such as pine or cherry, the cutter should be scraped off frequently with a knife. Titanium nitride bits have a gold-colored coating that prolongs edge life by four to eight times over steel by increasing the lubricity of the bit so that deposits do not stick as readily.

When the edge becomes dull or chipped, the cutter should be reground, preferably by a good sharpening shop. The best sharpeners remove only as much material as necessary to sharpen the bit. If a bit ever comes back from the sharpener out of balance, return it and ask for a refund. You may find that you can buy a new router bit for what it costs to get one sharpened, but I still think that sharpening bits is worth the effort. Maybe it's my thrifty Wisconsin heritage, but I hate to throw away a bit just because it's dull.

There's a fine line between spending enough and spending too much for a router bit. You don't actually need a huge variety of bits, even if you do a lot of different types of work. In a catalog that advertises 1,000 router bits, you probably need only 10. I would rather have 10 good bits than 100 mediocre ones. There's an economy of scale here, too. If you use a bit infrequently, you can get away with high-speed steel, as long as you keep the bit sharp. On the other hand, if you are doing a lot of work with one particular bit, or if you are a pro or semi-pro, then it's false economy to keep sharpening steel bits when you could be using carbide.

Just because a bit has carbide on it, don't assume it's of high quality. There are various grades of carbide, and there are various ways of attaching the carbide to the body. If the carbide falls off, the manufacturer should replace the bit. Also, unless I'm bouncing bits off the pavement or routing 10d nails, I'd want a replacement if a bit chips.

Cleaning the router

Taking good care of your router will prolong the life of vital parts and make it more dependable and pleasant to use. An ounce of router maintenance is worth a pound of service-center cure. To prolong the life of the motor, clean the router after every use by blowing out the inside with compressed air.

Periodically clean and lubricate the router base with a dry lubricant, such as Teflon® or wax. If you own a plunge router, remove the router from the base and clean the columns that allow plunging with an abrasive pad. Rub the columns with a dry lubricant, such as graphite or wax, before reassembling the router.

Shaper design

The shaper is a larger and heavier machine than the router and is designed to absorb the kind of side thrust typical of continuous heavy industrial production. All shapers have essentially the same design, though they vary in size, power and quality. Smaller shapers have an open stand, much like the contractor's table saw. The larger industrial models have an enclosed stand similar to the cabinet table saw. Some shapers have a sliding table, which helps move the workpiece past the shaper cutter smoothly. This feature makes it easier to cut raised panels or the end of a board.

The spindle, which protrudes through the center of the shaper table, holds the cutter in much the same way as the arbor holds the sawblade on a table saw. Unlike the table-saw arbor, however, the spindle is designed to be removable and interchangeable. There are different size spindles for different size cutters. The smallest spindle is usually ½ in. in diameter; size increases in ¼-in. increments.

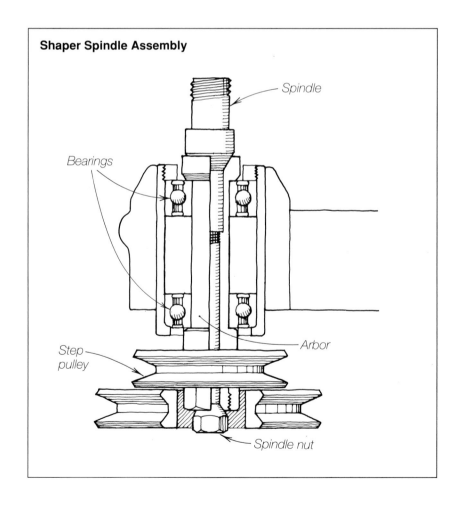

Shaper Spindle Assembly

Spindle

Bearings

Arbor

Step pulley

Spindle nut

Some large shapers, especially European machines, have a tilting spindle. This feature makes it possible to change the angle of the cutter so that you can use one cutter for more than one profile. Although the tilting-arbor shaper may be more expensive initially, in the long term it may save you money on cutters.

Shaper anatomy

The spindle fits in the hollow shaft of the arbor and is usually locked in place with a nut at the base of the spindle shaft. The cutters stack on the spindle and are locked in place by a spindle nut. The spindle assembly is held in place by a casting, which is usually attached to an elevating mechanism that raises and lowers the spindle assembly by means of a knob or handle on the side of the machine.

Most shapers have a belt-and-step-pulley mechanism for changing the speed of the spindle. Shaper cutters spin at either 7,000 rpm or 10,000 rpm—somewhat slower than a router. You can also change the direction of spindle rotation with a reversing switch. This feature allows you to flip the cutter over and feed the workpiece from the opposite direction. When the spindle is spinning in the opposite direction a special lock nut is usually used on top of the standard nut.

A recent development is the introduction of shaper tables with large table inserts, which allow you to mount panel-raising cutters up to 4 in. in diameter. A cast table insert usually fits around the cutter, and different size rings can be inserted to fill the space between the hole and the cutter.

The shaper speed-change mechanism changes the spindle speed from 7,000 rpm to 10,000 rpm.

Some shapers have table inserts, which allow use of cutters up to 4 in. in diameter.

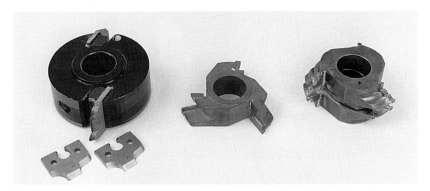

Shaper cutters: from left to right, a molding head with interchangeable steel knives, a solid cutter and a combination cutter.

Typical Cutter Setup

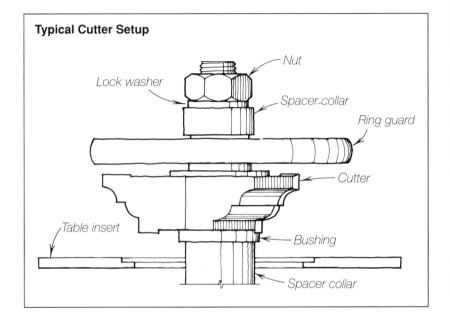

Nut

Lock washer

Spacer-collar

Ring guard

Cutter

Table insert

Bushing

Spacer collar

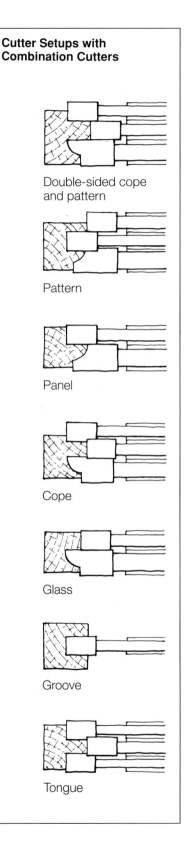

Cutter Setups with Combination Cutters

Double-sided cope and pattern

Pattern

Panel

Cope

Glass

Groove

Tongue

Shaper cutters

Shaper cutters are expensive, so it is best to try to get the most options with the fewest number of cutters. There are three basic designs, as shown in the photo at top. The least expensive is the cutter with interchangeable steel knives. The standard cutter is one solid piece, usually with carbide tips. The combination cutter has individual cutters whose position can be changed relative to one another, which means you can make more than one type of molding with one cutter (see the drawing at right).

The shaper spindle is long enough to allow the cutter and other devices such as spacer collars, bearings, bushings, shims and guards to be mounted on the shaft. The drawing above shows a typical setup of the cutter.

Use a dial indicator to check runout when a new spindle is installed.

Tuning the shaper

Most shapers do not have a collet mechanism, so much of the routine maintenance discussed for the router is unnecessary for the shaper. Shaper tune-up focuses instead on the bearings and the spindle shaft.

The two large bearings that hold the shaft in place should be checked often for roughness and play. There should be no sideways or up-and-down movement of the shaft, and it should rotate smoothly. If you detect movement or roughness, replace the bearings with the highest quality available. You can either do this yourself, or have the manufacturer's service department or a bearing house do it for you.

Follow the manufacturer's directions when changing the spindle shaft. Most spindles have a nut on the bottom that locks the shaft into the bearing assembly. It is important that the surfaces of the shaft and the mating bearing assembly are clean. Any dirt or debris will cause runout in the shaft and create an out-of-balance cutter, shortening bearing life and decreasing the quality of the cut.

To make sure that the spindle is running true, check runout when you install a new spindle. The amount of runout can be checked with a dial indicator or a feeler gauge, as explained in the section on checking router runout (see p. 165).

As with other woodworking machines, it is important to keep the moving parts of the shaper clean and well lubricated with a dry lubricant, especially the mechanism that raises and lowers the arbor.

Shaper safety

The shaper has a reputation as the most dangerous woodworking machine. Injuries are caused either by contact with the cutter or by kickback. Contact with the cutter is the more dangerous of the two and can be prevented with the use of proper guards. A recent innovation is a round plastic guard with a bearing that fits on the spindle on top of the cutter (see the photo below).

When using the shaper, you need to develop a feel for feed rate. Your goal is to keep your hand as far from the cutter as possible. A power feed gives a uniform feed rate and also keeps your hands a safe distance from the cutter. If you are making a narrow molding, shape the edge of a wide board and then cut off the molding.

Shaper accidents occur most often when a curved edge is shaped without a fence. To avoid accidents, keep the piece as large as possible for as long as possible. Make curved cuts first and straight cuts last. For example, if you are shaping two panels exactly the same size it is safest to shape both curved ends while the panels are still one board. Then cut the piece in the middle and shape the straight bottom ends with a fence.

There are two options for using the cutter: either running in the table below the work ("submerged") or on top of the work ("cutter over"). To prevent kickback, it is best to run the cutter in the submerged position. This way, if the stock lifts off the table, it won't move into the cutter and thereby risk kickback.

This plastic guard has a ball bearing in the center and is mounted on the spindle above the cutter.

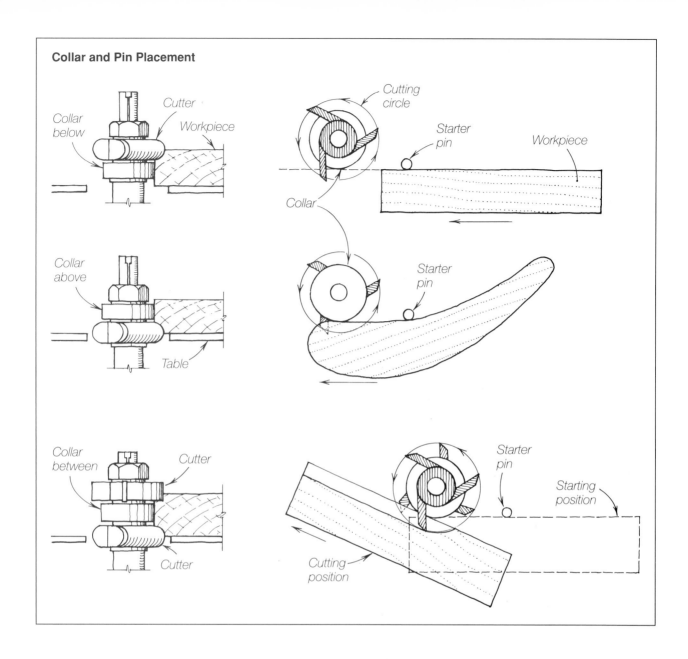

Collar and Pin Placement

Collar below

Cutter

Workpiece

Collar above

Table

Collar between

Cutter

Cutter

Cutting circle

Starter pin

Workpiece

Collar

Starter pin

Starter pin

Starting position

Cutting position

Kickback can also be prevented by using a starter pin, which is a piece of metal, usually a solid metal shaft, that can be screwed into the top of the shaper table near the cutter. The starter pin is used in conjunction with a bearing or collar that limits the depth of cut. Note that the collar can be above, below or between cutters. When shaping a curved edge, the pin should be on the same side of the workpiece as the cutter rotation, and the workpiece should contact the starting pin before the cutter. Essentially, the starter pin acts as a fulcrum and gives you more control over the workpiece.

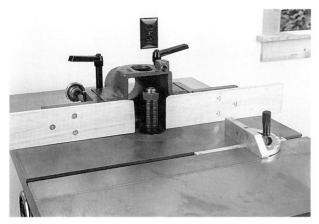

Use a fence and a miter gauge to control the work when making straight or angled straight cuts.

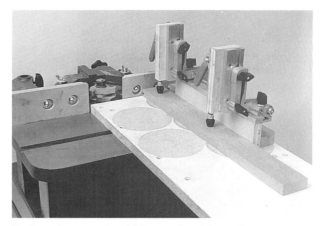

End-grain cuts should be made with a miter gauge or a sled jig. Here, a shopmade sled is used with clamps securing the workpiece.

Using the shaper

It is beyond the scope of this book to discuss all the jigs and fixtures that can be designed to hold and support the workpiece while you are shaping, but a few basic devices bear mention.

For straight cuts, use a fence and miter gauge, as shown in the left photo above. To control straight or angled straight cuts on end grain, such as rabbets, grooves or cope cuts, use a miter gauge or a sled jig. The best approach to shaping a curved edge is to have the workpiece in contact with a starter pin at the start of the cut, as discussed on p. 174.

Multiples of the exact same size are made by pattern shaping. Forms, jigs and fixtures hold pieces with odd or unusual shapes. In most cases the jig contacts the fence, the miter gauge or a bearing and/or collar. The pattern contacts the collar or bearing while the cutter cuts the edge of the board. In pattern shaping the cutter can either be straight or have a decorative profile.

A comprehensive book on using the shaper is *Shaper Handbook* (Sterling Publishing Co., 1990) by Roger Cliffe and Michael Holtz.

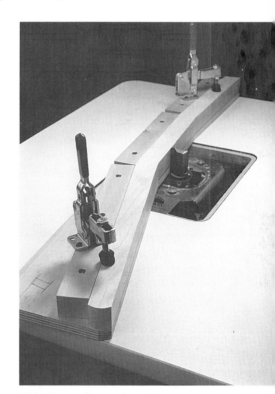

This fixture is used to shape the back leg of a chair. The work is clamped to a plywood base that contacts a bearing on the bottom of the cutter.

CHAPTER 7
Stock Preparation

The success of any woodworking project depends on the accuracy of stock preparation. This critical process, which is labor-intensive and time-consuming, involves much more than just cutting up the pieces for your project.

The first stage in stock preparation is planning. It clearly makes more sense to make your mistakes on paper than on an expensive piece of mahogany. Plans, working drawings and shopmade sketches help you to visualize the finished project. A cutting list, which is a detailed account of the number and size of the individual pieces, is imperative for most projects. An important part of the planning process is selecting appropriate stock for your project, which requires that you understand how wood behaves when it is cut.

There are two schools of thought about planning. The "cutting list" school dictates that wood is processed to the exact dimensions of the list, with little regard for the unique character of the individual pieces. A production kitchen cabinetmaker uses this approach. The opposite approach is to design a piece around the best features of a particular board, finding the best use for each plank—table top, door or interior parts. This is the approach taught by James Krenov and George Nakashima. Both attitudes have their appropriate time and place. A balance of the two is what most woodworkers are after, resulting in a well-designed piece that is sensitive to the nature of the wood and to the purpose for which it was made.

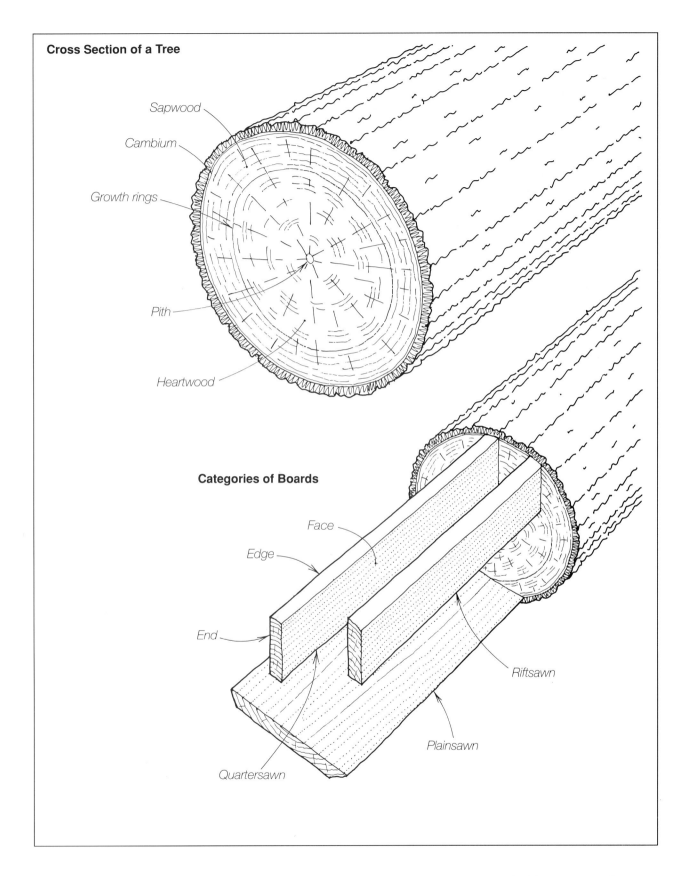

Cross Section of a Tree

Sapwood

Cambium

Growth rings

Pith

Heartwood

Categories of Boards

Face

Edge

End

Riftsawn

Plainsawn

Quartersawn

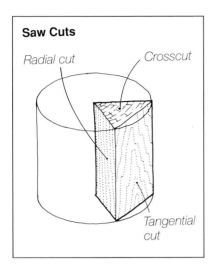

Saw Cuts

Radial cut

Crosscut

Tangential cut

The nature of wood

We like to think there is something "natural" about woodworking, but woodworkers are actually interrupting a natural process—the process of decay. It's more natural for a tree to decompose than to become a piece of furniture. The woodworker attempts to intervene in this natural process by drying wood, and then by trying to keep the wood dry with protective finishes. However, wood never really dries completely. It tries to remain at equilibrium with atmospheric relative humidity.

If wood were a static material, preparing accurate stock would be a simple matter, but wood is constantly changing. A number of factors affect a board's stability, chief among them fluctuations in humidity. Wood is a highly porous material, and a board shrinks as humidity decreases and expands when it increases. Expansion and contraction are an ongoing process and must be taken into consideration when wood is prepared. I like to bring wood into the shop for about a month before it is machined and allow it to equalize with the shop's humidity.

Another factor that affects the wood's behavior is the orientation of the grain. A tree's growth is visible in distinct annual rings, which create the design that is often referred to as grain or figure. A cross section of a log reveals the circular end-grain pattern. The layout of the growth rings in a board is determined at the sawmill. The cuts that the sawyer makes in the log have a dramatic effect on the appearance of the grain in each board, on the board's strength and on the way that it expands and contracts in response to humidity.

Hardwoods typically contain two types of wood, heartwood and sapwood (see the top drawing on p. 177). The heartwood, which forms the largest part of the trunk, is the inner part of the tree around the pith. The sapwood, which has a higher moisture content than the heartwood, is the outer part of the tree. The growth of the tree takes place in the cambium between the sapwood and the bark.

Sawing the log

There are several different ways to saw a log, each of which exposes the grain from a different orientation. If the cut exposes a surface from the pith to the bark, it is referred to as a "radial" cut and the resulting board is said to be "quartersawn." When the cut is at a tangent to the growth rings, it is called a "tangential" cut and the wood is "flatsawn" (in softwood) or "plainsawn" (in hardwood). I use the term plainsawn in this book because I work primarily with hardwood.

Quartersawn boards expose each growth ring and give a uniform pattern of closely spaced lines. The growth rings are about 90° from the edge of the board, as shown in the bottom drawing on p. 177. The pattern of the plainsawn board reveals a few widely spaced lines, with growth rings that are nearly parallel to the face of the board. Many boards will be neither quartersawn nor flatsawn but have growth rings that are about 45° from the edge of the board. These are known as rift-sawn boards.

Economics plays the most important part in determining how wood is sawn. Many years ago special sawing techniques were developed to yield a greater number of quartersawn boards from each log. The premier-quality oak that you find in turn-of-the-century furniture exists because sawyers made the extra effort to cut it. Few sawyers will quartersaw a log for you today, because the process is time-consuming and wastes more of the log.

If you've ever looked fruitlessly through a pile of boards for quartersawn wood, it's likely that the sawmill isn't producing much. Most logs today are cut in the fastest and most economical way possible, using a technique called "through and through" sawing (see the drawing below). All the cuts are parallel, which produces quartersawn boards in the middle, plainsawn boards on the outside and riftsawn boards between the middle and the edge. Sometimes the log is squared first to remove the bark on the edge of the board and provide a straight edge.

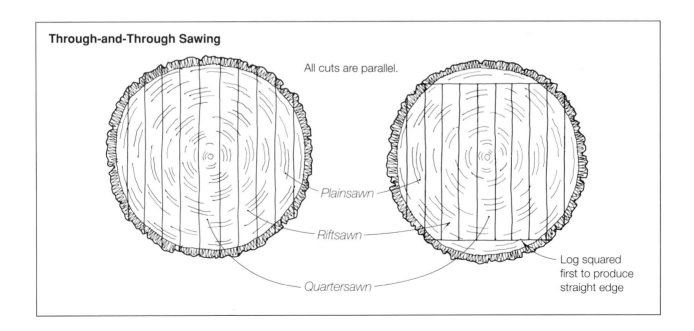

Through-and-Through Sawing

All cuts are parallel.

Plainsawn

Riftsawn

Quartersawn

Log squared first to produce straight edge

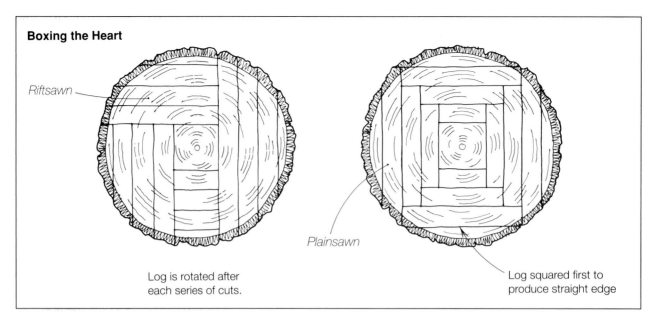

Boxing the Heart

Riftsawn

Plainsawn

Log is rotated after
each series of cuts.

Log squared first to
produce straight edge

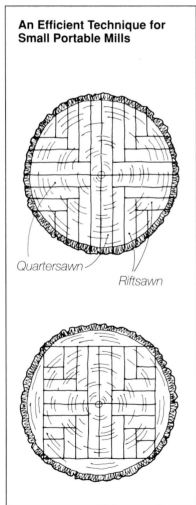

**An Efficient Technique for
Small Portable Mills**

Quartersawn

Riftsawn

Another quick sawing technique is "boxing the heart," which is shown in the drawing above. The log is rotated after each series of cuts, which means that all the boards are either plainsawn or riftsawn.

The various techniques that have been devised to yield more quartersawn boards from a log are shown in the drawing on the facing page. There is a direct correlation between the number of quartersawn boards that can be cut and the time and expense it takes to cut them. The most time-consuming technique (shown at bottom in the drawing) produces only quartersawn wood, but the wedge-shaped pieces are not practical for furniture making and are used almost exclusively as stock for musical instruments. The drawing at left shows two good compromise techniques that yield high-quality quartersawn and riftsawn material and are not too time-consuming. These techniques are favored by many Wisconsin woodworkers who have small portable bandsaw mills.

If you own land or have access to wooded land, harvesting your own lumber may be a realistic option. One way to harvest wood is to use a chainsaw rig, but, be warned, these machines are loud, dangerous and take a big bite of wood with each saw cut. Portable bandsaw mills (see the photo on p. 80) are better on a number of counts, but they are more expensive. Sawmill operation is beyond the scope of this book. I recommend Will Malloff's *Chainsaw Lumbermaking* (The Taunton Press, Newtown, Conn., 1982) if you are interested in reading more on the subject.

Cutting Techniques for Producing More Quartersawn and Riftsawn Lumber

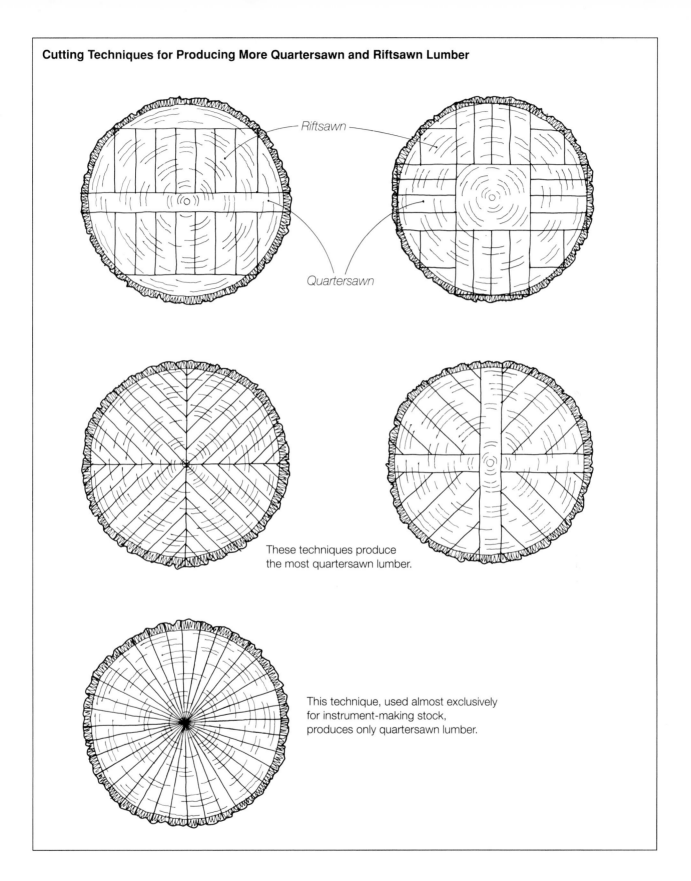

Riftsawn

Quartersawn

These techniques produce
the most quartersawn lumber.

This technique, used almost exclusively
for instrument-making stock,
produces only quartersawn lumber.

The first decisions in preparing stock are made at the sawmill. If you don't have your own mill, these decisions will have been made for you. Nonetheless, you should still be able to select appropriate stock. Look at a board and visualize where it was in the tree. It is more than just a question of aesthetics: The location of the board affects its rate of expansion and contraction and its resistance to deformation during the drying process.

Wood movement

How the wood is sawn affects not only the amount of shrinkage during the initial drying process, but also how much expansion and contraction occur after the board becomes part of a piece of furniture.

After the wood is sawn, the water in the board is exposed to air and the moisture evaporates. The board continues to lose moisture until it reaches equilibrium with the environment. Here in Wisconsin, it takes about a year for every inch of thickness for a board to air-dry, which is probably a good average figure. If you live in a really dry or wet climate, you will need to adjust that figure accordingly.

As wood dries, it shrinks in some dimensions more than others. Along its length, a board shrinks very little (only about 0.1%), whereas across its width it will shrink about 5% to 10%. Quartersawn boards shrink the least across their width, while plainsawn boards will shrink the most in width as they dry.

After the initial drying, a board expands as humidity increases or contracts as humidity decreases. Although dramatic daily fluctuations affect wood slightly, the greatest changes are seasonal. This is why doors

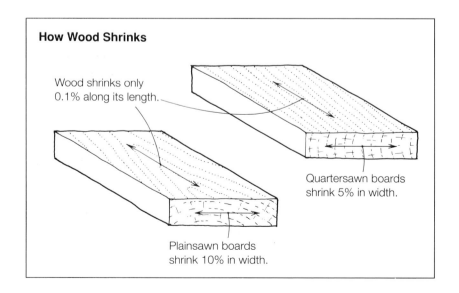

How Wood Shrinks

Wood shrinks only 0.1% along its length.

Quartersawn boards shrink 5% in width.

Plainsawn boards shrink 10% in width.

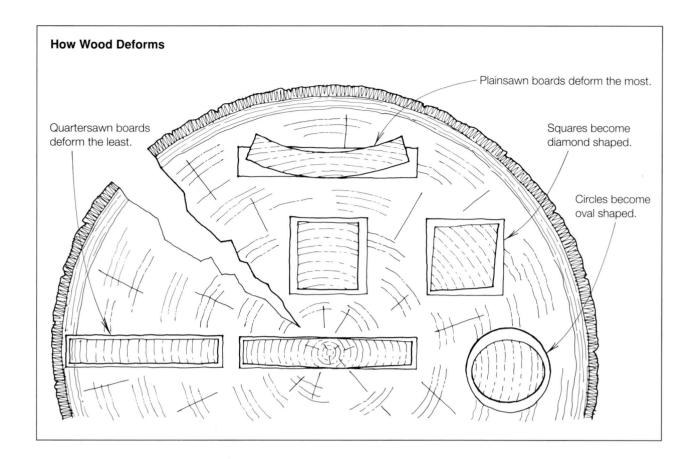

How Wood Deforms

Plainsawn boards deform the most.

Quartersawn boards deform the least.

Squares become diamond shaped.

Circles become oval shaped.

and drawers stick in summer and open smoothly in winter. Quartersawn wood is the best choice for such pieces as drawer sides, because there is a minimal amount of shrinkage.

How boards deform as they dry   As wood dries a number of changes take place in the shape of the board, as shown in the drawing above. Drying exerts tremendous force on wood. It is impossible to stop all deformation, but rapid drying causes the most stresses. If a log is not cut into boards, the force of the outside drying faster than the inside is enough to cause a deep split from the bark to the pith.

"Warp" is a general term used to describe the deformation of a board as a result of variable shrinkage in different directions. Quartersawn wood is most likely to retain its rough-sawn shape during the drying process. Quartersawn boards dry with very predictable changes, squares changing to diamonds and circles to ovals. Plainsawn boards warp the most as they dry. "Cup" is a form of warp across the width of a board. The direction of cupping is usually away from the center of the tree. Woodworkers often predict the direction of cupping by saying "growth rings straighten out."

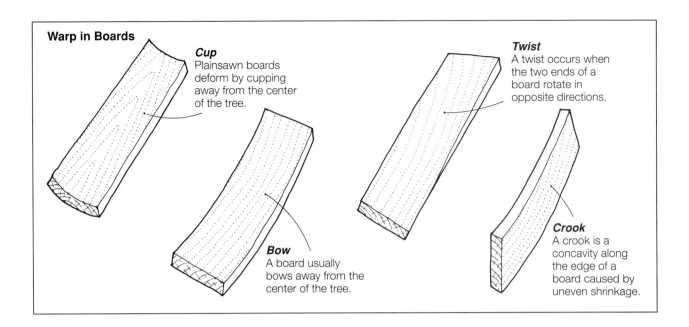

Warp in Boards

Cup
Plainsawn boards deform by cupping away from the center of the tree.

Bow
A board usually bows away from the center of the tree.

Twist
A twist occurs when the two ends of a board rotate in opposite directions.

Crook
A crook is a concavity along the edge of a board caused by uneven shrinkage.

Although a board is more stable in length than in width, changes do also occur in that direction during the drying process. A "bow" is a curvature from one end of a board to the other. As with cupping, plainsawn boards are most prone to bowing and the direction of bow is away from the center of the tree. A "twist" occurs when the ends of the board move in opposite directions. A "crook" is a concavity along the edge of a board caused by uneven shrinkage. This type of deformation is most common in quartersawn wood; the concave edge is toward the outside of the tree. By sighting down a corner of a board, you'll quickly be able to see how much and what kind of warp there is in a board.

Machining stock

For the craftsman, wood is usually available in three forms. "Rough lumber" has not been processed since it was cut at the sawmill. When you receive it, a rough-lumber board will likely be warped to some degree and have coarse surfaces. "Surfaced lumber" has been planed so that both faces of the board are parallel to each other and smooth. This is also known as "surfaced two sides" or "S2S." "Surfaced four sides" ("S4S") means that the board has been planed and the edges are square and parallel to each other. The subsequent treatment of either kind of surfaced wood in shipment and storage determines whether those surfaces remain smooth and parallel.

Man-made materials, such as plywood and particleboard, are the most stable materials available to the woodworker. Together with boards that are S4S, man-made materials are the most convenient to use because they are ready to be cut into the sizes required in the project cutting list. The drawback, of course, is that you have to pay a higher price for these boards and sheets. I prefer to surface rough lumber into S4S lumber.

Milling rough lumber

Rough lumber is usually oversized by about ¼ in., which means that a board that is surfaced to a finished ¾ in. is usually cut at a 1-in. or 1⅛-in. thickness at the sawmill. The extra ¼ in. or more is allowed for shrinkage and warpage. That extra ¼ in. of material may seem like a lot of waste, but you must remember that the board may lose ⅛ in. of thickness as it dries. A wide board may warp ⅛ in. or more during the drying process, too.

If the tree had a lot of internal stresses, ¼ in. excess material may not be enough to salvage a long board. I recently milled some oak planks from a tree on my farm that had warped so much during drying that the 1-in. boards I cut weren't thick enough for the long boards I needed. I was forced to cut the boards into shorter pieces to salvage them. Remember to reserve long straight pieces for the long parts of your project when you assess your wood pile.

Safety considerations   Machining rough lumber is one of the most dangerous woodworking tasks. The undulating surfaces of a rough-cut board and its unseen internal stresses can create serious problems. You can usually deal with the problem of warp fairly easily, but it is more difficult to predict the effects of internal stresses.

If stresses originated during the growth of the tree, they are often released when the board is cut at the sawmill. The board may peel away from the log, creating a gentle arc, or it may bend back toward the blade. These stresses will again be released when the board is ripped with the table saw or bandsaw. Drying stresses are likely if a board is cupped, twisted or has a crook. Usually the greater the warp, the greater the internal stress.

If you suspect a board has internal stresses, the bandsaw is the best tool for ripping because there is no danger of kickback. If you must rip a board that has internal stresses on the table saw, use a short fence and a splitter (as described on p. 40).

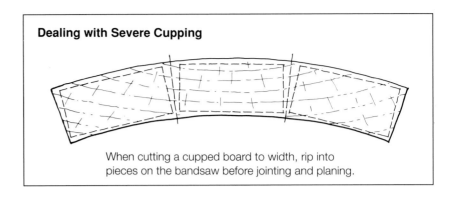

Dealing with Severe Cupping

When cutting a cupped board to width, rip into pieces on the bandsaw before jointing and planing.

Layout

Layout is the process of selecting and marking the desired pieces of the cutting lists on the board. The boards are usually first cut to length, leaving an extra 3 in. or 4 in. for trimming. A board that is 4 ft. long is the most manageable to machine. If the finished pieces will be short, leave them long for as long as possible and crosscut to length last.

When cutting stock to width, either surface (joint and plane) first or rip first. It is quicker to face-joint and plane first, but sometimes the stock won't allow it. For example, to get three 2-in. wide pieces from a severely cupped 7-in. wide board it's best to rip the board into individual pieces on the bandsaw first and then surface and plane them to final dimension.

The key to layout success is to plan ahead so that you can maximize the use of your lumber and your time. Every situation is different and requires a different solution. The determining factors that you must balance are the size of the pieces and the amount of warp.

Face-jointing

The first step in machining rough stock is to establish one flat face, usually on the jointer. This face becomes the straight and flat reference for making the opposite face parallel and the edges square and true.

To begin, inspect the wood. Obviously, if the wood is wider than the jointer, you'll have to establish the flat face in some other way, either by hand-planing or by ripping the stock into smaller pieces. Assuming the wood is sized appropriately for the jointer, check for twist. The traditional way to do this is with a pair of winding sticks, which are two identically dimensioned pieces of wood. Place the winding sticks at opposite ends of the board and sight down the board. Any deviation is obvious. You can also check for twist by laying the board on a flat surface. If the board rocks, it is twisted.

Next, check for flaws, warp, loose knots, checks, splits or other defects that may prove dangerous. Either cut these sections out of the rough stock on the bandsaw or table saw or glue the piece together with Superglue® or epoxy. When inspecting the wood, note grain direction. You should always surface with the grain when using the jointer or planer. Cutting against the grain lifts or tears the grain and leaves a rough surface. It's like stroking a dog. Stroked from head to tail, the hair lies flat, but stroked in the opposite direction the hair is raised and ruffled.

The standard approach is to look at the edge of the board to see which way the grain is running. However, this can be very time-consuming when you have a lot of boards to surface. Another approach is to observe the V-shaped surface figure on the face of the board. The V figure

Establishing the First Face

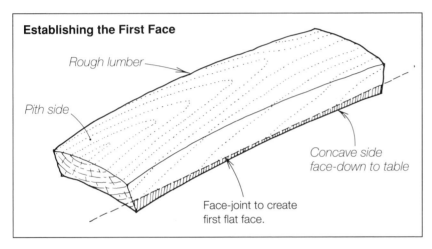

Rough lumber

Pith side

Concave side face-down to table

Face-joint to create first flat face.

Grain Direction when Jointing

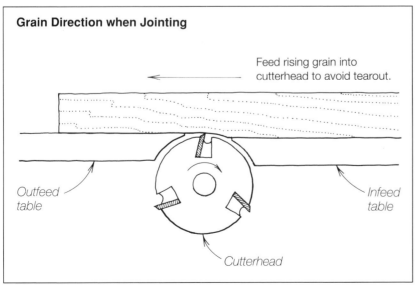

Feed rising grain into cutterhead to avoid tearout.

Outfeed table

Infeed table

Cutterhead

Detecting Warp with Winding Sticks

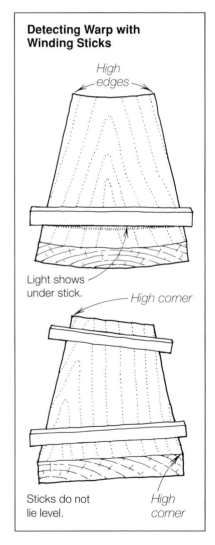

High edges

Light shows under stick.

High corner

Sticks do not lie level.

High corner

Jointing the Face

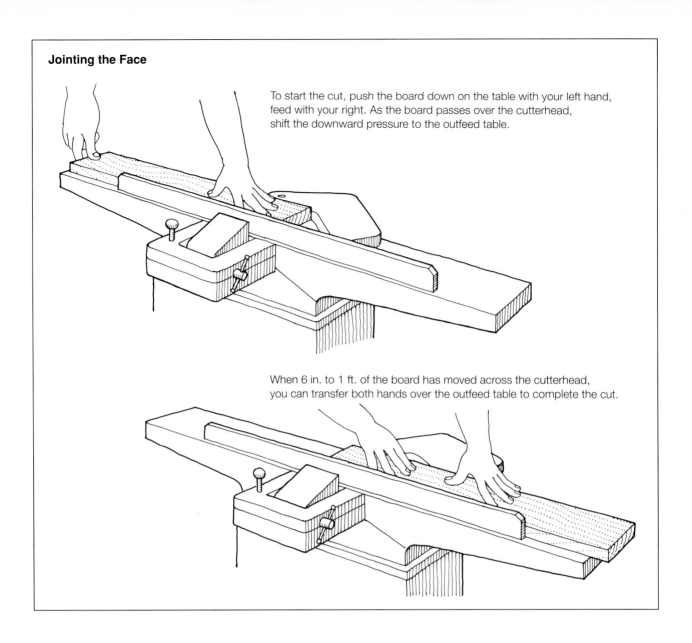

To start the cut, push the board down on the table with your left hand, feed with your right. As the board passes over the cutterhead, shift the downward pressure to the outfeed table.

When 6 in. to 1 ft. of the board has moved across the cutterhead, you can transfer both hands over the outfeed table to complete the cut.

indicates the direction of the grain if you are looking at the inside (pith side) of the board and opposite the direction of grain if you are looking at the outside (bark side). In Wisconsin we say, "inside with, outside against." Woods with distinct grain such as oak are easier to read than subtle or nondescript woods such as birch or maple. Grain direction is much less important in quartersawn boards than in plainsawn boards.

In selecting which face to joint, make sure that the concave side faces down to the table. This way you minimize the tendency of the board to rock from side to side as it is cut. If you have a hard time determining which side is the concave side, lay the board on a flat surface and see which side rocks less (this is probably the concave side).

A twisted board is harder to face-joint because it will have a tendency to rock back and forth on the table. Identify the opposite corners on which the board is rocking. You can probably hand-plane these opposite corners so that the board sits flat, or you can make successive light passes over the cutterhead until the board rests flat on the table. Don't try to remove too much material from the offending corners in one pass. Eventually the board will rest on all four corners and then you can be more aggressive with each cut.

Once the board is stable, start face-jointing the concave face to get the first flat side. The ends of the concave face of a bowed board are jointed first. Each successive pass removes material until the surface is perfectly flat. A number of factors affect the quality of the cut. The larger the diameter of the cutterhead, the faster the cutterhead speed, and the slower the feed speed of the wood the better the quality of the cut.

Woods such as bird's-eye maple and a number of exotic species can be difficult to surface because they often chip or tear out easily. I solve this problem by grinding a slight back bevel on the jointer or planer blades, as explained on pp. 133-134.

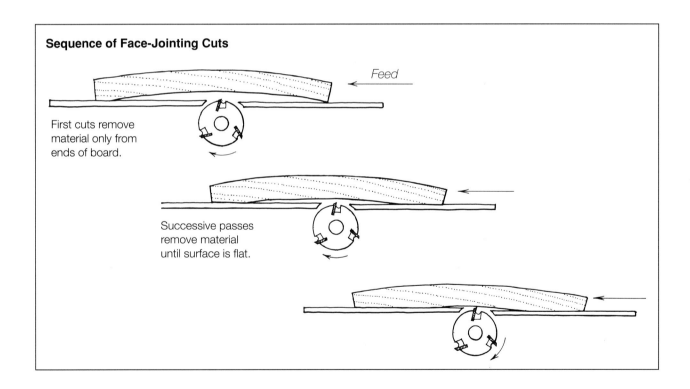

Sequence of Face-Jointing Cuts

Feed

First cuts remove material only from ends of board.

Successive passes remove material until surface is flat.

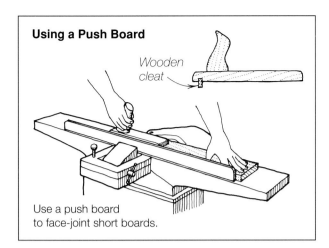

Using a Push Board

Wooden cleat

Use a push board to face-joint short boards.

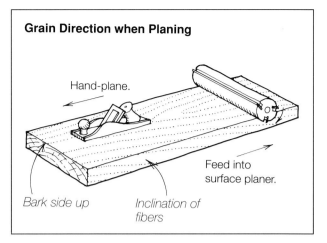

Grain Direction when Planing

Hand-plane.

Feed into surface planer.

Bark side up

Inclination of fibers

Always use the jointer guard and keep your fingers away from the cutterhead. Some people like to use push boards at the end of the cut, and they should always be used when jointing short boards. Never joint a board that is less than 12 in. long.

Thickness planing

Once you have established a true face, plane the opposite side parallel with the thickness planer. Place the jointed face down on the planer's infeed table, adjust the depth of cut and turn the board so that the grain faces the right direction. Occasionally the board may bow because planing releases tension on one side of the board. If it has bowed or cupped, joint the concave side again, but be careful not to remove too much material. Once you get a parallel and true second face, continue to plane the board to the appropriate dimension. Flip the board over after each pass so that you're planing both surfaces. The planer generally leaves a smoother finish than the jointer.

Jointing and planing may not only release tension in the board, but may also expose the interior of the board to the environment, which may have a different moisture content. The fresh surfaces may either release or absorb moisture, and the board may distort more than it did initially. Many experienced woodworkers allow the wood to settle by partially processing the wood and then allowing it to stabilize for a month in the shop before final machining. The wood is cut to size, planed to between $\frac{1}{16}$ in. and $\frac{1}{8}$ in. oversize and then stacked with stickers (small pieces of wood) between each board. Stacking the boards in this way allows air to circulate between the boards so that they have the same moisture content as the air in the shop. Once the boards have stabilized, they are jointed and planed again to remove any warp that appeared during the settling process.

Squaring the first edge

After you've surfaced each side of the board to the desired thickness, square an edge on the jointer, unless the edges are rough or crooked. If an edge is more than ¼ in. out of straight, it is faster to rip it off. One way of doing this is to nail or screw a straightedge to one edge of the board and run it along the rip fence as you rip off the wavy edge on the table saw (see the top drawing below). Don't rip severely cupped boards. On boards that are slightly cupped (less than ⅛-in. cup), rip with the concave side down, as shown in the bottom drawing below. Ripping with a straightedge against the rip fence works particularly

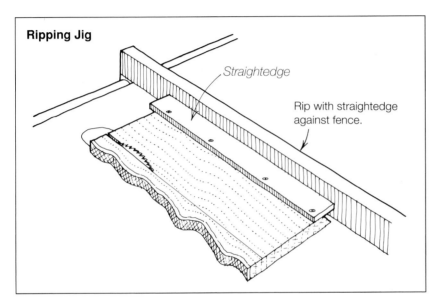

Ripping Jig

Straightedge

Rip with straightedge against fence.

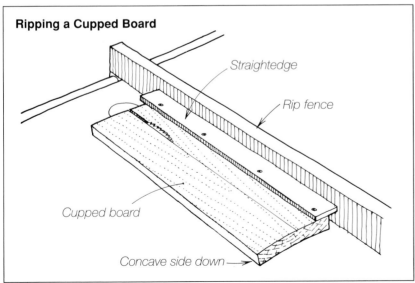

Ripping a Cupped Board

Straightedge

Rip fence

Cupped board

Concave side down

well on long boards, but for cutting short boards, tapers and odd angles use the simple jig shown in the top drawing below. You can also rip the first edge on the bandsaw. Whether you use the bandsaw or the table saw, joint the edge once it is straight.

Before jointing the edge, double-check to make sure that the jointer fence is square to the table. Keep pressure down onto the table and into the fence, as shown in the bottom drawing below. After you have made the first cut, check the edges for squareness.

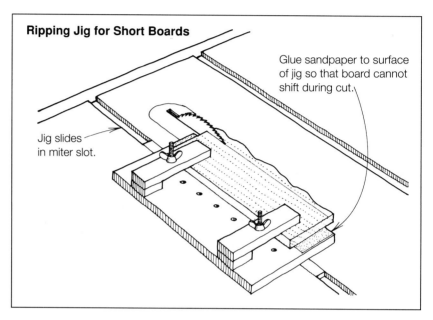

Ripping Jig for Short Boards

Glue sandpaper to surface of jig so that board cannot shift during cut.

Jig slides in miter slot.

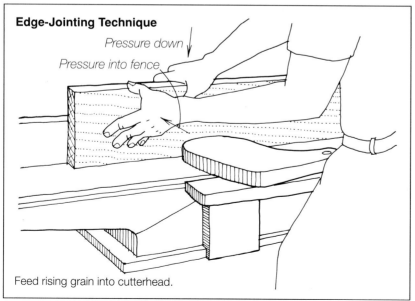

Edge-Jointing Technique

Pressure down

Pressure into fence

Feed rising grain into cutterhead.

Squaring the edge before surfacing

The advantage of thicknessing the stock before jointing is that you can place either side against the jointer fence so that you can always cut with the grain. But sometimes you have to square the edge before running the board through the thickness planer, for example, when you are working with square-shaped stock. In this case, it's most efficient to square a corner first and then run the opposite sides through the planer in two quick passes.

It is efficient to square an edge before surfacing when you have a lot of excess thickness to remove. For example, when jointing a board with excessive bow, you may end up with a board that is ⅞ in. thick on the ends but as much as 1⅛ in. thick in the middle. This means that you would have to remove ⅜ in. of material from the middle of the board to finish it to ¾ in. In such situations I save time, wear on the planer and electricity by ripping off the excessive waste on the bandsaw. One or two passes on the planer and I have my finished board and a piece of kindling rather than just another pile of sawdust.

Sawing the waste off a warped board on the bandsaw takes little time and saves wear and tear on the planer.

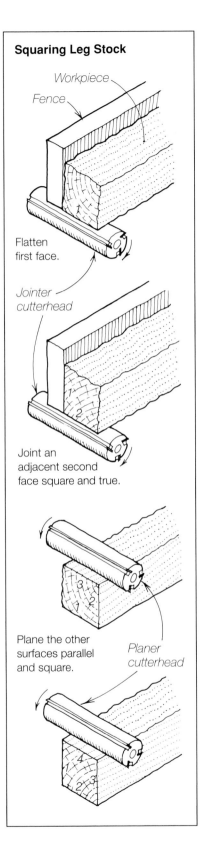

Squaring Leg Stock

Workpiece

Fence

Flatten first face.

Jointer cutterhead

Joint an adjacent second face square and true.

Plane the other surfaces parallel and square.

Planer cutterhead

Saw the board to width with the straight edge against the rip fence. Add about ¹⁄₁₆ in. to the finished dimension to allow for cleanup with the jointer.

Cutting to width

Once you have surfaced both sides of the board and jointed one edge, you are ready to cut the final edge to determine the width of the board. The first step is to rip a parallel edge on the board. The table saw doesn't leave an edge smooth enough for gluing, so a pass or two on the jointer is required to make the edge perfectly flat and square. When setting the distance between the rip fence and the sawblade, add about ¹⁄₁₆ in. for final jointing.

You can also rip the board on the bandsaw and then finish the edge with the planer. Install a ½-in., 3-TPI hook blade on your bandsaw for this operation. The new portable planers, affectionately known as "lunch-box planers," are ideal for planing parallel edges. If you are finishing the edge of the board with the planer, gang-plane three or four pieces at a time. Hold the group together as they are fed through the planer to prevent them from tipping. Double-check squareness after the cut. As a safety precaution, when planing more than one board at a time, don't stand behind the planer in case of kickback.

Cutting to length

Once the board has been surfaced on all four sides, the final stage is to crosscut the two ends square and to size. This is a two-step process: The first step is to cut one end square; the second step is to cut the second end square and to the required length.

I use my table saw and the miter gauge to crosscut boards that are less than 4 ft. long and the radial-arm saw or miter saw for stock longer than 4 ft. If more than one board is to be cut to the same length, use a stop block for accuracy (as explained in detail in Chapter 1).

When cutting large panels it is a good idea to reverse the miter gauge in the slot. The workpiece should be clamped to the auxiliary fence if you are not using a stop.

Making angled cuts

For straight mitered cuts the table and blade remain square and the miter-gauge head is angled. Add a plywood auxiliary fence (about 2 in. high) to support the workpiece. Raise the blade and cut the fence off once the angle is set. Don't use a fence that extends past the blade for an angled cut because the waste could be trapped by the blade and become a projectile.

Cutting tapers Tapers are angled cuts that are used for structural or design elements. The tapered leg of a Shaker table enhances the design and makes the table lighter without sacrificing strength. I like to cut tapers on the bandsaw because it is the safest tool to use without a taper jig. The surface of the cut made by the bandsaw is not smooth, but it can easily be finished with a jointer or hand plane. To cut tapers on the table saw, use one of the taper jigs shown on pp. 196-197. I strongly advise against using a taper jig on the radial-arm saw: If the workpiece slips relative to the jig, or vice versa, or binds on the blade, kickback can occur with amazing speed. I know someone who atomized the windshield on his wife's car by cutting tapers on a radial-arm saw.

There are four types of jigs used to cut tapers. The simplest jig is a tapered piece of wood that has a brass screw as a stop. The stop can be used in front or back of the workpiece.

The second jig is a jig with stepped notches. To make this jig, mill a straight and true piece of wood about 1 in. by 3 in. by 24 in. and cross-cut three pieces about 3 in. long off the end. Glue the pieces together so that each step is about ¼ in. Tapers are usually described as ratios, such as "1 in. per ft." If you make the distance from the first step to the end of the jig 12 in., the jig will automatically cut tapers at 1-in. and 2-in. per foot ratios. Vary the step thickness to make other taper ratios.

To use this jig, first mark the start of the taper. Place the workpiece on the first step and then start the cut. Some designs require two tapers. For the second taper rotate the workpiece to an adjacent side and make another cut. If you want to make a taper on the opposite side or on a leg with all four sides tapered, use the second step.

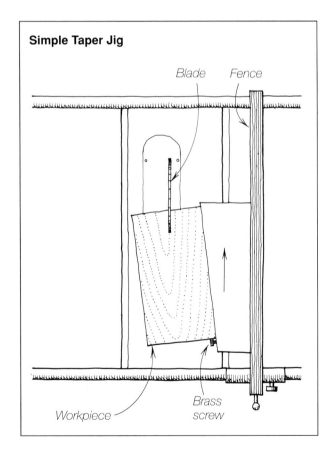

Simple Taper Jig

Blade *Fence*

Workpiece *Brass screw*

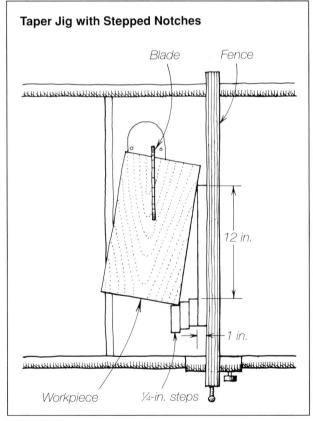

Taper Jig with Stepped Notches

Blade *Fence*

12 in.

1 in.

Workpiece *¼-in. steps*

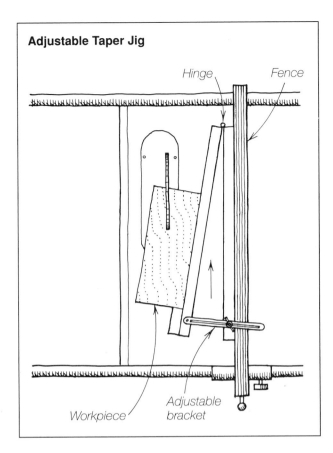

Adjustable Taper Jig

Hinge

Fence

Workpiece

Adjustable bracket

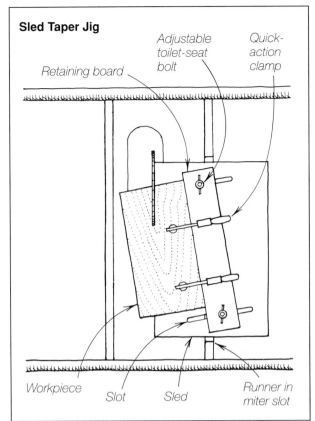

Sled Taper Jig

Adjustable toilet-seat bolt

Quick-action clamp

Retaining board

Workpiece

Slot

Sled

Runner in miter slot

The third type of taper jig is an adjustable jig that is sold commercially. This design is hinged on one end and has a gauge for setting the angle in degrees.

The most complicated taper jig to make (but the safest to use) is a sled jig that slides in the miter-gauge slot. There are a number of ways to make this jig. The easiest method is to nail or screw the retaining board onto the platform. To make a jig that is adjustable, you have to make a slot on the front and back edge. Toilet-seat bolts hold the retaining board in place and are easy to adjust. With either type of sled jig quick-action clamps should be used to hold the workpiece on the jig during the sawing process.

CHAPTER 8
Joinery

Joining wood is a fundamental woodworking skill. Centuries ago, before reliable glues were available, interlocking joints such as the mortise and tenon and the dovetail were developed to hold furniture together. When modern adhesives, properly dried materials and traditional joinery are combined, the furniture created should last several lifetimes.

In this concluding chapter, I explain how to make traditional woodworking joints using the machines discussed in this book and a number of inexpensive shopmade jigs and fixtures. Once you build these jigs and practice the techniques outlined here, you'll be able to make mortise-and-tenon joints, dovetails and other woodworking joints quickly and accurately, and with the pleasure of knowing that you did it yourself. Many of the jigs and injection-molded plastic gadgets that are available commercially promise quick and easy woodworking. In reality, using these products is more frustrating and time-consuming than learning how to make the joints without them. There are no easy shortcuts: With my system, you have to take the time to practice until you get the techniques right and they become a habit for you. Consider this your apprenticeship.

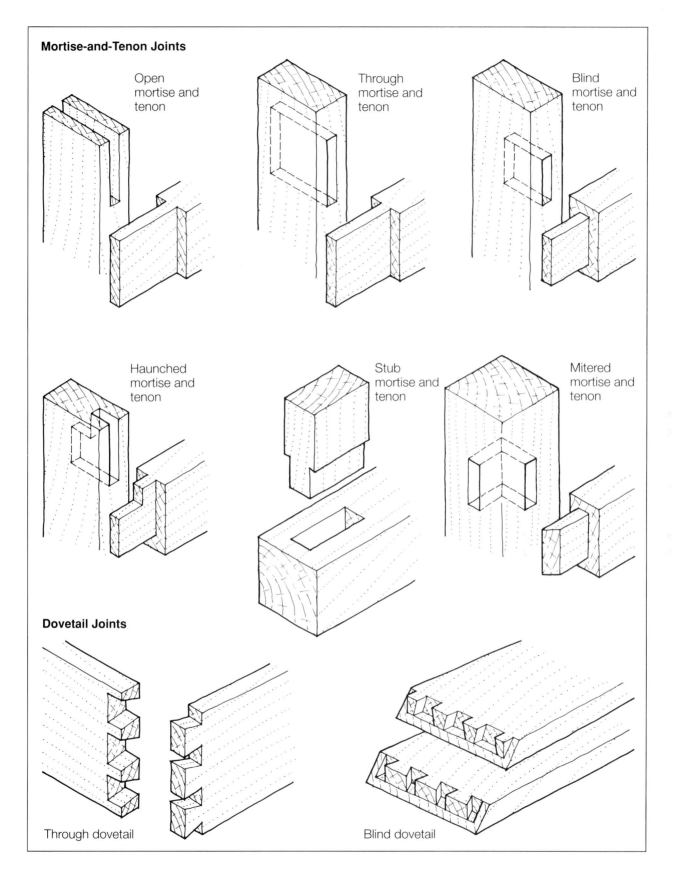

Mortise-and-Tenon Joints

Open mortise and tenon

Through mortise and tenon

Blind mortise and tenon

Haunched mortise and tenon

Stub mortise and tenon

Mitered mortise and tenon

Dovetail Joints

Through dovetail

Blind dovetail

Shopmade joinery jigs

The jigs described in this chapter are made from ¾-in. plywood, which is used because of its dimensional stability. You can use scrap, but the higher the quality of the plywood the better. It's a good idea to finish the jigs with oil, wax or varnish, although I must admit that I'm often so anxious to start using the jigs that I often don't get around to finishing them. I usually use ¼-in. bolts with a variety of head styles for my jigs. I have a collection of about 10 bolts for each size, so I don't have to go to the hardware store every time I want to make a new jig. When a bolt must slide in a groove, as with the bandsaw dovetail jig (see p. 222), I use a toilet bolt with a rectangular head and round corners. These are available in various lengths in the plumbing department.

Universal table-saw jig

The basic table-saw jig is a board about 4 in. high that attaches to the face of the miter gauge. Variations of this type of jig support the workpiece when it is on its edge for making tenons (see pp. 207-213), dovetails (pp. 218-230) and finger joints (pp. 239-241). It is important that the board be able to move back and forth for fine adjustments. The best jig I've come up with is a two-part system, which has a base board screwed to the miter gauge and a jig board attached to the base board with two bolts (see the drawing on the facing page). A ¾-in. dado with a ¼-in. through slot in the jig board supports a ¼-in. by ¾-in. by 7½-in. piece of wood. This piece houses two bolts that attach the jig board to the base and allow microadjustment of the jig.

A table-saw jig that works just like the shopmade universal jig is available commercially, and contrary to my comments about commercial jigs, it has some distinct advantages. This jig is a precision aluminum extrusion that can be screwed to the back of any board, so changing fixtures is a quick process. It also has a microadjuster that allows precision tweaking, which is handy when making dovetails or finger joints.

Mortise-and-tenon joints

Interlocking and mechanical joints, such as the mortise and tenon and the dovetail, have evolved over centuries and are still favorites for high-quality work. Because of its strength and resistance to racking and twist, the mortise-and-tenon joint is ideal for frame construction, such as chairs, cabinets and frame-and-panel doors. Once a well-fit mortise-and-tenon joint is glued, the mechanical contact and the large gluing surface area of the mating long-grain faces make it a very strong joint. Its only real weakness is that the tenon can be pulled straight out of the mortise fairly easily. This can be controlled by good gluing and, in demanding situations, by using a locking pin.

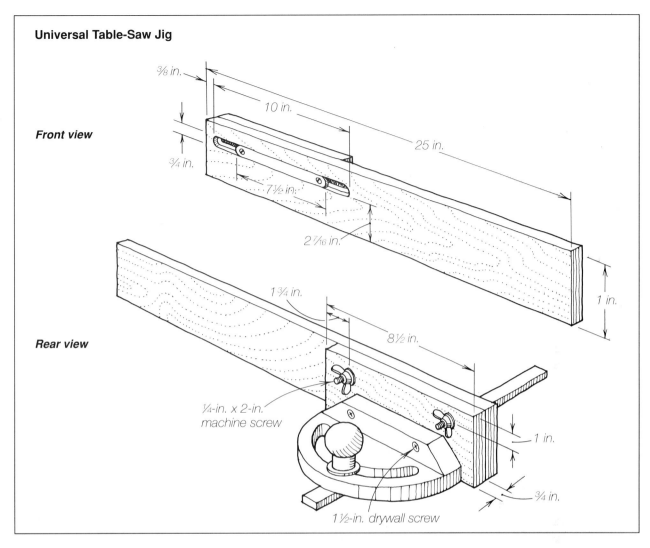

Universal Table-Saw Jig

Front view

⅜ in.

10 in.

25 in.

¾ in.

7½ in.

2⁷⁄₁₆ in.

1 in.

Rear view

1¾ in.

8½ in.

¼-in. x 2-in.
machine screw

1 in.

¾ in.

1½-in. drywall screw

This commercially available table-saw jig works in the same way as the shopmade universal jig shown above.

Types of mortise and tenon

Anyone who repairs old furniture knows that there are a large number of variations of the mortise-and-tenon joint. These joints were traditionally cut by hand, but, like many things in modern life, the mortise-and-tenon process has been simplified and standardized for machine production. Glue is stronger now, and locking mechanisms such as pins or wedges are not as important as they once were for longevity of the joint.

Joints with structural tenons that extend all the way through the mortise piece are called *through mortise and tenons.* Wedges are often used to expand and lock the tenon and, in some instances, to add a decorative element. The *blind mortise and tenon* does not extend through the member. The *haunched mortise and tenon,* used on corner joints, adds extra surface area for gluing and resists twisting. The haunched mortise is usually square, but it can be sloped if the appearance of the haunch is undesirable. This joint is often found in door construction in conjunction with dadoes for panels. The *stub tenon* is a short tenon, which is usually given extra support with a screw or peg. A *mitered mortise and tenon* is used for the corners of a chair or a table. All of these joints can be made with machines, although the sloped haunch is usually made by hand because of the complex and time-consuming machine setup required.

Mortise-and-tenon proportions

Traditionally, mortise-and-tenon joints are proportioned so that the thickness of the tenon is one-third the thickness of the stock; for example, a ¼-in. thick tenon would be appropriate for ¾-in. stock. The

Mortise-and-Tenon Proportions

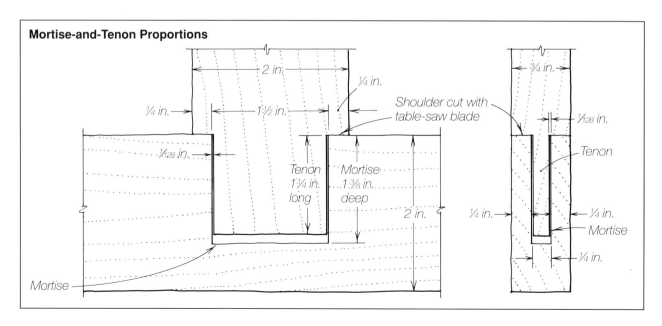

deeper the mortise, the stronger the joint because of the increased contact area between the two pieces. On 2-in. wide stock, I make the mortises 1⅜ in. deep, which is about the limit of a plunge-router cut. I cut the tenons 1¼ in. long, which leaves ⅛-in. clearance at the bottom of the mortise. In this case, members with tenons on both ends need to have an extra 2½-in. length, which makes the math easy. On a 1-in. wide frame, I'd make the mortise ⅞ in. deep and the tenon ¾ in. long.

Although the rule of thirds works well in most cases, it should be changed as the situation demands. If the load is only downward and there is very little twisting or racking, the tenon size could be increased and the width of the mortise walls decreased, or vice versa.

Making mortise and tenons with specialized machines

Mortise-and-tenon joints are made in the same sequence whether they are cut by hand or machine: The mortise is made first and then the tenon is cut to fit the mortise. In industry, mortises are cut with a mortising machine. This specialized machine is similar to a drill press, except that it usually features a foot or pneumatic feed. Additionally, American mortisers are fitted with a hollow square chisel, inside of which rotates an auger bit. These machines are called square-chisel mortisers and are usually of cast-iron construction. The chain mortiser is a similar machine, with a chainsaw cutter that cuts rectangular holes. Any kind of mortiser works well when properly maintained and set up, but I don't use these machines because there are easier and simpler approaches for my limited production runs. In addition, new mortisers are expensive.

European mortisers feature a fixed horizontal cutter. The work can be advanced in two directions. This type of mortiser is either a separate machine or is sometimes found as an additional feature of a table saw or jointer/planer. The horizontal travel of the bed is adjustable to regulate the width of the mortise (which is round-cornered rather than square). This system is simpler and much more trouble-free than the square-chisel or chain technology.

There are now a number of American-made machines, like the Multi-router®, that cut both the mortise and the tenon. These machines are similar in design to the European mortisers, except that they are powered by a router. A template is used to size the tenon, and the mortise is adjusted to the size of the tenon, which is the reverse of the traditional method. The expense of these machines usually limits their use to professional shops. Some joints, such as the compound-angle mortise and tenon commonly found in chair construction, are particularly easy to make on this sort of machine; indeed, it would be very time-consuming to make the joint any other way.

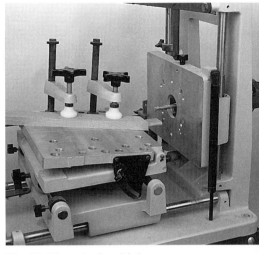

The Multi-router®, which uses a router as the power plant, cuts both the mortise and the tenon with a following template.

Mortising with the drill press

The drill press can be used to make the mortise, and many models are available with a hollow-chisel mortising attachment that mimics the industrial mortiser (see pp. 153-154). The chisel chops into the wood as you pull down on the feed lever. The square sharp corners compress the wood and force it into the auger bit, which removes the waste.

The mortise is chopped by making a series of plunges. It is usually best to make the corners first and then waste the material in the middle of the mortise. Some people prefer to remove the bulk of the material with a series of drill holes first, particularly in harder woods. The outside of the square fixture should be polished and waxed for easy withdrawal. The fixture should never be honed in such a way that it creates a taper, because a tapered chisel is likely to stick. As with many drilling operations, frequent withdrawal helps to remove the waste and prevent sticking. Waxing the chisel frequently helps too, but even with these precautions the chisel is often hard to withdraw from hardwoods. Many people who prefer a mortiser get an extra drill press and keep it set up for mortising.

Another way of mortising is to use a spiral-flute router bit in a drill press, as discussed on p. 154, or to drill the holes with a drill and then use the router bit to remove the waste.

Mortising with the router

The router is capable of performing most woodworking tasks and is particularly well suited to making mortises because of its ability to remove material cleanly with the appropriate jig. I use a plunge router with an up-cut spiral bit to make mortises. Most routers are hard to control because they are top-heavy, so I replace the standard router base with a special auxiliary base fitted with two adjustable fences. These fences fit snugly on either side of the workpiece during mortising, which aligns the cut on the thickness of the stock and stabilizes the router atop the edge of the workpiece. Although I have made bases out of wood, I now use a clear plastic base and fence system made by Woodhaven, 5323 West Kimberly Road, Davenport, IA 52806; (800) 344-6657. The clear base makes it easy to see alignment marks on the workpiece.

The plunge router and plastic base work in conjunction with a shop-made holding-and-referencing jig to cut slot-type mortises (that is, mortises with rounded ends). The mortising jig holds the workpiece steady and provides stops for limiting the cut of the router. The jig, which takes about an hour to assemble, consists of a ¾-in. thick plywood base with a strip dadoed into the underside for clamping in a bench vise. A shallow dado in the top of the base holds two fences.

The inside ends of the fences serve as stops for the router-base fence. Once the stops have been set, the fences lock to the base with bolts riding in slotted holes.

Two plywood wedges, each tapered and beveled at a 15° angle, secure the workpiece during the mortising process. One wedge is fixed (bolted to the base through a slot) and the other wedge is free-moving (see the drawing below). The tapered edges are driven against each other by

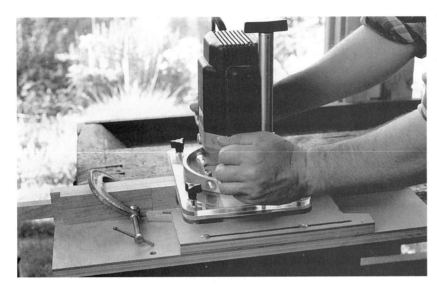

This plywood jig is used when making mortises with a plunge router. A Plexiglas® fixture rides on top of the jig. A stop lock clamps in place to locate the distance between the end of the board and the mortise.

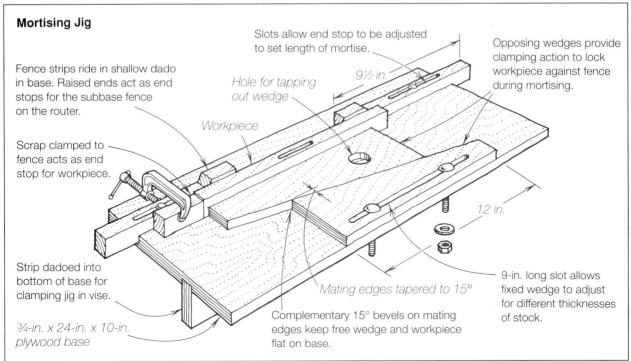

Mortising Jig

Fence strips ride in shallow dado in base. Raised ends act as end stops for the subbase fence on the router.

Scrap clamped to fence acts as end stop for workpiece.

Slots allow end stop to be adjusted to set length of mortise.

Hole for tapping out wedge

Workpiece

9½ in.

Opposing wedges provide clamping action to lock workpiece against fence during mortising.

Strip dadoed into bottom of base for clamping jig in vise.

¾-in. x 24-in. x 10-in. plywood base

12 in.

Mating edges tapered to 15°

Complementary 15° bevels on mating edges keep free wedge and workpiece flat on base.

9-in. long slot allows fixed wedge to adjust for different thicknesses of stock.

tapping the free wedge with a hammer, forcing the workpiece against the fence. A hole in the free wedge provides a spot to tap for separating the work after mortising.

An end stop the same width as the workpiece is clamped or screwed to the router stop to locate the end of the workpiece relative to the position of the router. Thus the distance between the mortise and the end of the workpiece can be accurately set for cutting corner joints. Only those frame members with mortises in the center need to be marked and positioned before mortising. In this case, I mark out the two ends of the mortise, put the router against one stop and then move the stock so that one of the layout marks is aligned with the bit. After clamping the stock, I move the other stop to align the router bit with the second layout mark.

For efficiency, I follow a definite sequence in setting up the router and jig for mortising. First, I center the mortise, and then set the depth of cut of the router's bit. Finally, I set the fence stops for the length of the mortise. The mortises must be exactly centered on the stock. It may take a little extra time setting up the fences on the router base, but you'll save time later when the tenons are made and fitted. The best way to check the position of the mortises is to make a plunge cut on one edge of a scrap piece, turn the piece over and make another cut on the other side. If the cuts line up, the mortise is centered.

The up-cut spiral bit that I use for mortising cuts makes a clean slotted mortise. Flutes on an up-cut bit are similar to a drill bit: They pull the waste up and out of the cut. Although end mills are capable of taking up to a $\frac{3}{8}$-in. deep cut per pass, you'll get the best results with many small passes, taking $\frac{1}{8}$ in. or less per pass. Move the router back and forth with a slow rhythmic motion and plunge slightly deeper on each pass until you reach the desired depth.

Avoid making heavy cuts. Overtaxing the bit produces chatter or vibration that leaves the sides of the mortise irregular and rough and may cause bit slippage, which can rapidly wear the collet. A worn collet not only results in mortises that are too deep, but can also be dangerous if the bit slips out. Guard against this by placing an ink mark on the bit and the collet; if the marks move during mortising, the bit is slipping and it may be time to order a new collet. If you do a lot of mortising, you might consider using solid carbide bits instead of high-speed steel bits: A sharp bit has much less of a tendency to vibrate than a dull one.

If you're using a variable-speed plunge router, you should set it to run at about 12,000 rpm. Slower speed and light passes are best for smooth, clean mortises, especially with a small bit or a hard wood such as maple. Experiment on scrap stock before deciding on the best router speed.

The length of the mortise is set by adjusting the mortise jig's stops. With my system, the mortise is cut shorter than the width of the tenon stock because the tenons are later trimmed. In this case, the stock is 2 in. wide and the mortise is 1½ in. long (see the drawing on p. 202). Once the stops are adjusted, you're ready to run your batch of mortises.

When machining wide stock, such as a chair or table leg, the router can slide directly on the edge of a single member. But when mortising narrow stock, such as a ¾-in. face frame, clamp two members side by side for a wider, more stable base for the router to prevent it from tipping. After you've mortised all the necessary workpieces, mortise two extra scrap pieces for setting up subsequent operations.

Sawing the tenon

After all the mortises have been made, the tenons are cut to fit them. There are a number of ways to do this, but I prefer to use the table saw, the radial-arm saw and the bandsaw in combination. Why all three machines? If I have three cuts to make for a tenon and can set up a saw for each, I only have to reset one machine if I make an error on one of the cuts. If I were using only one machine, I might have to make three setups again.

Tenons are cut in three stages. First, a shallow kerf is crosscut all the way around the end of the workpiece, to define the tenon shoulder. Second, the face cheeks of the tenon are cut, and then the edge cheeks are cut. If I have round-cornered mortises, the edges of the tenon itself are chamfered with the bandsaw to fit the round-cornered mortise (see pp. 211-212). I use the table saw or the radial-arm saw to make the initial cuts and the bandsaw for the cheek cuts.

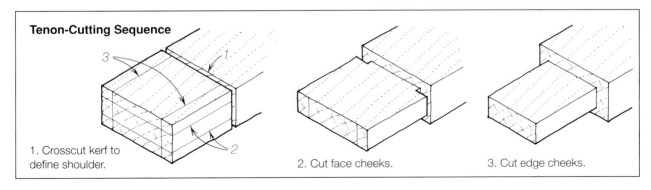

Tenon-Cutting Sequence

1. Crosscut kerf to define shoulder.

2. Cut face cheeks.

3. Cut edge cheeks.

The tenon shoulder is crosscut on the table saw using the miter gauge. The rip fence acts as a stop.

Cutting the shoulders On boards less than 4 ft. long, shoulder cuts are easy to make using the table saw and the miter gauge. I prefer to use a sharp crosscut or combination blade, which yields a crisp cut without tearout. The saw's rip fence can be used as a stop for setting the length of the tenon. As a rule, you shouldn't use the fence and the miter gauge together, but in this situation it is safe to do so because you don't have to worry about a cut-off piece binding between the blade and the fence. To ensure a perfect tenon shoulder all the way around, square the miter gauge (see pp. 16-17) and then set the fence square to the miter gauge. In addition, it's important for the face of the fence to be square to the table: Otherwise, when you rotate the stock for the various cuts, the wood will contact different parts of the fence and the shoulder cuts won't match all the way around.

Make all four shoulder cuts with the blade at the same height. Crosscut one of the extra mortised pieces through its mortise, place it next to the blade and set the blade to be about $\frac{1}{32}$ in. higher than the wall thickness. If you use a $\frac{1}{4}$-in. router bit centered in $\frac{3}{4}$-in. stock, the wall thickness is $\frac{1}{4}$ in., which means that the height of the blade should be $\frac{9}{32}$ in. Rotate the blade back and forth to make sure you are setting the saw height with the tooth at top dead center. This extra depth of cut ensures that the shoulder cut is deep enough but will not weaken the tenon.

If the workpiece is longer than 4 ft., I crosscut tenons on the radial-arm saw. This requires two series of cuts with the blade at a different height for the face and edge shoulders.

Cutting the face cheeks Once I have completed the shoulder cuts, I use the bandsaw to cut the tenon cheeks. The bandsaw has some distinct advantages over the table saw or radial-arm saw for this job. The demanding end-grain cut is easier on the bandsaw because the blade cuts a narrower kerf. In addition, the cheeks are cut with the stock horizontal on the bandsaw table; using a tenoning jig on the table saw, the stock stands upright, and the length of stock you can tenon is limited. A further advantage is that frame pieces don't need to be clamped to a jig, which saves time when cutting dozens of tenons. For accurate, repetitive cuts on the bandsaw, use a rip fence. If your bandsaw doesn't have a rip fence, make one from wood scraps and carriage bolts (as shown in the drawing on p. 109).

Although it doesn't make a great deal of difference which bandsaw blade you use, I prefer a ¼-in., 4-TPI or 6-TPI blade. The bandsaw must be properly adjusted for this technique to work. To prevent the blade from fluctuating sideways, the guides are positioned so that they actually touch the blade. I use Cool Blocks® (see p. 101) to decrease the friction created by metal-to-metal contact.

Set up the fence on the bandsaw with the tenon between the blade and the fence, so that as the cheeks are cut the waste doesn't get trapped between blade and fence. Use one of the scrap mortises as a gauge to set the fence-to-blade distance (in the same way you set the

Use a shopmade fence for cutting the tenon on the bandsaw. Position the tenon so that the waste is away from the fence.

depth of the shoulder cuts). With the mortise scrap against the fence, the blade should cut the first sample tenon about 1/64 in. oversize. Adjust the fence closer to the blade by inserting paper shims between the fence and the subfence and make another cut. Remember that the amount you move the fence will be doubled because you're taking that amount off each side of the tenon. Also, use a new piece of scrap for each new adjustment; if you use the previously cut piece, the bandsaw blade will deflect and you will not get a true reading.

If you do not have a bandsaw, you can use a dado blade on the table saw or radial-arm saw to cut the face cheeks. Alternatively, if the boards to be tenoned are relatively short, a tenoning jig holds the work vertically over the table-saw blade with a good deal of precision and safety. A bar mounted in the base of the jig slides in the miter-gauge slot on the table saw.

The easiest way to set the tenoning jig is to use a sample mortise as a guide. The corner of the blade should just touch the outside edge of the mortise. Slide the jig, with the board clamped in place, through the blade and back again to make the cut. After the first cut, unclamp the board and turn it for the second cut. This technique will center the tenon.

The tenoning jig holds the wood upright as it passes over the table-saw blade.

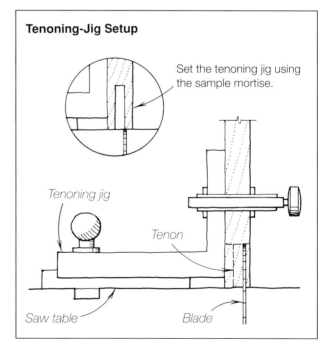

Tenoning-Jig Setup

Set the tenoning jig using the sample mortise.

Tenoning jig

Tenon

Saw table

Blade

Ideally, the tenon should fit into the mortise with about 0.004 in. extra on each side, which is the thickness of a layer of glue. To check the fit use a dollar bill; with the bill in place, the tenon should fit snugly.

Cutting the edge cheeks Once the face cheeks have been cut, trim the edge cheeks of the tenon back to the shoulder on the bandsaw. This requires that the fence be reset so the blade will take about ⅛ in. off each edge of the tenon. If the corners of the mortise are square, this is also the step for fitting the tenon into the mortise. Make the tenon a hair oversize and then use sample cuts to fit the joint, making adjustments similar to those made for the face cheeks.

If you don't have a bandsaw, cut the edges off the tenon on the table saw using a miter gauge with an extension board. Clamp a stop block to position the board and make final adjustments with paper shims between the tenon board and the stop block.

If the mortise has round corners, follow the same procedure as described previously but remove material until the tenon is about ¹⁄₁₆ in. narrower than the mortise. In the case of a 1¾-in. wide mortise, the tenon will be 1¹¹⁄₁₆-in. wide. The ¹⁄₁₆-in. space enables you to fit the tenons by chamfering the corners rather than fully rounding the tenon.

Chamfering tenons for round mortises If you used a router bit to make the mortise, the corners of the mortise are round. Since the tenon corners are square, the tenon won't fit unless you chisel the mortise corners square or the round the tenons. After years of experimenting, I've decided that it's easiest to chamfer the tenons at a 45° angle. The chamfers allow a small space between the flat surface of the tenon and the round surface of the mortise and ensure a perfectly mating joint because the space allows glue squeeze-out. If there is too much glue in the mortise, the space releases the hydraulic pressure, allowing air or glue to escape.

Although you can easily chamfer a few tenons by hand, it's better to use a machine if you have a lot to cut. To chamfer on the bandsaw, set the table to 45° and adjust the fence so that the saw cuts off a small portion of the tenon's square edge while the face of the workpiece is against the fence (see the drawing on p. 212). You may want to take the corners off a scrap tenon by hand and trial-fit it into a mortise to get an idea of how much material has to be trimmed. Once set, chamfer all pairs of opposite edges on each tenon. Next, reset the fence to chamfer the tenon while the face of the workpiece is against the table and repeat the cuts. Alternatively, to chamfer with either the table saw or the radial-arm saw, clamp a V-block so the wood is held at a 45° angle.

The mortise cut with a standard router bit has round ends. A tenon with chamfered corners can fit into the rounded mortise.

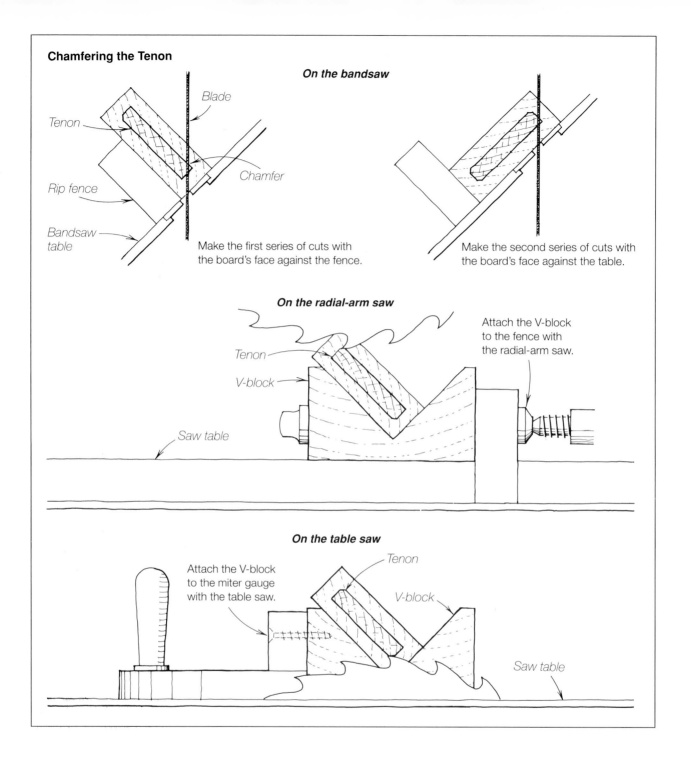

Chamfering the Tenon

On the bandsaw

Blade

Tenon

Chamfer

Rip fence

Bandsaw table

Make the first series of cuts with the board's face against the fence.

Make the second series of cuts with the board's face against the table.

On the radial-arm saw

Attach the V-block to the fence with the radial-arm saw.

Tenon

V-block

Saw table

On the table saw

Attach the V-block to the miter gauge with the table saw.

Tenon

V-block

Saw table

Fitting the joint If you have been careful with your cutting, you should have a close but not-too-close fit between the mortise and the tenon. If the joint is too loose, the inside contact between the two pieces is insufficient for good gluing. If it's too tight, you may crack the frame members during glue-up or starve the joint of glue and leave it weak.

Making an open mortise and tenon

An open mortise and tenon can be cut quickly on the table saw with just a single setting on the tenon jig. Plane, rip or resaw a wooden shim the same thickness as the saw cut. Place a board in the tenoning jig and set the jig to make a cut one-third of the way in from the edge. Make the first cut at this setting. Turn the board around and cut the other side at the same setting. Next, clamp the tenon piece in place with the wooden shim beside it. Make one cut, flip the board and make the next cut. The shim displaces the board to the right the thickness of the saw cut. As a result, the tenon and the open mortise match perfectly. The shoulders of the tenon should be cut off using the miter gauge, as described on p. 208. Clean out the middle of the mortise with several passes on the table saw or using an ⅛-in. blade on the bandsaw.

The open mortise and tenon can also be cut on a bandsaw with a series of cuts. The ⅛-in. blade is best for this procedure, because curved cuts are required to remove the waste for the mortise.

Open Mortise and Tenon on the Table Saw

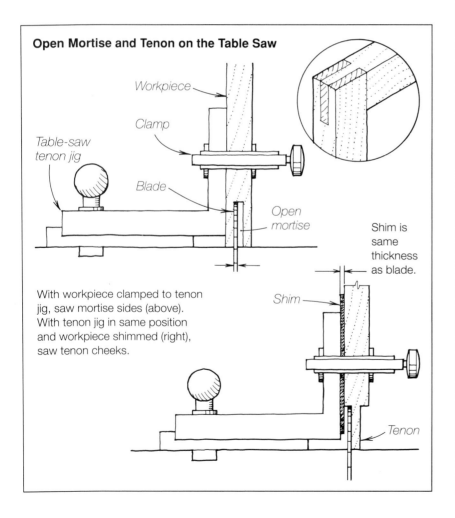

With workpiece clamped to tenon jig, saw mortise sides (above). With tenon jig in same position and workpiece shimmed (right), saw tenon cheeks.

Open Mortise and Tenon on the Bandsaw

Cut the mortise with the first series of cuts.

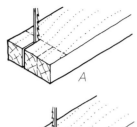

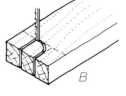

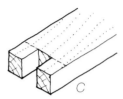

Cut the tenon with the second series of cuts.

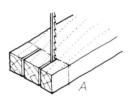

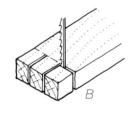

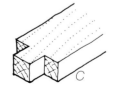

The dovetail is an ancient technique for joining wood and is still the strongest way to form a 90° angle. These through dovetails were made in minutes using spacer blocks and a shopmade jig.

Dovetail joints

The dovetail is the strongest and most attractive joint for carcase joinery. This classic joint is the hallmark of quality craftsmanship, and mastering dovetailing is a major step in learning the craft of woodworking. There's an attitude that real woodworkers do dovetails. This kind of pressure sells a lot of plastic jigs and fixtures, but many of them are overcomplicated and expensive. The one I like the least is simply a spacing jig that moves a fence in increments of ⅟₃₂ in. At the opposite end of the scale, the high-end router jigs with micrometer-controlled adjustments, such as the Keller and the Leigh, are well designed and are worth the money if you are doing production dovetails.

The alternative to using dovetail jigs is to cut dovetails by hand, but this traditional method requires skill and patience. It's slow work, and unless you have considerable hand skill it is not a very practical method. I have always felt that there was a missing link between the tedium of hand-cutting dozens of dovetails and the faster method of producing monotonous-looking joints with router jigs. With that in mind, I developed a spacer-block dovetail method (see pp. 219-230) that combines hand-tool flexibility with power-tool speed and accuracy.

My dovetail system is fast, accurate and easy to use, costs next to nothing and allows for design flexibility. I can either make dovetails on the bandsaw and the table saw in combination or I can make them on the bandsaw alone. The key problems of making accurate dovetails are maintaining the correct angle of cut and accurately spacing the cuts. The simple shopmade jig that I devised maintains the angle and accurately spaces the saw cuts with spacing blocks. Spacing blocks in combination with the jig allow repeatable, accurate cuts without guesswork. Once the entry cuts are made, the waste is removed with an ⅛-in. bandsaw blade or chopped out by hand.

With this technique, you can vary both the width and the spacing of the pins and tails for virtually any aesthetic effect. The blocks that set the spacing are self-centering and produce perfect-fitting, interchangeable joints, eliminating the need to mark boards so that individual joints will fit, as is necessary with hand-dovetailing.

Dovetail design

The dovetail has been used in one form or another for everything from small boxes to log barns for at least 5,000 years. The exposed dovetail is both structurally sound and aesthetically pleasing. However, the relationship between design and technique is complex. Just because you have dovetails that are technically sound doesn't mean that the piece is well designed. Design without technical skill or consideration is superficial, and technical virtuosity without an eye for design may result in a joint that is plain ugly.

The dovetail is a locking joint with two elements, the pin and the tail. The pin and tail fit together from only one direction and hold together without glue. The single dovetail joint can either be a complete pin or a complete tail. The multiple dovetail usually ends with a half pin at each corner; the half tail is usually avoided at the ends of the joint because it can break off. Tail boards are interchangeable. Each side is identical and can function as either the inside or the outside of a box. The pin-board sides are not identical, and thus not reversible. The outside of the pin board is the side toward which the pins are tapered.

The dovetail angle provides a mechanical lock. The angle of the pin mates with the angle of the tail, and the contact point is the foundation of the joint. If the angle is too slight, the pin can slide between the tails and the locking mechanism is inadequate. If the angle is too great, the wood at the corner is too fragile and breaks easily under stress.

The ideal dovetail angle is approximately 80°. It does not matter if this angle is a couple of degrees off either way, but what is important is that the pin and tail have the same angle and fit closely without gaps.

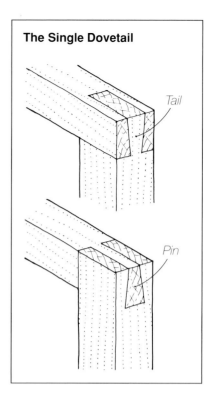

The Single Dovetail

Tail

Pin

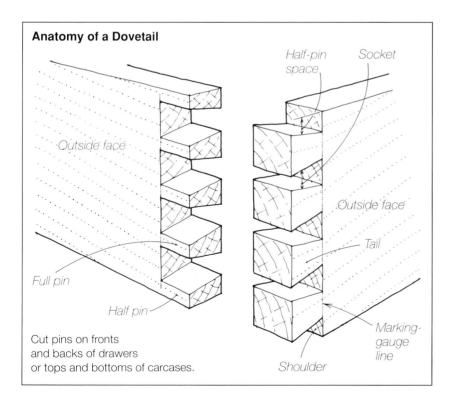

Anatomy of a Dovetail

Outside face

Full pin

Half pin

Cut pins on fronts
and backs of drawers
or tops and bottoms of carcases.

Half-pin space

Socket

Outside face

Tail

Marking-gauge line

Shoulder

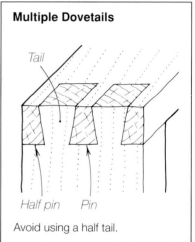

Multiple Dovetails

Tail

Half pin   Pin

Avoid using a half tail.

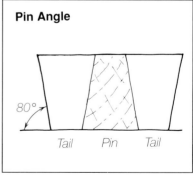

Pin Angle

80°

Tail   Pin   Tail

On some softwoods, such as pine, an angle of 82° to 83° is preferable. Most dovetail router bits are ground at an angle of 14°. This angle is not the strongest, or the most attractive, but the large surface area of the many pins and tails creates a strong joint. When using the 14° router bit be careful that you do not break the corners of the pins off, particularly in hardwoods. The tendency for the corners to chip is especially disturbing when the tails show, as with through dovetails.

Pin spacing   The spacing of the pins across the board is an important design consideration. The spacing is best measured from the center of the pin. If you take the measurement from the outside corner of the pin, the pins will be bigger than the tails. If you measure from the inside corner of the pin board where the pin is widest, the tail will be bigger than the pin.

To avoid a mechanical look, space pins so that the tails are unequal in size. The drawing at left below shows a number of possible arrangements. The design created should be consistent with the need for structural strength. If the pins are not evenly spaced, as shown in C, they should be closer to the edge of the piece as in D and E. The close proximity of the pin to the half pin on the corner provides extra strength. A dovetail usually fails on the corner rather than in the middle, so it makes good sense to reinforce the corner. If the pins are too close to the middle of the board, as shown in A, they provide little more strength than a large single pin. I find example D the most visually interesting.

Variable Pin Spacing

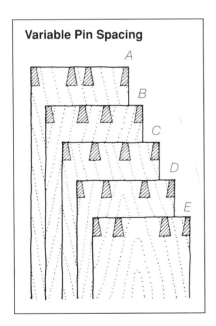

Pin-Spacing Ratios

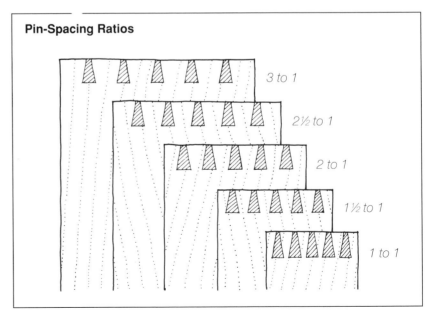

Pin-to-Tail Ratios

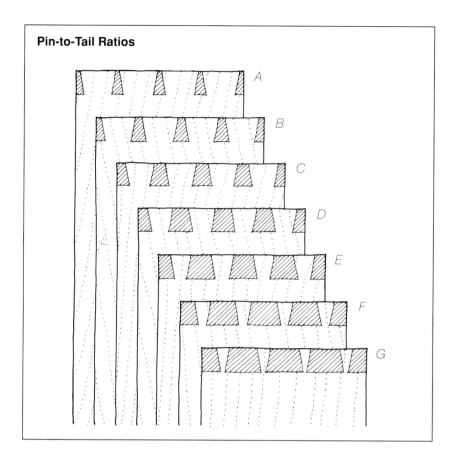

The drawing at right on the facing page shows various pin-spacing ratios. The 1:1 ratio of the pins and tails is very mechanical looking. This is the type of joint created by a router and jig or an industrial dovetail machine, and its mass-produced look is not consistent with high-quality work. The 1:1 ratio is often used for kitchen cabinets. I find the other pin-spacing designs much more attractive, and the 2½:1 ratio the most pleasing.

The drawing above shows various size ratios of the pins (shaded) and the tails. The strongest joint is example D, because the pins and tails are similar in size and are therefore equally strong. The weakest joints are examples A and G, the two extremes. The small pins of A and the small tails of G would both break easily under stress. Small pins, such as in example A, were in vogue for a time on expensive European cabinets. They were considered elegant looking but went out of fashion when it was discovered that the drawers required frequent repair. Examples B and C combine the strength of D and the appearance of A. Examples E, F and G would probably not be used because the tail is traditionally larger than the pin.

Dovetail Tails on the Table Saw

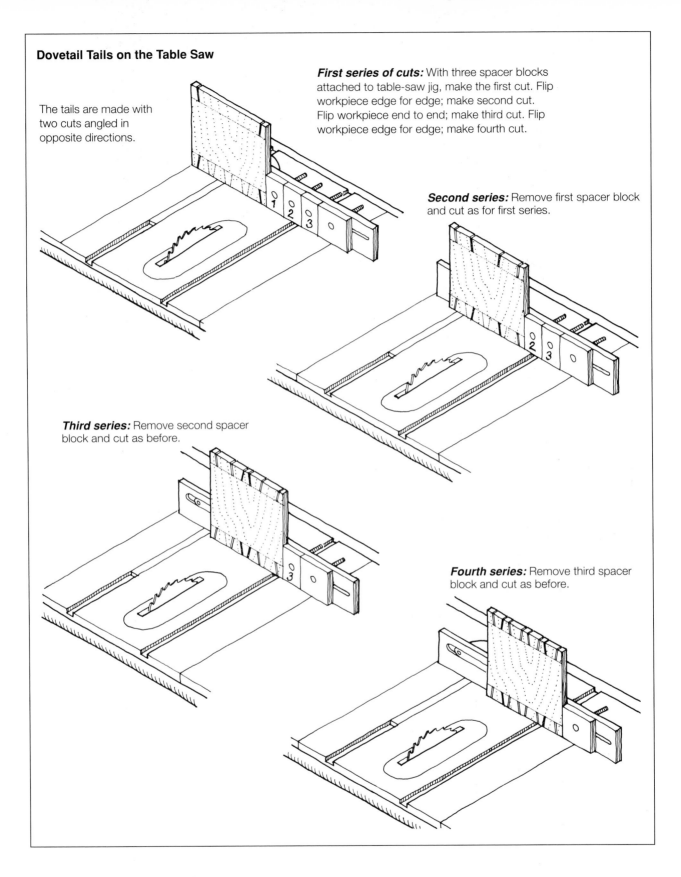

The tails are made with two cuts angled in opposite directions.

First series of cuts: With three spacer blocks attached to table-saw jig, make the first cut. Flip workpiece edge for edge; make second cut. Flip workpiece end to end; make third cut. Flip workpiece edge for edge; make fourth cut.

Second series: Remove first spacer block and cut as for first series.

Third series: Remove second spacer block and cut as before.

Fourth series: Remove third spacer block and cut as before.

The spacer-block dovetail system

It took about five years of experimenting to develop the spacer-block system that I now use to cut dovetails. Initially, I marked out the joints and then cut them freehand on the table saw or the bandsaw. Jigs held the wood at the correct angle. To facilitate the correct spacing of the cuts, I started using plywood spacer blocks. Now, when used with a simple guide, these blocks space the angled dovetail cuts precisely. The blocks must be of consistent width, so I crosscut them from the same ripping, then sand or plane off any fuzzy corners so that they'll line up with no gaps.

Spacing the cuts   The blocks and the workpiece are positioned on or against the universal table-saw jig, as shown in the drawing on the facing page. Whether you use the bandsaw or the table saw, the tails are always cut before the pins. A cut is made in each corner of the board, and after each series of four cuts one spacer block is removed and another series of cuts is made.

The drawing below shows the relationship between the blocks and the saw cuts. Each block spaces the distance from the corner of one tail to the corner of the next tail. For the sample piece shown in the drawing at left, the pins are spaced equally for the 4¼-in. wide drawer

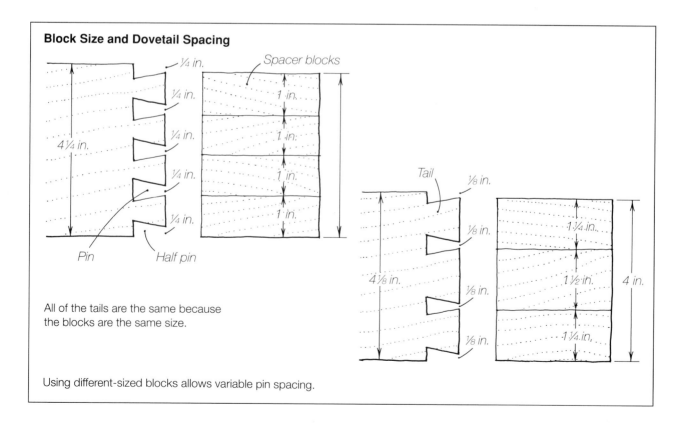

Block Size and Dovetail Spacing

¼ in.

Spacer blocks

¼ in.

1 in.

¼ in.

1 in.

4¼ in.

¼ in.

1 in.

¼ in.

1 in.

Pin   Half pin

All of the tails are the same because
the blocks are the same size.

Tail   ⅛ in.

⅛ in.

1¼ in.

4⅛ in.

1½ in.   4 in.

⅛ in.

⅛ in.

1¼ in.

Using different-sized blocks allows variable pin spacing.

part. The difference between the total width of the four blocks (4 in.) and the width of the workpiece (4¼ in.) determines the size of the pin and the half pin (¼ in.). Both of the examples shown in the drawing use a total of 4 in. of spacer blocks, yet the designs are completely different. Variable pin spaces are made with different-size spacer blocks.

Tail size is also determined by block size. One block is equal to the size of the tail plus the size of the pin. When you use tails of different sizes, you affect the design of the joint. You can change the design by altering the block sizes and the width of the workpiece.

Limitations of the block system   All woodworking systems have advantages and disadvantages, and the spacer-block dovetail system is no exception. One factor that limits the use of this system is the size of the workpiece. It is not practical to have a piece more than 2 ft. long standing on edge on your table-saw top. However, it is possible to cut the tails on the end of a 3-ft. board on the bandsaw. The tails are usually located on the longer piece of wood, so use the bandsaw if the tail board is long.

The only limitation to cutting pins on the bandsaw is the throat size of the bandsaw. You cannot cut a board wider than the distance between the column and the blade. I usually cut the pins on the table saw when the pin board is wider than 6 in.

If you need to make dovetails on boards wider than 12 in. or longer than 3 ft., I suggest you use the Leigh or the Keller router-jig system (for production work) or cut the dovetails by hand (for single pieces). Most router-dovetail systems make only through dovetails. If you are using a router jig for drawers, you'll have to add a front piece if you don't want the joint to show.

It requires some study and experimentation to master the spacer-block system, so don't expect expert results the first couple of times that you try this technique. The more you use the system, the better you will get at it.

Bandsaw versus table saw   Cutting dovetails with a bandsaw has several important advantages. It is a quieter and safer machine than the table saw and, in my opinion, more enjoyable to work with. I recommend the bandsaw for your first dovetails.

The beauty of the spacer-block system, however, is that you can make the joint completely on the bandsaw or completely on the table saw if you do some chisel work. If you have a bandsaw, you can remove the waste between the table-saw cuts with a ⅛-in. blade, eliminating the need for hand work. You also can cut one half of the joint with one ma-

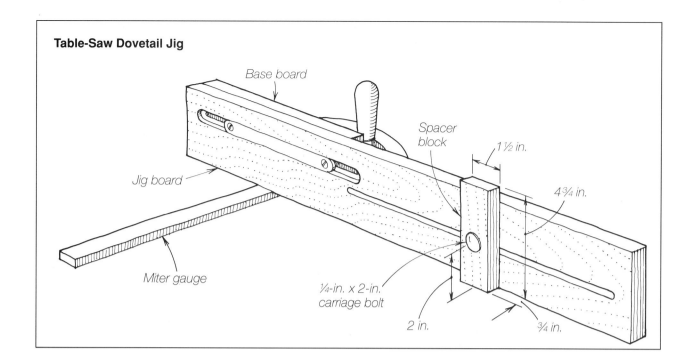

Table-Saw Dovetail Jig

Base board

Spacer block

Jig board

1 ½ in.

4 ¾ in.

Miter gauge

¼-in. x 2-in. carriage bolt

2 in.

¾ in.

chine and the other half with the other machine, but if you opt for this method rip the blocks for each machine at the same time. Close doesn't count in dovetails.

Making the dovetail jigs

The jigs that are used with the spacer-block system should be made of ¾-in. plywood. They need to be adjustable for different thicknesses of stock. If you make both the table-saw jig and the bandsaw jig, you will need two ¼-in. toilet bolts and 2-in. long stove bolts with wing nuts and washers for each jig. The table-saw jig also requires a 2-in. by ¼-in. carriage bolt with a washer and wing nut for each block that you use.

The table-saw jig A single jig is used to cut both the tails and the pins on the table saw. It is a piece of plywood about 4 in. high that attaches to the miter gauge. The jig has to allow sideways adjustment of the jig board for the final positioning of the workpiece after the miter angle is set. On p. 201 is a drawing of a universal table-saw jig. To convert it to a dovetail jig, add another through slot for the bolts that hold the spacer blocks in place, as shown in the drawing above.

Bandsaw Tail Jig

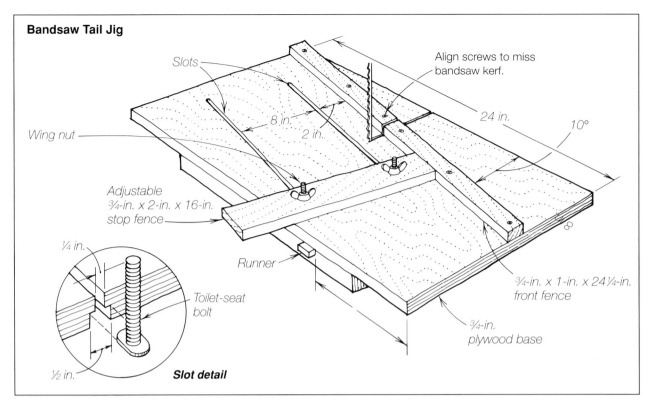

Slots

Align screws to miss bandsaw kerf.

Wing nut

8 in.

2 in.

24 in.

10°

Adjustable
¾-in. x 2-in. x 16-in.
stop fence

Runner

8

¾-in. x 1-in. x 24¼-in.
front fence

¼ in.

Toilet-seat
bolt

½ in.

Slot detail

¾-in.
plywood base

Bandsaw Pin Jig

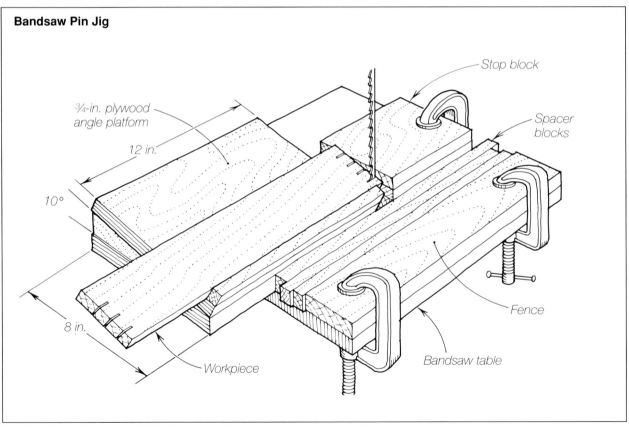

Stop block

¾-in. plywood
angle platform

Spacer
blocks

12 in.

10°

8 in.

Workpiece

Fence

Bandsaw table

Bandsaw jigs One jig is required to cut the tails on the bandsaw. This jig is used to move the workpiece into the blade at a 10° angle and to hold the spacer blocks. The jig is a plywood platform with a runner that slides in the miter slot on the bandsaw table. A board is attached at a 10° angle to the front of the jig, and an adjustable board is positioned at 90° to the fixed board (see the top drawing on the facing page). The blocks and the workpiece are positioned in the corner where the boards meet.

If you have a bandsaw with a table that tilts 10° toward the column, you can cut the pins without a jig, but you will need a rip fence. If your saw table does not tilt 10° in both directions, you will need to make a jig to support the workpiece and the blocks while cutting the pins. The jig consists of two pieces of plywood with two 10° wedges between them, as shown in the bottom drawing on the facing page.

Cutting the tails

Before cutting the tails, first square the ends of the boards to be joined. Take your time with this step because inaccurately prepared stock virtually guarantees sloppy results. To mark the depth of the tail and pin cuts, set your marking gauge to the thickness of the stock. Scribe a line on the face and edges of the tail board and on the faces of the pin board. Then pencil the starting mark, which is the difference between the width of the blocks and the workpiece.

The tails are created by making two cuts angled in opposite directions. Both angled cuts are made with one setup by turning and rotating the board after each cut. All of the tail boards will be a mirror image and will be interchangeable with each other. Since one face is exactly the same as the opposite side of the board, either face can function as the inside or the outside of a box or drawer.

Mark the difference between the total width of the blocks and the workpiece. The difference here is about ⅜ in., which will be the width of both the half pin and the pins. The pencil mark indicates where the first cut will be made.

Cut all four corners of both tail boards. Remove a spacer block and repeat the cuts. Next, move the workpiece away from the block and widen the saw kerf between the tails so that it is wide enough to accept an ⅛-in. sawblade.

Bandsaw tails An ⅛-in. blade seems to work best for bandsawing the tails. Tilt the top saw wheel back far enough so that the blade rides against the thrust bearing. This prevents the blade from wandering forward over the gauge line. To prevent side deflection make sure there is no space between the guide blocks and the blade: Use fiber replacement guide blocks (Cool Blocks®), as discussed on p. 101.

It is a good idea to use a piece of scrap when setting up the bandsaw to cut the tails. Position the blocks and the workpiece on the jig, placing the blocks on the side of the workpiece. The edge of the blade should be lined up with the pencil mark so that the body of the blade cuts into the waste area between the line and the edge of the board.

Make the first cut to the line you scribed with the marking gauge and then place a stop on the table so that the jig cannot go back any farther. Next, turn and flip the board so that all four corners are cut. Remove a spacer block and repeat the process.

The next step is to widen the saw kerf between the two inside cuts. This helps you remove the waste later with a crosscut against the fence. Some people prefer to remove the waste the traditional way, that is, with a chisel.

Table-saw tails Use a standard table-saw blade to make the entry cuts for the tails. A good-quality carbide-tipped blade saws crisp tails and pins, but set at an angle it leaves a small triangle of waste at the bottom of the cut that must be removed later with a chisel or a small bandsaw blade. I like to use an 1/8-in. wide carbide-tipped blade because it allows me to use an 1/8-in. bandsaw blade to saw out the waste. I prefer a flat-bottomed cut, so I don't use the triple-chip grind because it leaves a pointed kerf.

Cut the tails with the saw arbor (or table) tilted to 80°. Set the miter gauge at 90°. A bevel gauge set at 80° can be used to set both the saw-blade for the tails and later the miter gauge for the pins. An option is to cut a piece of scrap plywood at 80° for use as a setup guide.

Position the table-saw jig (see the drawing on p. 221) in the middle of its lateral adjustment. Attach the spacer blocks and the stop block to the jig fence so that the edge of the blade aligns to the pencil starting mark. Make sure that the blade is cutting into the waste area between the mark and the edge of the board. Make the final adjustment by moving the jig. Raise the sawblade after each sample cut until it cuts right to the gauge line. With all the blocks in place, make the first cut. After the first cut, make all four corners by flipping the board edge-for-edge and end-for-end. Continue this process, removing a spacer block after each series of cuts, until all the tails are cut (see the drawing on p. 218).

Remove the tail waste on the bandsaw with a 14-TPI, 1/8-in. blade and the rip fence, as shown in the photo below. The microadjustable fence is very handy for this operation. Alternatively, you can remove the waste by hand with a sharp chisel.

Cut the waste between the tails with the end of the board positioned against the rip fence. For the inside cuts place the blade in the wide kerf and crosscut the waste. Flip the piece over and trim the opposite corner.

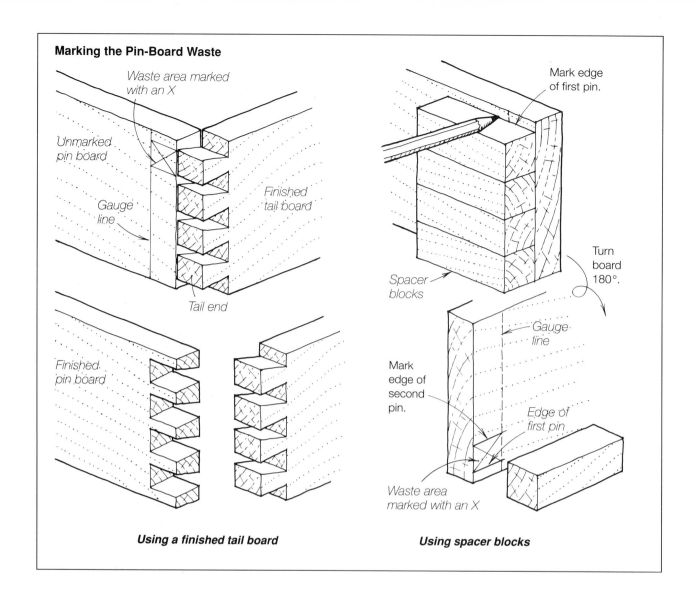

Marking the Pin-Board Waste

Waste area marked with an X

Unmarked pin board

Gauge line

Finished tail board

Tail end

Finished pin board

Using a finished tail board

Mark edge of first pin.

Turn board 180°.

Spacer blocks

Gauge line

Mark edge of second pin.

Edge of first pin

Waste area marked with an X

Using spacer blocks

Cutting the pins

Once the tails have been cut, clamp the finished tail board to an unmarked pin board and scribe either of the outermost tail ends onto the pin board. Mark the wood to be removed with an X, as shown at left in the drawing above. You can either clamp the tail board in a vise or clamp the two together on a flat surface. A small Japanese clamp is perfect for the job. Take care that the edges of the boards are aligned. An alternative method is to use the spacer blocks to mark the pin-board waste, as shown at right in the drawing above. Use all the spacer blocks to mark the edge of the first pin. Then flip the board over and use one block to mark the edge of the second pin. With either method, only one waste area need be marked; the spacer blocks will automatically take care of the others.

Cutting the pins is a two-step process. The first cutting series is made with the board angled at 10°; the next series is cut with the board tilted 10° in the opposite direction. The cutting sequence for the pins is different than that for the tails: Start the pin cut on one side and progress to the opposite side by removing spacing blocks.

The outside face of the board, the outside of the box, should always be face-up on the bandsaw table and away from the jig on the table saw. I usually make a mark on the outside face to remind me which way the board faces during the cut.

Bandsaw pins If your bandsaw table does not tilt 10°, use the 10° platform shown in the drawing on p. 222. Line up the corner of the blade inside the scribed line. Cut in the waste area. Start the first cutting sequence without a spacer block. In this sequence, blocks are added instead of subtracted. A stop (a square block of wood works well) should be used to prevent the forward progress of the pin board. You can also clamp the jig to the saw table if you are using one.

Make the first series of cuts on all the pin boards and one test board, cutting opposite corners rather than all four corners as when cutting the tails. Widen the cut on the waste side to make it easier to remove the waste later with the bandsaw blade. Then add a block to space the next cut, and repeat the cutting sequence until one side of each pin is cut.

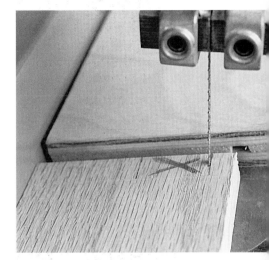

Make the first cut without the spacer blocks. Line up the corner of the blade on the inside of the pencil mark.

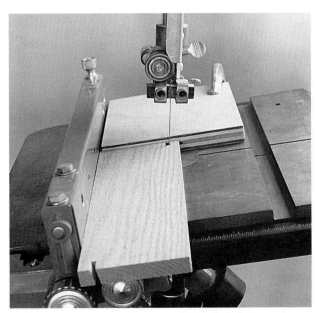

The first series of cuts is made with the bandsaw table tilted 10°. If you plan to remove the waste with the bandsaw, widen the kerf to accept the 1/8-in. blade.

Add a block for the next series of cuts.

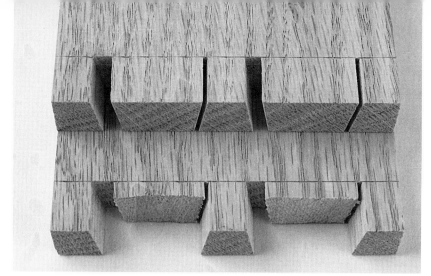

The second series of cuts is made with the bandsaw table or jig angled in the opposite direction. The single cuts shown here are those made in the second series. The bottom piece shows the final step, which is removing the waste with a coping saw to test whether the joint fits.

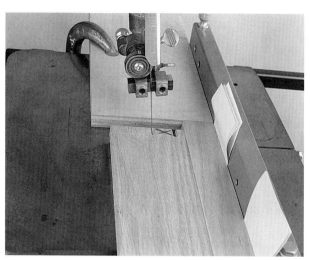

Line up the blade so that it is just shy of the pencil mark. Place paper shims between the block and the fence.

Fit the dovetails with a test piece. To fit the joint, remove the paper shims or use a microadjuster on the fence. When you remove the shims, the area that accepts the tail is enlarged.

Make the second series of pin cuts on the test board with the bandsaw table or the jig tilted in the opposite direction. Align the blade so that it is just short of the tail corner or the pencil mark — you can always take more off later. Use the spacer block for this cut. With this series of cuts, you are making the final fitting for the entire batch of dovetails. Make one test cut to see whether the dovetail fits. If it does, finish the rest of the cuts. If it doesn't fit, make the final fitting by using a paper shim to move the test board a hair. If the fit is too tight, use another paper shim to make the adjustment.

After completing the second series of pin cuts on the test board, cut off the waste with a coping saw and fit the tails to the pin board. If the fit is too tight, make another cut. Take a hair off with a paper shim.

When the joint fits, finish the cutting series with all of the pieces. Cut off the waste using the rip fence on the bandsaw, as shown in the photo on p. 225, or a chisel. You may have to tilt the piece slightly to start and end the waste cut.

Table-saw pins To cut the pins on the table saw, first return the arbor or table to 90° and adjust the miter gauge to 80°. With all the spacer blocks in place, reset the stop block so that, with the outside face of the board positioned away from you, the first cut will be made just to the inside of the pencil line. Make sure that the board is positioned correctly, or else you'll end up cutting the pin angle in the wrong direction. Make the first cut, flip the board end-for-end and cut only the opposite corner. Then remove the first block and repeat the process until one side of each pin is cut.

For the second series of cuts, reset the miter gauge to 80° in the opposite direction, replace the spacer blocks and reset the stop block so that the blade cuts just inside the other pencil line. Make the final adjustment by moving the jig board.

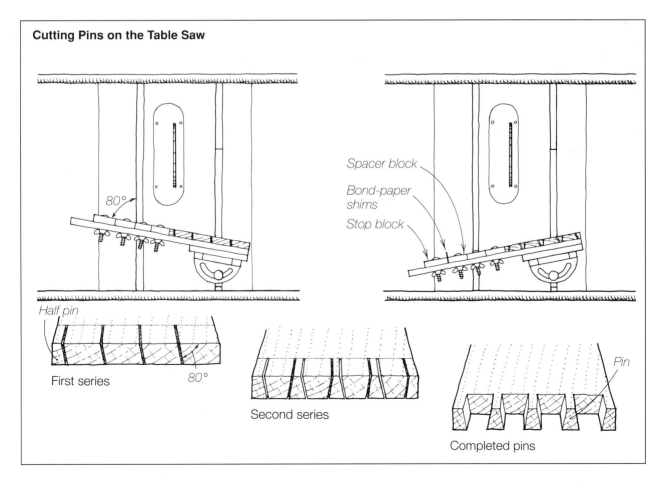

Cutting Pins on the Table Saw

80°

Spacer block
Bond-paper shims
Stop block

Half pin

First series   80°

Second series

Pin

Completed pins

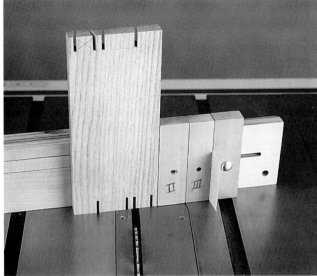

After the first two cuts have been made on opposite corners, remove one spacer block and repeat the two cuts on opposite ends of the board (left). For the second series of cuts, rotate the miter gauge in the opposite direction to 80° (right). Before making the final adjustment, add four paper shims between the last spacer block and the stop block. Position the blade inside the pencil mark and repeat the series of cuts. Do not use the number 1 block for the second series of cuts.

Make the second series of cuts in the same way as the first series, but before proceeding, slip three or four strips of paper (dollar bills work well) between the last spacer block and the stop block. These paper shims work just like a microadjuster and are used to position the workpiece for the final fit.

Complete the second series of cuts on a test piece. Then saw out the waste on the bandsaw and try the joint. If the joint is too tight, remove one or more paper shims, repeat the cuts and try again. When the test piece fits, you are ready to finish the cuts on the rest of the pin boards.

With practice you will be able to make perfect joints using this block system. The first couple of times there may be excess material in the bottom of the joint. Pare any tight spots with a chisel, and you're ready to glue up.

Other woodworking joints

The simpler joinery of the Machine Age, such as miters, dadoes, rabbets, finger joints and lap joints, is dependent on the use of modern glues and fasteners. For the most part, these joints were developed or adapted for mass production and are less desirable for fine furniture, although they are used.

Miter joints

The miter joint is the bane of picture framers, box makers and other such desperate folks. It's a notoriously weak joint. Two problems must be solved to make successful miters: The angles at the end of the boards must be accurate, and the length of the pieces must be exact.

The workpiece can be cut in either the closed (acute-angle) or open (obtuse-angle) position. I prefer the open position because the workpiece can be supported with an auxiliary fence and a stop. The sawing pressure pushes the wood against the stop, and the cut is therefore more accurate. In the closed position the sawing force pulls the wood away from the stop and compromises the accuracy of the angle and the total length of the workpiece. You can minimize the inaccuracy by clamping the workpiece against the stop or gluing sandpaper on the auxiliary fence to prevent slippage. Even with these precautions, however, the closed position is still less accurate than the open position. In addition, it is easier to support a long board in the open position.

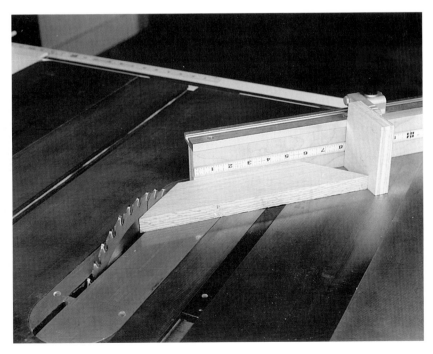

Mitering is more accurate in the open position than in the closed position.

Adjust the miter gauge to 45° with a combination square.

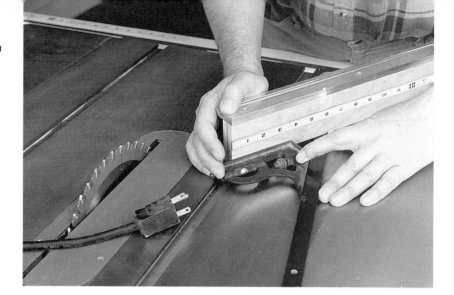

Use a special square for six- or eight-sided objects. The square allows precision adjustment in either the closed or the open position.

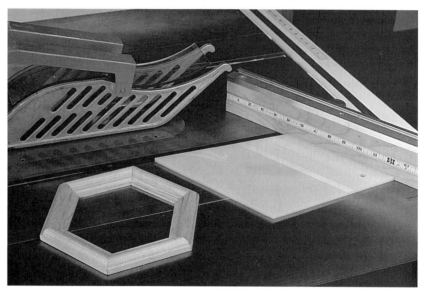

Miter angles   A four-sided object requires a 45° angle on the miter gauge. Although the protractor on the miter head has a scale, you get more accurate angles if you measure with an adjustable bevel gauge or an adjustable drafting square. Resist the temptation to adjust the miter head with a square against the blade because this approach is only accurate if the miter slot is perfectly parallel to the blade and if the blade has no runout. Place the square between the miter bar and head as shown in the top photo above. The head of a combination square is good for adjusting the miter to a 45° angle. A special square is made for adjusting the fence for six- and eight-sided objects; it allows the correct angle to be set in either the open or closed position. If you use a thin square, such as a drafting square, elevate the bar slightly by putting pennies in the miter slot. Alternatively, set the miter gauge with an adjustable bevel gauge. Adjust the angle on the bevel with a protractor. Divide the number of sides into 180° to find the miter angle for a flat frame with any number of sides.

Cutting accurate miters   A square or rectangular mitered object requires eight highly accurate cuts: two 45° cuts at each end of four boards. For successful miter joints, each angle and length must be exact. Any error is multiplied eight times, so even slight errors are obvious. Always plan your work. Molded or routed stock requires different techniques than square or rectangular stock.

Make a sample frame from scrap wood to test the miter angle before making a finished product. Check the accuracy of a cut with a miter square or put two 45° cuts together and check them with an accurate square, as shown in the drawing at right.

The most economical way to miter is to cut from a single board and flip the board over after each cut, as shown in the drawing below. The drawback of this technique is that the grain of the wood is not continuous on the same side of the object. However, if the wood will be painted or if the visual continuity of the grain is not important, this technique works well.

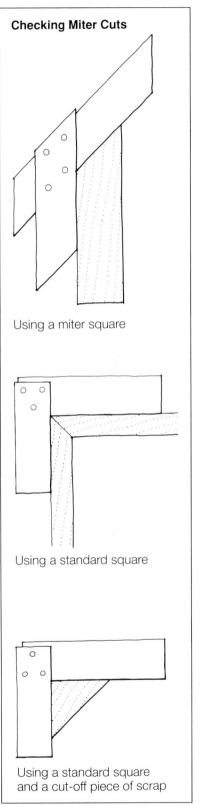

Checking Miter Cuts

Using a miter square

Using a standard square

Using a standard square
and a cut-off piece of scrap

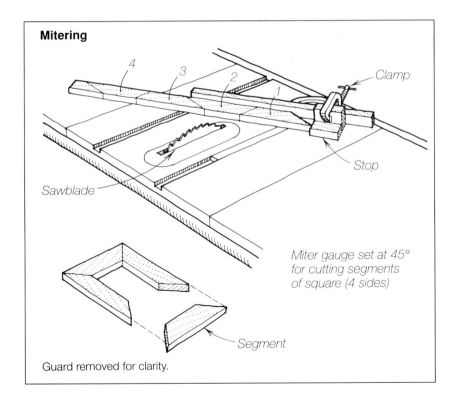

Mitering

Clamp

Stop

Sawblade

*Miter gauge set at 45°
for cutting segments
of square (4 sides)*

Segment

Guard removed for clarity.

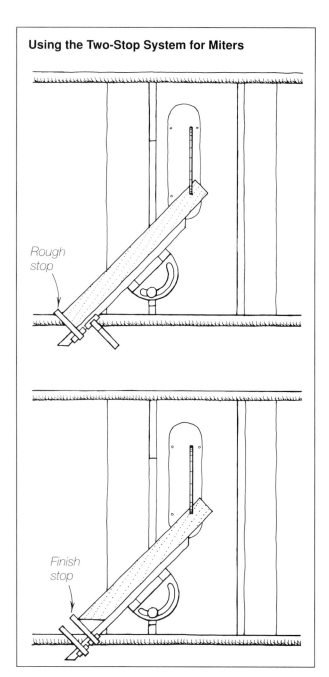

Using the Two-Stop System for Miters

Rough stop

Finish stop

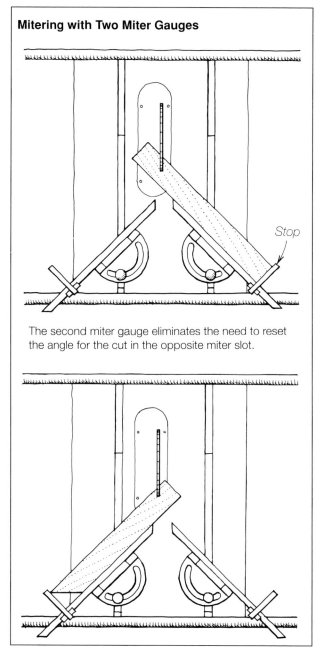

Mitering with Two Miter Gauges

Stop

The second miter gauge eliminates the need to reset the angle for the cut in the opposite miter slot.

When continuity of grain is important, cut the wood to length and then miter each end. Using the two-stop system, you can cut both ends quickly and accurately (see the drawing at left above). Make the first cut against the outside (rough) stop and the finish cut against the inside stop. Another option that saves time is to make the first cut to length at the desired angle.

If you make a lot of picture frames, particularly with moldings, you may want to use a second miter gauge to facilitate the job, as shown in the drawing at right on the facing page. The second miter gauge eliminates the need to reset the angle for the cut in the opposite miter slot. Put a stop on each miter gauge to ensure identical lengths.

Miter gauges and sled jigs The standard miter gauge is limited by the size of the workpiece it can support. For this reason, a number of after-market miter gauges are manufactured, which make miters on large work possible. The problem with these miter gauges is that they are simply larger versions of the standard gauge. In fact, one version with a 90° fence is very dangerous because one of the miter cuts must be made on the back of the gauge with the operator's hand placed close to the blade.

An alternative to the miter gauge is to use a shopmade sled jig, as shown in the drawing below. This device has two runners that fit in the miter slots and a plywood platform with fences that support the work. The whole unit slides through the blade during a cut. The fences can be adjusted and function like dual miter gauges. Make the fences out of plywood with 120-grit sandpaper underneath them. Attach the fences to the table with countersunk ¼-in. carriage bolts. The bolt hole nearest the blade on either side should be ¼-in. and the other holes should be ½ in.; the difference in hole diameter allows the fence to be rotated slightly for minute adjustments.

Sled Jig for Cutting Miters

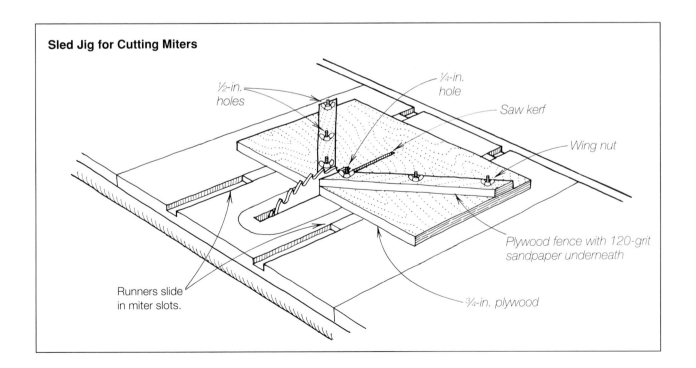

½-in. holes

¼-in. hole

Saw kerf

Wing nut

Plywood fence with 120-grit sandpaper underneath

¾-in. plywood

Runners slide in miter slots.

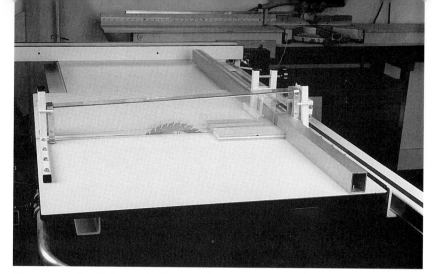

Biesemeyer's sliding cut-off table is an accurate alternative to the miter gauge.

Commercial versions of the sled jig are also available; one of the best, manufactured by Biesemeyer, is shown in the photo above. The Biesemeyer jig has a plastic guard and metal fence with a stop. A metal bracket at the front and back supports each half of the plywood top so the blade can cut all the way through the jig. A shopmade version of this type of jig is not difficult to make.

Compound miters   For compound miters, both the miter gauge and the blade are angled. Refer to the table on the facing page to determine the desired slope and the necessary miter and blade angle to produce an angled object with four, six or eight sides.

Set the miter gauge in the right-hand slot, and attach a short auxiliary wooden fence to the right side of the fence as a stop (see the drawing on the facing page). Remember that the workpiece should no longer be in contact with the auxiliary fence by the time the cut is completed. After making the first angled cut, make a series of cuts, turning the board and reclamping after each cut. This is the most economical way to make an object with compound angles, but the grain is not continuous from piece to piece.

If you want the grain to run continuously around the object, you need to use a different technique. I usually make two series of cuts. The grain will not match perfectly because a wedge-shaped piece is cut off. The match will be better at the bottom of the assembled object because there is less material missing between the mating pieces. Place the miter gauge set at the correct angle in the left-hand slot and make the first series of cuts. Cut the required number of pieces. Then reverse the miter gauge and place it in the right-hand slot; set a stop to space the second series of cuts accurately.

The best way to connect the pieces to each other is with a spline cut in each mating edge. The spline holds the pieces together and prevents slippage when they are glued. To make the spline cut, leave the blade or table at the same angle used to cut the pieces. Attach a high fence (see pp. 38-39) to the rip fence when making the cut.

Compound-Miter Table

	4-sided miter		6-sided miter		8-sided miter	
Slope	Blade tilt	Miter gauge	Blade tilt	Miter gauge	Blade tilt	Miter gauge
5°	44¾°	85°	29¾°	87½°	22¼°	88°
10°	44¼°	80¼°	29½°	84½°	22°	86°
15°	43¼°	75½°	29°	81¾°	21½°	84°
20°	41¾°	71¼°	28¼°	79°	21°	82°
25°	40°	67°	27¼°	76½°	20¼°	80°
30°	37¾°	63½°	26°	74°	19½°	78¼°
35°	35¼°	60¼°	24½°	71¾°	18¼°	76¾°
40°	32½°	57¼°	22¾°	69¾°	17°	75°
45°	30°	54¾°	21°	67¾°	15¾°	73¾°
50°	27°	52½°	19°	66¼°	14¼°	72½°
55°	24°	50¾°	16¾°	64¾°	12½°	71¼°
60°	21°	49°	14½°	63½°	11°	70¼°

Compound-Angle Miter

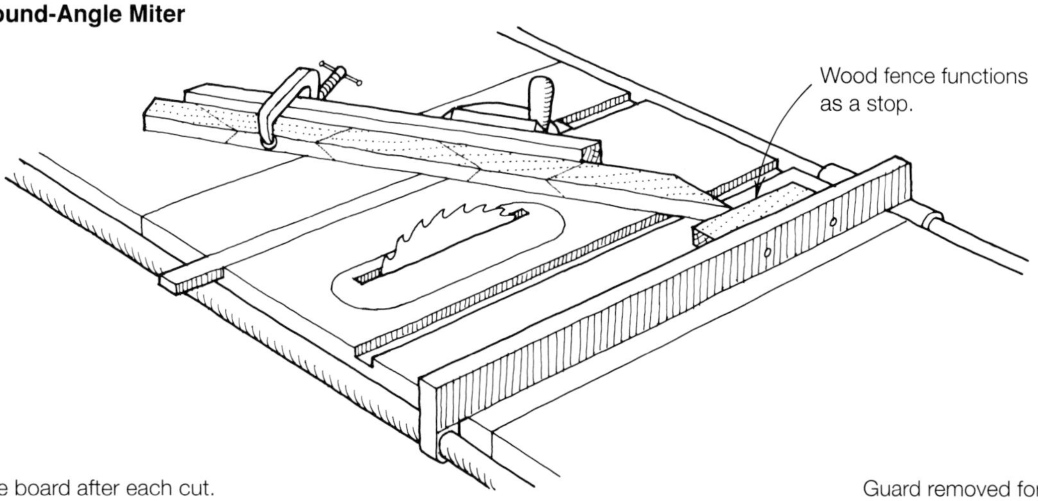
Wood fence functions as a stop.

Turn the board after each cut.

Guard removed for clarity.

Dadoes

Dado blades make wide cuts such as grooves, dadoes and rabbets in a single pass. They can also be used to make finger joints and tenons. Because a lot of wood is removed in one pass, the workpiece is more likely to kick back. For this reason, more downward and feed pressure and a slower feed rate are required. This is particularly true when the cut is deep and wide and the wood is hard. Dadoing is also more dangerous because it requires removal of the guard. Consequently, working with a dado blade calls for a heightened sense of awareness.

The dado set   The dado set, also known as a dado head, contains a number of blades. The outside blades have teeth like traditional blades with the addition of a series of wide gullets. The middle blades are chippers with swaged cutting edges. There are two teeth per chipper. The chipper tooth is placed in the gullet of the outside blades. The number of chippers determines the width of the cut. Paper shims inserted between the blades help make fine adjustments possible.

The dado set is a number of blades that are used in combination to cut a wide groove in a board at a single pass.

The adjustable dado is a one-piece cutter that can be set at any width between ¼ in. and ¹³⁄₁₆ in.

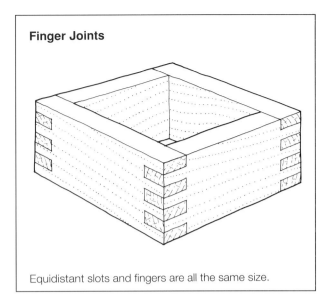

Finger Joints

Equidistant slots and fingers are all the same size.

The adjustable dado   An alternative to the dado set is the adjustable dado, which allows infinite settings between the minimum width of ¼ in. and the maximum width of ¹³⁄₁₆ in. This cutter is also called the wobble dado because its single blade is tilted on the arbor and has the appearance of wobbling to and fro as it cuts. The amount of tilt on the arbor determines the width of the cut.

Finger joints

Finger joints are interlocking joints used at corners of boxes and drawers. The fingers fit into the empty spaces of the mating piece, and the large gluing surface makes for a very strong joint. Finger joints are attractive and are often left exposed on finished furniture.

The table saw is the best tool to use for making finger joints. The joint is made by cutting out the negative space between the fingers with a dado blade or an industrial groover (a solid cutter that makes a clean flat bottom kerf). A jig positions the workpiece in relation to the cutter. Use the shopmade universal table-saw jig or the commercial fixture shown on p. 201. The miter-gauge head should be set at 90° for the entire operation.

A small pin the same width as the saw kerf protrudes from the front of the jig board (see the drawing at left on p. 240). The width of the cutter determines the size of the space between the fingers. The distance between the pin and the sawblade controls the width of the finger. The fit of the joint is adjusted by changing the size of the fingers.

Start by making and adjusting the pin. Make a cut in the jig board with the blade or dado head set to the desired width and slightly higher than the board is thick. Plane a piece of wood to fit snugly into the cut and glue it in place. Fast-drying glues speed the jig making process. Leave the pin protruding about ¾ in. and cut off the excess, which is saved for setting up the jig. Adjust the position of the jig with the waste from the pin material between the pin and the blade (see the drawing at right below).

The depth of the fingers should equal the thickness of the stock. Make a knife line this distance from the end of each board. The knife line will make setup easier and will also prevent tearout. Make practice cuts on a piece of scrap and adjust the height of the blade to the knife line.

Test the setup with two scrap boards. Place the side of the first board against the pin and make the first cut. For the second cut, place the opening made by the first cut over the pin, press the workpiece against the side of the pin and make the cut. Each cut is made by placing the pin against the side of the cut just completed.

If the corner of the first board is a finger, the corner of the second board should be a space. To cut the second board, rotate the first board and position the first finger cut over the guide pin. Press the side of the piece to be cut against the side of the finished piece. In this way the first cut will be at the very edge of the board, creating a negative space that will mate exactly with the first finger of the adjoining board. For the second cut remove the set-up piece and continue to make the series of cuts.

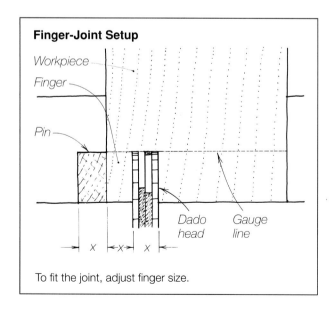

Finger-Joint Setup

Workpiece

Finger

Pin

Dado head

Gauge line

X X X

To fit the joint, adjust finger size.

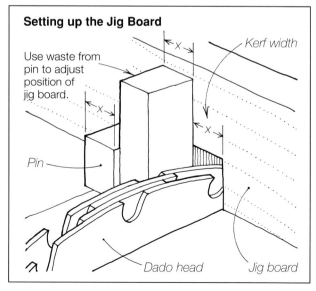

Setting up the Jig Board

Kerf width

Use waste from pin to adjust position of jig board.

X

X

X

Pin

Dado head

Jig board

Finger-Joint Cutting Sequence

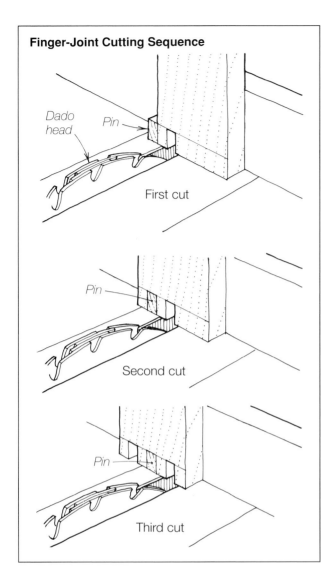

Dado head

Pin

First cut

Pin

Second cut

Pin

Third cut

Setup for Second Board

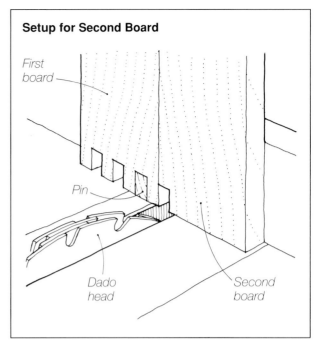

First board

Pin

Dado head

Second board

Once you have made the two end cuts, test the fit. The joint should fit so that one board will fall out of the other with the force of gravity. You should be able to insert a 0.004-in. feeler gauge between the fingers. If the joint is too tight, you will have problems getting the joint together after the glue is applied.

Since you cannot change the size of the saw kerf, the joint is adjusted by changing the size of the fingers. If the fit is too loose, increase the size of the fingers by shifting the jig board to the right. If it's too tight, shift the jig to the left. The amount that you move the jig is doubled, because you are removing that much material from each finger. The universal jig with its microadjuster is particularly handy for making this adjustment.

INDEX

Editor: ANDY SCHULTZ

Designer/Layout Artist: HENRY ROTH

Illustrator: VINCE BABAK

Photographer, except where noted: MARK DUGINSKE

Copy/Production Editor: PETER CHAPMAN

Typeface: GARAMOND

Paper: WARREN PATINA MATTE, 70lb., NEUTRAL pH

Printer: ARCATA GRAPHICS/HAWKINS, NEW CANTON, TENNESSEE